SCULPTURE

SCULPTURE

Some Observations on Shape and Form
from Pygmalion's Creative Dream

JOHANN GOTTFRIED HERDER

Edited and translated by
JASON GAIGER

THE UNIVERSITY OF CHICAGO PRESS
Chicago & London

Johann Gottfried Herder (1744–1803) was the leading figure of the *Sturm und Drang* literary movement and an innovator in the philosophy of history and culture.

Jason Gaiger is a lecturer in the Department of Art History at the Open University.

The University of Chicago Press, Chicago 60637
The University of Chicago Press, Ltd., London

Printed in the United States of America

11 10 09 08 07 06 05 04 03 02 1 2 3 4 5

ISBN: 0-226-32753-1 (cloth)
ISBN: 0-226-32755-8 (paper)

Library of Congress Cataloging-in-Publication Data

Herder, Johann Gottfried, 1744–1803.
[Plastik. English]
Sculpture : some observations on shape and form from Pygmalion's creative dream / Johann Gottfried Herder ; edited and translated by Jason Gaiger.
p. cm.
Includes bibliographical references and index.
ISBN 0-226-32753-1 (alk. paper) — ISBN 0-226-32755-8 (pbk. : alk. paper)
1. Art—Philosophy. 2. Sculpture—Philosophy. 3. Aesthetics. I. Gaiger, Jason. II. Title.

N64 .H6813 2002
701—dc21

2002022829

♾ The paper used in this publication meets the minimum requirements of the American National Standard for Information Sciences—Permanence of Paper for Printed Library Materials, ANSI Z39.48-1992.

CONTENTS

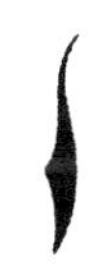

ILLUSTRATIONS

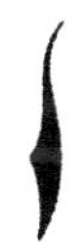

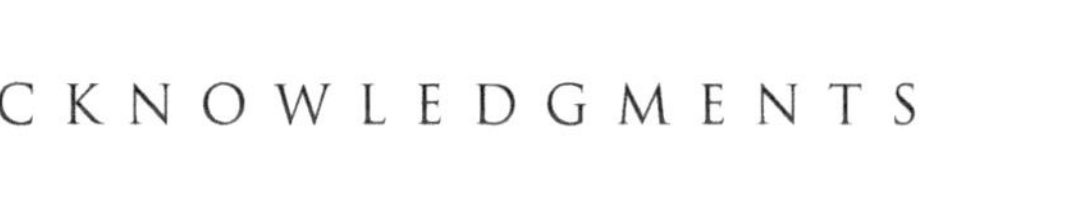

ACKNOWLEDGMENTS

I would like to offer my warmest thanks to the following people for their help in preparing this edition: Katerina Deligiorgi, Haydn Downey, Gordon Finlayson, Katrin Flikschuh, Charles Harrison, Alex Potts, and Nicholas Walker. I would also like to thank the British Academy for the award of a research grant to cover the costs of the illustrations.

INTRODUCTION

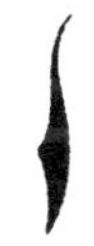

On the third of June, 1769, Johann Gottfried Herder boarded a ship at the Baltic Sea town of Riga and embarked upon a journey across Europe without knowing where his travels would take him or how long they would last. By his own admission he was fleeing his life in the Russian protectorate, where he had served as a teacher and a pastor for the past five years, and was seeking a new beginning. Although he had already made a significant contribution to German letters through the publication of his *Fragments on Recent German Literature* and the first three of his *Critical Groves,* he could still fear that he was "an inkwell of learned scribbling, a dictionary of arts and sciences that I have not seen and do not understand."[1] Herder originally intended to disembark at Copenhagen to meet the poet Friedrich Klopstock, but a friend

1. Herder's *Fragments on Recent German Literature* were published anonymously in 1776–77. A partial English translation appears in Johann Gottfried Herder, *Selected Early Works, 1764–1767,* ed. Ernest A. Menze and Karl Menges, trans. Ernest A. Menze with Michael Palma (University Park: Pennsylvania State University Press, 1992). Herder's *Critical Groves* [*Kritische Wälder*], published in 1769, are a series of polemical essays that address contemporary debates in German literature and the arts. Their title is derived from Quintilian's "sylvae." The quotation is from *Journal meiner Reise im Jahre 1769* [Travel journal of 1769], in Johann Gottfried Herder, *Sämtliche Werke,* ed. Bernard Suphan (Berlin: Weidmannsche Buchhandlung, 1878), 4:347. This edition of Herder's works will henceforth be cited as *SW.* Herder's travel journal was first published in 1846.

on board persuaded him to travel on as far as France. On the sixteenth of July he arrived in Nantes, where he reworked the fourth of his *Critical Groves* and immersed himself in recent French literature and philosophy in preparation for a visit to Paris. In the French capital he was able to discuss his ideas on aesthetics and the psychology of sense perception with d'Alembert and Diderot. He also devoted considerable time to exploring the art collections in Paris, including the important sculpture collection at Versailles. Built up by Louis XIV, this collection contained copies of many of the most celebrated antique sculptures found in Rome. Though few of the sculptures were Greek or Roman originals, they exercised a powerful impact upon Herder, who previously had enjoyed only limited opportunities to view sculpture in the round. In a large number of sketches and fragments dating from this period, he recorded his responses to what he had seen, testing and revising his earlier views and exploring new avenues of interpretation.[2] *Sculpture* arose out of this highly productive encounter. It bears witness not only to Herder's sustained meditation on problems of art and aesthetics, but also to his willingness to modify and extend his views in the face of his own powerful responses to works of art.

While still in Paris Herder received an offer of employment as tutor and travel companion to the sixteen-year-old son of the prince-bishop of Lübeck. He accepted the offer and traveled on to Eutin via Brussels, Antwerp, and Amsterdam. He also broke his journey at Hamburg in order to meet Gotthold Lessing, whose *Laocoön: An Essay on the Limits of Poetry and Painting* (1766) had been the subject of the first of Herder's *Critical Groves.* Herder wrote the unfinished first version of *Sculpture* in Eutin between March and July while preparing to depart for Italy with the prince.[3] He succeeded in bringing the first three chapters to near-completion in a relatively short time, but was forced to discontinue work on the project on July 17, when he accompanied the prince's lavish ceremonial procession out of the city. It would be 1778 before the work was complete. Although the 1770 version of the manuscript remained the basis for the finished work, Herder's ideas had undergone considerable revision in the intervening eight years, and the published version reflects important changes.

Herder accompanied the prince on his journey as far as Strasbourg,

2. These sketches and fragments, which remained unpublished in Herder's lifetime, are gathered together as *Studien und Entwürfe zur Plastik* in *SW* (8:88–115). The longest and most important is entitled "Von der Bildhauerkunst fürs Gefühl (Gedanken aus dem Garten zu Versailles)" [On Sculpture for the Sense of Touch (Thoughts from the Garden at Versailles)].

3. The 1770 version of *Sculpture* appears in *SW* (8:116).

visiting the Walmonden art collection in Hannover, the Kunsthaus in Kassel, and the renowned Antikensaal, or sculpture gallery, in Mannheim. After Versailles, Mannheim provided Herder with his second great experience of classical sculpture, long before he was finally able to visit Rome itself in 1788. It is worth considering the gallery in some detail, not only for what we can learn about the particular works Herder saw, but also for what it reveals about the conditions and expectations under which antique sculpture was viewed in Germany in the last third of the eighteenth century. The collection consisted almost entirely of casts from antique sculptures and busts. It had been built up in Düsseldorf in the previous century by the elector Johann Wilhelm, but fell into neglect after his death in 1716. Interest in the collection was reawakened by the new enthusiasm for antique sculpture that swept across Germany and the rest of Europe after the publication in 1755 of Johann Joachim Winckelmann's *Reflections on the Imitation of Greek Works in Painting and Sculpture*. The collection was subsequently transferred from Düsseldorf to the court at Mannheim, where individual pieces were at first displayed in private houses. In 1767 the elector Carl Theodor created a dedicated sculpture gallery as part of the new Drawing Academy. The sculptures were reunited under conditions specially created to show them to their best advantage and to present them as objects of serious study. The gallery was designed according to the instructions of the director of the academy, Peter Anton Verschaffelt. Not only could the plentiful light be controlled with adjustable curtains, but the sculptures themselves were mounted on movable sockets so that they could be viewed from every side. When Goethe visited the collection in October 1769 he was struck by this "forest of statues" arranged throughout the room rather than lining the walls.[4]

The collection consisted of some forty figure sculptures together with a large number of busts. In the absence of a catalog it is not possible to establish the exact contents with any certainty. However, comparisons of the numerous reports left by contemporary visitors, together with a 1731 inventory of the sculptures at Düsseldorf, have led to the identification of a significant number of the works on display at Mannheim.[5] These include casts of the Apollo Belvedere, the Laocoön,

4. Johann Wolfgang Goethe, *Aus meinem Leben: Dichtung und Wahrheit* (Munich: Carl Hanser Verlag, 1985), 535 (bk. 11).

5. The inventory of 1731 has been published, with a commentary by Claudia Braun, in the catalog to an exhibition held by the Department of Archaeology at the University of Mannheim (November 22, 1982–December 10, 1982). See Jürgen Voss, Dirk Kocks, and Horst Meixner, *Der Antikensaal in der Mannheimer Zeichnungsakademie, 1769–1803* (Mannheim: Gesellschaft der Freunde Mannheims und der Ehemaligen Kurpfalz, 1984), 21–29.

the Belvedere Torso, Castor and Pollux, the Dying Gladiator, the Farnese Hercules, the Farnese Flora, the Borghese Gladiator, the Apoxyomenos, the Borghese Hermaphrodite, Venus de Medici, the Thorn Puller, the Wrestlers, the Faun with Cymbals, the Idelfonso Faun, Antinous, Niobe, a Dying Niobid, Idolino, and Psyche and Cupid. Visitors to the gallery could thus see, gathered together in one place and presented under the most advantageous conditions, an assembly of the most highly considered sculptures that had survived from classical antiquity. As Haskell and Penny have shown, from the period of the most spectacular finds at the beginning of the sixteenth century through to the end of the eighteenth century, a relatively small number of antique sculptures were held to be representative of the finest products of human art and to provide exemplary standards of taste and value.[6] Herder is typical of his generation in regarding these works as an unparalleled realization of sculptural form. His responses should be placed alongside those of figures such as Goethe and Schiller, both of whom left vivid accounts of the impact the Mannheim collection made upon them.[7]

Herder arrived in Strasbourg on September 3, 1770, and remained there until April of the next year. Unhappy with his position in the prince's entourage, he had decided to relinquish his post and stay on in the city to undergo an eye operation. The operation, performed by Johann Lobstein, was a failure, and Herder was obliged to spend several months confined to his room. Shortly after his visit to Mannheim he had written to Johann Heinrich Merck to say that he was "dreaming darkly of new elucidations to *Sculpture.*"[8] But in September he conceded to his publisher, Johann Hartknoch of Riga, that "Strasbourg does not appear to be a place where one can think about sculpture."[9] Instead he pursued other interests, completing his prize-winning *Treatise on the Origin of Language* for the Berlin Academy and deepening his knowledge and understanding of the diversity of national literatures. He was able to communicate his ideas to Goethe, who was a regular visitor during his convalescence, and to establish contact with a number of young writers in Strasbourg, including Jung-Stilling and

6. See Francis Haskell and Nicholas Penny, *Taste and the Antique: The Lure of Classical Sculpture, 1500–1900* (New Haven, Conn.: Yale University Press, 1981).

7. For Goethe's description of his visit to the Antikensaal in Mannheim, see *Dichtung und Wahrheit,* 535 (bk. 11). Schiller gives his account in "Briefe eines reisenden Dänen (Der Antikensaal zu Mannheim)," in *Schillers Werke,* Nationalausgabe (Weimar: Hermann Böhlaus, 1962), 20:101–6.

8. Letter to Johann Heinrich Merck, August 28, 1770, in Johann Gottfried Herder, *Briefe,* ed. Wilhelm Dobbek and Günther Arnold (Weimar: Hermann Böhlau, 1977), 1:195.

9. Letter to Johann Hartknoch, September 5, 1770, in Herder, *Briefe,* 1:204.

the playwrights Lenz and Wagner. Herder's insistence on the expressive resources of the German language and his claim that literature should be seen as an integral part of the culture of a people served as a catalyst for the emergence of the *Sturm und Drang* [Storm and Stress]. This short-lived but explosive movement was an attempt to overcome the restrictive dependence on classical models in German literature and to regenerate German art and literature on the basis of individual and national genius. With *On German Style and Art,* published in collaboration with Goethe in 1773, Herder provided the movement with its "manifesto." While still in Strasbourg he received and accepted an offer of a post as court preacher in the north German town of Bückeberg. On April 28, 1771, he presented himself before his new employer, the count of Schaumberg-Lippe. Although he remained isolated and unhappy at this provincial court, his duties allowed him to devote considerable time to writing, and it was here that he produced several of his most important theological and historical works, including *The Oldest Document of the Human Race* (1774) and *Yet Another Philosophy of History for the Education of Humanity* (1774).

We know from Herder's letters that he continued to think about the book on sculpture during this period and that he sought to assimilate and interpret subsequent experiences in light of the earlier study. However, work on the final version did not begin until his move in October 1776 to Weimar, where he took up a position as general superintendent (chief pastor) that Goethe had arranged for him. By 1778 Herder had completed two more chapters, to be added to those written in Eutin, and he had subjected the entire manuscript to a thorough revision.[10] He handed the manuscript over to his publisher in March of that year. Like so many of Herder's early writings, it appeared anonymously. Although the published text was littered with a large number of printer's errors, it was the only edition to appear in his lifetime. While *Sculpture* can be shown to have influenced contemporaries such as Goethe, Novalis, Heinse, August Wilhelm Schlegel, and Alexander Humboldt, it was not until after Herder's death that it began to receive serious critical attention.

Herder himself did not succeed in building on the ideas he had developed in *Sculpture.* The recent publication of Herder's notebook detailing his responses to the artworks he saw on his visit to Rome in 1788 reveals an assiduous application of concepts he had already formed

10. He also had completed the final version of another essay on which he had worked for several years, *On Knowledge and Sensation in the Human Soul,* a study of the sources of human knowledge that contained ideas closely related to *Sculpture.*

rather than a new productive encounter with plastic art.[11] His major work on aesthetics in his later years is *Kaligone,* published in 1800. *Kaligone,* however, is largely devoted to criticism of Kant's *Critique of Judgment* and is far removed from the content and spirit of the earlier study. To appreciate the originality of *Sculpture,* we must turn to the development of Herder's thought in the period leading up to his visit to Paris in 1769. It is only in the context of his inquiry into more general problems of art and aesthetics that the real import of his writings on sculpture can be understood.

Herder's Aesthetics

Herder's early philosophical training took place at the University of Königsberg in East Prussia, where he came under the formative influence of two of the most important, but opposed, thinkers of the age: Immanuel Kant and Johann Georg Hamann. Although Kant had yet to embark upon his great project of a "critique of reason," he imbued Herder with a powerful sense of the vocation of philosophy, schooling him in the analytic method of ascending to general principles only on the basis of secure and verifiable evidence, while encouraging him to trust in the human capacity for rational reflection and self-determination. From Hamann, Herder learned to emphasize the importance of feeling and to recognize the irreducible contributions of language and of local and historical context to the supposedly universal claims of reason. Herder pursued a lifelong struggle to reconcile the opposing views of his teachers, critically reflecting upon the limits of the Enlightenment view of reason, while refusing to abandon the analytic method of philosophy that he had learned from Kant. In the period leading up to the publication of *Sculpture* in 1778 aesthetics played a special role in his thought, for he believed that many of the central problems of philosophy, including issues of history, language, and cognition, could be brought into focus by concentrating on this domain. Since works of art were themselves the products of a multiple interaction of our intellectual, physiological, and psychological capacities, their analysis offered the possibility of addressing the real complexity of human knowledge and experience. Herder was equally familiar with both the rationalism of Leibniz and Wolff in Germany and the sensualism and empiricism

11. Johann Gottfried Herder, *Bloß für Dich geschrieben. Briefe und Aufzeichnungen über eine Reise nach Italien 1788/9,* ed. Walter Dietze and Ernst Loeb (Berlin: Ruetten and Loening, 1980).

pursued by figures such as Locke in Britain and Condillac and Diderot in France. Like Kant, he sought to bring together rationalism and empiricism and to arrive at a position that could overcome the respective deficiencies of both schools of thought.

The term "aesthetics" was first employed in its modern sense by the German philosopher Alexander Gottlieb Baumgarten in his *Meditationes philosophicae* of 1735.[12] It is derived from the ancient Greek word *aisthesis,* which means "perception" or "sensation." Baumgarten uses it to describe the "science of perception in general," a science that also encompasses "philosophical poetics," or the study of artworks. Fifteen years later, at the mid-point of the eighteenth century, he published the first volume of his *Aesthetica,* an ambitious project to develop a "science of sensible knowledge."[13] This was conceived as a philosophical analysis of knowledge gained through the senses, with works of art as the "perfected presentation of sensate representations." To grasp the originality of Baumgarten's work, it is necessary to recall the distrust with which sensory knowledge had been regarded by philosophers in a rationalist tradition that reached back at least as far as Plato. At the beginning of the modern period, Descartes argued that, unlike rational reflection, the information given by the senses was indistinct and unreliable and could not provide a secure basis for knowledge. In *Meditationes philosophicae,* Baumgarten upholds this long-standing distinction between things that are known by the mind *(noeta)* and things that are perceived by the senses *(aistheta).* Where he departs from his predecessors, however, is in suggesting that just as there is a discipline of "logic" that is concerned with the operations of reason, so there ought to be a new discipline of "aesthetics" that is concerned with what is learned through the senses. Whereas logic analyzes complex ideas into simple parts, the new science of aesthetics is directed toward the plenitude and complexity of sensations. The particular character of sensory knowledge resides in the richness and vividness of its representations, something that is revealed in an exemplary fashion in works of

12. Baumgarten's *Meditationes philosophicae de nonnullis ad poema pertinentibus* [Philosophical meditations on some matters pertaining to poetry] has been translated into English by Karl Aschenbrenner and William B. Holther as *Reflections on Poetry* (Berkeley and Los Angeles: University of California Press, 1954). This edition also contains the original Latin text.

13. Baumgarten's *Aesthetica* has not been translated into English. A facsimile edition of the original 1750 edition is published by Georg Olms Verlagsbuchhandlung (Hildesheim, 1961). Hans Rudolf Schweizer has produced a parallel Latin/German edition of the most important sections, entitled *Theoretische Ästhetik* (Hamburg: Felix Meiner Verlag, 1983). The short "Prolegomena" is translated by Susan Halstead in *Art in Theory: 1648–1815,* ed. Charles Harrison, Paul Wood, and Jason Gaiger (Oxford: Blackwell, 2000).

art. Although Baumgarten identified sensory knowledge as confused and imperfect, he maintained that it possessed intrinsic value and was worthy of study in its own right.

In the fourth of his *Critical Groves,* Herder acknowledges the significance of Baumgarten's work and praises his achievement in introducing the term "sensible," or "sensuous," *(sensitivus)* into his definition of aesthetics.[14] At this stage in his development, Herder tended to present his own ideas through critical analyses of the works of other, more established writers. Although the fourth *Critical Grove* was written as a polemic against the now largely forgotten figure of Friedrich Just Riedel, it contains the clearest and most extensive account of Herder's aesthetics prior to *Sculpture.* In criticizing what he saw as the errors, falsehoods, and mistaken assumptions governing Riedel's *Theory of the Fine Arts and Sciences,* published just two years earlier (1767), Herder is obliged to elucidate his own ideas as to the proper form that such a theory should take. It is in his discussion of Baumgarten, however, that the lineaments of Herder's theory emerge most clearly. In effect, Herder pleads for a reorientation of aesthetics that both continues and extends Baumgarten's project. Whereas Baumgarten sought to incorporate aesthetics as a second domain of inquiry *alongside* logic, Herder recognized that this new "science" had important consequences for logic itself. Rather than functioning as an ancillary discipline, the study of aesthetics ultimately subverts the attempt to keep the two domains apart. For Herder, a theory of ideas conceived in abstraction from the operations of the senses must necessarily be deficient.

Herder's first line of criticism is to show that Baumgarten's conception of aesthetics remains oriented to the "higher" faculty of ideas and is thus based upon an inappropriate model. Sensible knowledge cannot be grasped as an "analogy of reason," nor can the categories through which it is analyzed be taken from traditional logic. Instead, we need to effect a reversal of approach, replacing the "nominal" definitions of logic with a philosophy that traces our ideas back to their origins in sensation and experience. The senses do not provide merely raw data that is worked up through the operations of reason. Rather, they pro-

14. Herder's fourth *Critical Grove* was written in 1769, but published only posthumously, in 1846. For Herder's discussion of Baumgarten, see *SW* 4:22–27 and 4:132–33. Baumgarten's definition of aesthetics in terms of sensible knowledge is given in section 1 of the *Aesthetica* as "Aesthetica (theoria liberalium artium, gnoseologia inferior, ars pulchre cogitandi, ars analogi rationis) est scientia cognitionis sensitivae" [Aesthetics (the theory of the liberal arts, the logic of the lower faculty of cognition, the art of thinking beautifully, the art of the analogue of reason) is the science of sensible knowledge]. See Schweizer, *Theoretische Ästhetik,* 3.

vide our fundamental modes of access to the world, actively disclosing things in a way that merits the closest philosophical attention. In a fragment dating from this period, entitled "On the Meaning of Feeling," Herder rejects the Cartesian account of self-knowledge as something that can be grasped in abstraction from any concrete relation to the external world. In place of Descartes' *cogito ergo sum* [I think therefore I am], he asserts, *"Ich fühle mich! Ich bin!"* [I feel! I am!].[15] Our embodied, sensuous existence provides the indispensable condition for genuine self-awareness. For this reason, philosophy must place human knowledge and experience at the center of its inquiries.

Herder's second line of criticism is closely related to the first. He argues that Baumgarten conceives the discipline of aesthetics in too general a fashion and that as a consequence he neglects to study the specific characteristics of each of the five senses. He fails to reflect upon the differences between the various forms of art and the media through which they operate. An aesthetics that is genuinely concerned with "sensible knowledge" must attend to the unique properties and characteristics of the different senses and show how these shape our experience of the world. Each of the various art forms such as poetry, painting, sculpture, and music have a different relation to the five senses and each calls for its own independent study. Rather than starting from the top down, with definitions of the most general terms such as "beauty" and "art," we need to undertake a "physiology of the senses" that can gather together and order the phenomena that are subsumed under these collective terms. Herder contrasts his method, which starts "from below," with Baumgarten's method "from above." Whereas Baumgarten begins with rigorous definitions of the most general or abstract concepts, Herder seeks to identify the *origins* of these concepts in experience. True to Kant's precritical teaching, he insists that philosophy must proceed by "strict analysis," examining as many different examples of art and beauty as possible before ascending to more general conclusions.

Finally, Herder criticizes Baumgarten for including in his definition of aesthetics the "art of thinking beautifully" *(ars pulchre cogitandi)* and for suggesting that aesthetics can fulfill an educative role. Herder is insistent that aesthetics must remain a descriptive discipline and that it cannot provide rules or instruction for what connoisseurs or artists ought to do. Its task is to discover the laws of art and beauty through

15. "Zum Sinn des Gefühls," *SW* 8:96. The full text of this fragment, of which Suphan provides only a part, has been rediscovered by Hans Dietrich Irmscher. See his essay, "Aus Herders Nachlaß," *Euphorian* 54 (1960): 281–94.

observation and reflection, not to direct us toward the right or appropriate way of doing things: "The essence of philosophy is to bring to the surface ideas that lie within us, to illuminate truths that we know only obscurely, and to develop proofs that we have not grasped clearly in all their intermediate stages."[16] Aesthetics should enable us to recover the complex web of experience that informs our most primitive concepts and to locate the origin of these concepts in the activity of the senses. In doing so it fulfills an important function, generating new insights and bringing our knowledge to a degree of clarity or evidence that it previously lacked. Aesthetics neither can nor should, however, impose rules on artistic creativity, which remains entirely free of the ruminations of philosophers.

Taken together, Herder's criticisms provide a clear statement of the direction that the fledgling discipline of aesthetics should take. If it is to remain true to the radical impulse behind Baumgarten's work, it must analyze the contributions of the different senses while integrating the results of this analysis into a study of the differences among the arts. This investigation, in turn, should have implications for a more general theory of knowledge. Aesthetics forms part of a "first psychology," the task of which is to trace the supposedly independent operations of the mind back to their origins in experience.[17] In pursuit of this goal, Herder turned to the writings of philosophers working outside the rationalist tradition, principally in Britain and France. As early as 1690, in his *Essay concerning Human Understanding,* the English philosopher John Locke had rejected the theory of innate ideas and had argued that sense impressions provided the most basic or fundamental components of human knowledge. Locke's starting point was not general truths of reason, but the information given through sensation. In the tradition of empiricist and sensualist philosophy, Herder is interested, above all, in the methodological isolation of the contributions made by the different senses. The golden thread that allows him to pursue this question through the work of figures such as Berkeley, Voltaire, Condillac, and Diderot is provided by Locke's discussion of the so-called Molyneux Problem. This discussion is contained in the fourth edition of the *Essay concerning Human Understanding,* published in 1700.[18]

16. *Viertes Wäldchen, SW* 4:12.

17. *Journal meiner Reise, SW* 4:445. Herder's notion of "first psychology" places a polemical spin on the traditional notion of *prima philosophia* or "first philosophy."

18. A detailed discussion of the Molyneux Problem, with transcriptions and translations of many of the key documents in the debate, is provided in Michael J. Morgan's *Molyneux's Question: Vision, Touch, and the Philosophy of Perception* (Cambridge: Cambridge University Press, 1997).

In considering the experience of a blind person who gains the use of his sight, Locke's *Essay* initiated a highly fruitful inquiry into the discrete contributions of the senses. The significance of this discussion for Herder resides in the methodological isolation of the sense of touch from the sense of sight. For if it can be shown that the different senses reveal the world to us in different ways, then aesthetics can begin where Herder believed it should: in an analysis of the physiological and imaginative capacities that we bring to bear in responding to and interpreting the world around us and of the distinctive ways in which we draw upon these capacities when considering works of art.

Molyneux's Problem and the Analysis of the Senses

William Molyneux was a Dublin lawyer and the author of a treatise on optics, the *Dioptica nova* of 1692. He had written to Locke with the following question: Suppose a man was born blind and had learned by his sense of touch to distinguish between a cube and a sphere. Could such a person, later gaining his sense of sight, identify these objects visually before he had learned to correlate his sense of sight and his sense of touch? Molyneux and Locke were in agreement that the answer must be no: "For though he has obtain'd the experience, of how a Globe, how a Cube affects his touch; yet he has not yet attained the Experience, that what affects his touch so or so, must affect his sight so or so."[19] The newly sighted person must first *learn* to coordinate the information provided by the two senses. The consensus between Locke and Molyneux was given against the background of a shared opposition to the notion of innate ideas. In order for this newly sighted person to identify a cube and a sphere simply by looking at them, he would need to possess an idea in his mind that was common to touch and vision but dependent on neither. Such an idea would clearly not be a simple "sensory impression," but would be prior to sensory experience. A positive answer to the question would thus appear to endorse the existence of "innate ideas," precisely the notion that Locke's *Essay* had refuted.

Philosophical speculation on this issue was given added interest when, in 1728, the surgeon William Cheselden reported on a cataract operation in which he had succeeded in restoring the sight of one of

19. John Locke, *An Essay concerning Human Understanding*, ed. Peter H. Nidditch (Oxford: Clarendon, 1975), 146 (bk. 2, chap. 9, para. 8).

his patients.[20] Here it seemed was a chance to test empirically the conclusions at which Molyneux and Locke had arrived by theory alone. Cheselden's patient suffered from cataracts in both eyes that prevented him from distinguishing anything other than light, dark, and patches of color. While Cheselden did not directly try out the experiment Locke discussed, his description of the patient's recovery appears to bear out the philosopher's conclusions. The patient could not immediately connect the new information he received through his eyes with what he knew by touch. Rather, he had to engage in a long and arduous process of learning, teaching the two senses to work in agreement with one another. In a passage that Herder cites in the opening section of *Sculpture,* Cheselden describes what happened when he showed the patient a painting: "We thought he soon knew what pictures represented, which were shewed to him, but we found afterward we were mistaken: for about two months after he was operated upon he discovered at once, they represented solid bodies; when to that time he considered them only as brilliantly-coloured planes, or surfaces diversified with a variety of paints. But even then he was no less surprized, expecting pictures would feel like the things they represented. He was amazed when he found those parts, which by their light and shadow appeared now round and uneven, felt only flat like the rest." At first, then, Cheselden's patient saw a painting as a mere colored surface. Only by learning to coordinate the information given by the two senses could he begin to "read" the images as depictions of objects. Even then he was still astonished that when he reached out to touch the painting his hand encountered something flat rather than a three-dimensional object. This apparent conflict between the senses led him to ask, "Which is the lying sense, seeing or feeling?" as if each offered him different and incompatible access to the world.

In his *Essay towards a New Theory of Vision,* published in 1709, George Berkeley had argued that the primary sensations of light and color that are received on the retina cannot on their own allow us to perceive the existence of three-dimensional objects. We can only make sense of space as something *oriented,* and for us this orientation takes place through awareness of our own bodies. Were it not for our sense of touch and for our capacity actively to intervene in the world, we would be unable to develop an awareness of the spatial characteristics of objects. From earliest childhood we learn to associate visual data with tactile experience, but the patterns of light and shade that are communi-

20. Cheselden's report was published in *Philosophical Transactions of the Royal Society of London,* no. 402 (1728), 447–50. It is reprinted in Morgan, *Molyneux's Question.*

cated to us by light do not themselves give us access to bodies. Berkeley reached the radical conclusion that "we never see and feel one and the same object" and that "the objects of sight and touch are two distinct things."[21]

The key elements of this debate were carried over to France with the publication of Voltaire's *Elements of Newton's Philosophy* (1738). The responses of Condillac and Diderot, both of whom exercised an important influence on the development of Herder's ideas, are significant. Condillac's most celebrated work, *Treatise on Sensations* (1754), is an elaborate thought experiment inspired by the mythical story of Pygmalion and Galatea. Pygmalion is said to have fallen in love with a statue he had carved of Galatea; in response to his prayers, Venus allows the statue to come to life. The myth of Pygmalion provides Herder's *Sculpture* with its subtitle *(Some Observations on Shape and Form from Pygmalion's Creative Dream)*, and Condillac's interpretation resonates throughout the book. Condillac sets out to demonstrate that the higher cognitive faculties of the mind are built upon the receipt of data given through the senses. In order to isolate the specific contribution of each of the senses, he imagines a statue's senses being activated one by one, beginning with the sense of smell. He accords special attention to the sense of touch, for it is only with the acquisition of this capacity that the statue is able to develop concepts of space, extension, and solidity. Indeed, it is only when it is endowed with the sense of touch that the statue becomes conscious of itself as something distinct from its own representations. Unlike Berkeley, however, Condillac maintains that the senses can learn to work in cooperation with one another to produce accurate knowledge of the external world. The coordination of the sense of sight with the sense of touch allows us to develop a capacity for *spatial seeing* in which visual data are interpreted in terms of three-dimensional objects. Condillac distinguishes between passive "seeing" and active "looking," arguing that "the eyes of the statue must learn to *look.*"[22]

Of equal importance for the genesis of Herder's *Sculpture* was Diderot's *Letter on the Blind for the Use of Those who can See* (1749). This essay, published in the form of a letter to an anonymous addressee (referred to simply as "Madam") earned Diderot a period of imprison-

21. George Berkeley, *An Essay towards a New Theory of Vision*, sect. 49, reprinted in Colin Murray Turbayne, ed., *Works on Vision* (Indianapolis, Ind.: Bobbs-Merril, 1963), 41.

22. Etienne Bonnot de Condillac, *Treatise on Sensations*, trans. Michael J. Morgan, in *Molyneux's Question*, 76.

ment at Vincennes for its defense of atheism. The essay begins with a discussion of psychology that contrasts the perceptual and sensory experiences of the blind with the experiences of the sighted. Drawing on the writings of Nicholas Saunderson, a blind professor of mathematics at Cambridge, and his own conversations with a congenitally blind man from Puisseaux, Diderot argues that we should not consider the blind simply as lacking something that the sighted possess. The extreme tactile refinement that arises from dependence on the sense of touch enables a blind person to make distinctions and to recognize qualities in things that would otherwise remain opaque. The blind experience the world in a way that is *different* from that of the sighted, but which should not be judged better or worse. This is eloquently expressed in the observation of the blind man from Puisseaux that if he could wish for an increase in his senses, it would not be for eyes to look upon the moon but for longer arms to feel its surface.[23] Diderot goes on to argue, however, that although the blind can judge symmetries extremely well, they do not possess a concept of beauty: "[W]hen [a blind person] says, 'That is beautiful,' he is not making an aesthetic judgement, he is simply repeating the judgement of those who can see. . . . Beauty is only a word for the blind, when it has no useful application; and since they lack one of the senses, the utility of many things is hidden from them."[24]

These remarks form part of a larger argument that is ultimately intended to undermine the supposedly "natural" or given character of our moral and religious judgments. However, Herder takes issue with Diderot's suggestion that the concept of beauty is restricted to objects of vision alone. In one of the Paris fragments dating from 1769 he maintains that the blind take "genuine, immediate pleasure in beautiful touch."[25] In the same fragment, he argues, "The sense of touch perceives only bodies; the sense of sight only surfaces. What then is beauty for the sense of touch? It is not colours! Nor is it light and shadow. [It is] bodies!"[26] Herder maintains that there is a specific concept of beauty accessible to the sense of touch, one that is quite distinct from the beauty of things seen. While reflection on the experiences of the blind can help us to identify its constituent elements, this beauty is, in fact, accessible to all of us. Beauty derived from touch forms an integral

23. Denis Diderot, *Letter on the Blind,* trans. Michael J. Morgan, in *Molyneux's Question,* 35.

24. Ibid., 33.

25. "Über die schöne Kunst des Gefühls," *SW* 8:94.

26. Ibid., 94.

part of our experience of the world but remains obscured by the dominance of vision over the other senses.

To show that this is the case, Herder reverses Diderot's basic question. He does not ask: What can the blind perceive without the use of sight? but rather: What could the sighted perceive without the use of touch? What could we actually see if we had been permanently deprived of the ability to grasp things with our hands and to intervene physically in the world through our own bodies? His answer to this question is: far less than most of us think. Drawing on the writings of Locke, Cheselden, Berkeley, and Condillac, he argues that we gain an awareness of three-dimensional space only through our sense of touch, and that concepts such as solidity, mass, volume, and depth cannot be derived from vision alone. Other animals, such as birds, horses, and fish—creatures without hands which cannot grasp things or touch them—cannot know the world as we do. Our knowledge of the world, even when we simply look upon it, is fundamentally codetermined by our tactile knowledge of volume and mass, and by the kinesthetic experience of touching and manipulating bodies in the round. Sight on its own can give us access only to surfaces, that is, to images arranged on a plane. Bodies, or three-dimensional forms, are first revealed to us through our sense of touch. For Herder, sight is dependent upon touch but naturally forgetful of its more fundamental role. In more modern language we might say that we suffer from an *optical bias* in our experience of the world, a bias that enters into our concept of beauty.

Herder concludes that this optical bias, this privilege accorded to the sense of sight, has led to a neglect of what distinguishes sculpture from painting.[27] Instead of speaking of the visual arts in general, or subsuming sculpture under painting, we need to recognize that sculpture obeys quite different laws and principles. It is an art that exists in the round, that occupies space and depth rather than being arrayed across a surface, for which a concept of beauty is derived from a different sense. Herder's *Sculpture* is his most sustained attempt to rehabilitate the sense of touch and to defend its legitimate claims over the sense of sight. It goes beyond his earlier writings, however, in its range of arguments and the diversity of material on which it draws in order to identify the specific beauty of sculptural form. Whereas the fourth *Critical Grove* issues in a general typology or system of the arts, *Sculpture*

27. At the time Herder was writing, it was widely assumed that sculpture was properly a monochrome art form. The use of color in antique statuary was first accorded widespread public attention after the publication of Quatramère de Quincy's *Le Jupiter Olympien, ou l'art de la sculpture antique, considerée sous un nouveau point de vue* in 1815.

offers a detailed investigation of the inherent resources and possibilities of just one art form.

Spatial Seeing and the Anamnesis of Touch

Thanks to the work of Paul Oskar Kristeller, it is now widely recognized that the eighteenth century witnessed not only the birth of aesthetics as a philosophical discipline, but also the very notion of the "fine arts" as a generic term that encompasses the five principal arts of sculpture, painting, music, literature, and architecture.[28] In common with other philosophers of his time, Herder sought to investigate the normative basis of these distinctions and to establish the laws and principles specific to each of the different forms of art. Although he consistently argues for an aesthetics from below, the fourth *Critical Grove* does not issue, as one might hope, in a detailed analysis of the physiological and imaginative resources that are brought into play in the production and appreciation of art, but in a new typology that grounds the relation between the arts in a different way. Herder's pursuit of this typology, the lineaments of which are still present in *Sculpture,* results in exactly that form of philosophizing from above that elsewhere he so forcibly rejects. This *esprit de système,* so characteristic of eighteenth-century philosophy, results in a series of strained and unworkable distinctions that ultimately serves to obscure the depth and subtlety of his thought.

Herder's analysis of the relation between the arts should be seen as an extension, but also as a criticism, of Lessing's procedure as set forth in *Laocoön* (1766). Lessing's principal insight was to recognize that the internal ordering of an artwork does not necessarily correspond to any given order in the subject matter it depicts, and that different forms of art draw upon different resources in order to create drama and coherence. In particular, he sought to show that poetry and painting order their constituent elements in distinct ways. Painting operates through arrangements of figures and colors on a plane, while poetry operates through articulated sounds in time. Whereas painting employs signs that are arranged alongside one another and coexist in space, poetry employs signs that succeed one another in time. The sequentiality of the one is static and spatial, whereas the sequentiality of the other is dynamic and temporal. This has important consequences for what can

28. See Paul Oskar Kristeller, "The Modern System of the Arts: A Study in the History of Aesthetics I–II," *Journal of the History of Ideas* 12 (1951): 496–527; 13 (1952): 17–46.

and cannot be done within each of these different media. For example, whereas a poem or a play can recount a continuous sequence of events, a painting or a sculpture can present us with only a single moment. Similarly, a literary text cannot present all the details of the visual appearance of a person or an object, and so must be highly selective in what it reveals. Herder offers two important revisions to this account. First, whereas Lessing speaks of the visual arts in general and subsumes sculpture under painting in order to form a single contrast to poetry, Herder insists that sculpture must be treated as a separate art form, operating through its own distinctive medium with its own constraints and possibilities. Second, whereas Lessing identifies the differences between poetry and painting on the basis of the different type of sign that each employs, Herder analyzes the differences between the arts in terms of their specific modes of "address." In place of Lessing's semiotic grounding, Herder offers a theory of the arts that is based on an account of our human embodied existence and of the sensual and imaginative capacities through which we experience and interpret the world.

In the fourth *Critical Grove,* Herder extends these insights to draw up a typology of the arts that relates each of the principal art forms to just one of the senses. Since he excludes smell and taste, this leaves just three "higher" senses on which to build the complete system.[29] This can be carried out with relative facility for the arts of painting, sculpture, and music. Painting is related to sight: it is concerned with shapes and figures on surfaces and presents things arranged alongside one another. Sculpture is related to touch: it is concerned with bodies in space and presents things in depth or in the round. Music is related to hearing: it is concerned with sounds and presents these in succession.[30] Herder is also concerned, however, with other, less amenable art forms, such as dance, architecture, and landscape design. While he is able to assimilate dance into his schema by regarding it as "music made visible," he is obliged to reject architecture and landscape design as "merely beautified mechanical arts."[31] Finally, in an argument that anticipates Hegel's views in the *Lectures on Aesthetics,* he describes poetry as an art form that incorporates elements from all the other arts without enjoying a special relationship to any one of the senses in particular. Poetry is addressed directly to the mind rather than to the senses.[32]

29. *Viertes Wäldchen, SW* 4:54.

30. Ibid., 61–62.

31. Ibid., 120–21, 123–25.

32. Ibid., 129ff. Cf. Georg Wilhelm Friedrich Hegel, *Lectures on Aesthetics,* trans. T. M. Knox (Oxford: Clarendon Press, 1975), 88–99, 959ff.

The problems besetting Herder's account are revealed most clearly in his treatment of music. Having identified music with the succession of sounds in time, he is obliged to argue that melody should be valued higher than polyphony and harmony, since the latter depend upon the temporal coexistence of sounds.[33]

Herder's effort to distinguish and delimit the arts provides the background against which his analysis of sculpture should be understood. As I have already suggested, however, his real achievement resides in his detailed exploration of the conditions of representation specific to sculpture and of the way in which these conditions sustain a distinctive form of engagement on the part of the viewer. The schematic correlation of painting with sight and sculpture with touch can even lead to a crude literalization of Herder's position, as if he were advocating that we need actually to reach out and touch a sculpture in order to appreciate it properly. Careful reading of his argument, however, both in the fourth *Critical Grove* and in *Sculpture,* shows that he is concerned with touch only as it is incorporated into our psychological and imaginative engagement with three-dimensional objects. Literal touching of cold marble or bronze would destroy the constitutive illusion of animate life on which figurative sculpture depends. In our everyday lives, the abbreviation of the other senses that takes place through the sense of sight is highly advantageous. To judge the distance of an object or to be aware of what lies hidden from view, we do not need to recall the contribution of touch to our knowledge of depth and form. But in contemplating a work of free-standing sculpture we are required to attend to features such as volume, mass, solidity, and extension. What distinguishes the medium of sculpture from painting and drawing, and from all other forms of representation upon a flat surface, is that it is an art of three-dimensions that occupies its own physical space. Despite the self-evidence of this claim, Herder maintains that its consequences have been but little explored.

Herder elaborates his position by considering in some detail the orientation of the viewer in relation to painting and sculpture, and the nature of the activity that each art form requires. A painting can be studied from a single viewpoint. Although we scan the surface with our eyes and move closer to appreciate specific details or back to appreciate the total effect, the depiction is contained on a single plane. In the language of the French art theorist Roger de Piles, the image as a whole

33. *Viertes Wäldchen, SW* 4:112ff.

should be accessible in a single *coup d'oeil.*[34] When we contemplate a sculpture, however, no single viewpoint is sufficient. Any one view offers us only a part of the whole; we must constantly alter our position if we are to take in the complete work. Herder observes that a sculpture has as many viewpoints as a circle that can be drawn around it has points. It is the task of the imagination to combine all these partial views in order to create something unified. We are able to recognize a sculpture as a body, rather than as a discrete plurality of surfaces, only by assimilating and coordinating the information given through our eyes and by drawing upon the knowledge of mass, volume, and three-dimensional form that we derive from our sense of touch.[35] The conditions of representation of sculpture are different from those of painting and call upon a different set of responses. We still look, but we look in a different way. Herder expresses this in highly figurative language: "The eye that gathers impressions is no longer the eye that sees a depiction on a surface; it becomes a hand, the ray of light becomes a finger and the imagination becomes a form of immediate touching."[36] The argument, however, is clear: we are only able to sustain recognition of the three-dimensionality of sculptural form through reference to our tactile knowledge of mass and volume. We fail to *see* a sculpture as a sculpture if we regard it merely as a series of views.

In a passage that is repeated with minor variations in the fourth *Critical Grove* and in both versions of *Sculpture,* Herder identifies Winckelmann's celebrated description of the *Apollo Belvedere* as an attempt to overcome the dominance of sight and to enter into a more profound relation to sculptural form.[37] Like a lover who constantly circles his beloved, Winckelmann strives to make the object of his admiration fully present, to turn his sight into touch and to *feel* what he sees before him. Above all, Herder praises his sensitivity to the motility of contour: the essence of sculpture resides not in any "mere proportion of the parts regarded as surfaces" but in the "beautiful elliptical line" that encircles the entire form.[38] Like Hogarth's "line of beauty," this line cannot be inscribed on a flat surface; we should imagine it, rather, like

34. See Roger de Piles, *Cours de peintures par principes* (Paris: J. Estienne, 1708), 58ff.

35. For a more recent defense of this position, see Susanne K. Langer, *Feeling and Form* (London: Routledge and Keegan Paul, 1953), 69–103.

36. *Viertes Wäldchen, SW* 4:66.

37. See ibid., 65–66; *Die Plastik von 1770, SW* 8:12; *Plastik, SW* 8:126; and this translation, p. 41.

38. *Viertes Wäldchen, SW* 4:64.

a fine wire twisting around an object and curving through three dimensions. In tracing this line we bring into unity the manifold variety of views that a sculpture affords, and we reconstitute it as an integral whole.

Inka Mülder-Bach has described Herder's account of the role played by the sense of touch in the appreciation of sculpture as a *restitutio ad integrum* that reverses the deception of the senses effected through the dominance of sight.[39] Herder himself speaks of returning to the sense of touch its "ancient rights": although touch has traditionally been categorized as belonging to the lower senses, it offers us our securest and most reliable knowledge of the external world. Sight, by contrast, is the "coldest" and most "philosophical" of the senses: it allows us to perceive things at a distance and to take everything in at a single glance.[40] The slowness of touch possesses a thoroughness and intimacy that is sacrificed by the independence and immediacy of sight. Herder frequently overstates his case, confusing the rigor of methodological isolation with the exigencies of accounting for the actual complexities of experience. He attributes to touch and denies to sight perceptions that are only achieved through a continual process of exchange and cooperation between the senses. His positive evaluation of the "obscurity" and "slowness" of touch in contrast to the "clarity" and "distinctness" of sight, however, offers a powerful challenge to the metaphorics of light and vision that characterizes Enlightenment conceptions of reason. The task of *Sculpture* is to effect a process of anamnesis, or recollection: it should enable us to recover the contribution of tactile knowledge to the appreciation of sculptural form while encouraging us to reflect upon the dominance of vision in our apprehension of the phenomenal world.[41]

Historical Understanding

Up to this point, we have considered these issues solely in relation to the particular individual, as if the "forgetting" of touch were something rooted in invariant human nature. As the argument of *Sculpture* proceeds, however, it becomes clear that these processes have a cultural

39. Inka Mülder-Bach, "Eine 'neue Logik für den Liebhaber': Herders Theorie der Plastik," in *Der ganze Mensch: Anthropologie und Literatur im 18. Jahrhundert* (DFG-Symposion 1992), ed. Hans-Jürgen Schings (Stuttgart: J. B. Metzler, 1994), 360.

40. *Viertes Wäldchen, SW* 4:44ff.

41. Cf. Mülder-Bach, "Eine 'neue Logik für den Liebhaber,'" 347ff.

and a historical dimension as well as a merely individual one. Herder himself appears to have become aware of this only in the course of his inquiries. As Bernhard Schweitzer has argued in some detail, Herder's ideas underwent a significant transformation in the eight years that elapsed between the first version of *Sculpture* in 1770 and the completion of the published text in 1778.[42] It was in the middle of this period, in 1774, that Herder published his programmatic essay, *Yet Another Philosophy of History for the Education of Humanity,* a work that Schweitzer describes as "the first burning manifesto of modern historical consciousness."[43] This enormously influential essay challenged the static and absolutist conception of history that underpinned Enlightenment historiography. Many of Herder's key arguments, such as his insistence that we should strive to achieve an internal understanding of past cultures rather than impose our own purportedly universal values and ideals, were already present in his *Fragments on Recent German Literature.* With the first of his major writings on history, however, these insights were embedded in a conception of historical change that extended to cover almost every aspect of human social and cultural activity.

Herder's *Yet Another Philosophy of History* was a caustic attack on the complacency of Enlightenment historiographers who assumed that the values of their age were universal and eternal and that they could be used to evaluate the achievements of other times and peoples. Herder rejected the idea of a universal human nature, arguing that character is to a large part shaped by environment. Other cultures, whether they are historically or geographically remote from our own, need to be understood in terms of their own standards and ideals. This form of nonreductive explanation requires sensitivity toward the particular features of other societies. Herder sought to cultivate a catholicity of understanding and appreciation, and to show that artworks, like actions and events, need to be interpreted in their cultural and historical context. Herder's theory of history was not, however, intended to issue in cultural relativism. He continued to defend a teleological and progressivist view of history, rooted in Rousseau's notion of *perfectibilité.* While each culture possesses its own individual worth or value and

42. See Bernhard Schweitzer, "J. G. Herders 'Plastik' und die Entstehung der neueren Kunstwissenschaft: Eine Einführung und Würdigung," in Bernhard Schweitzer, *Zur Kunst der Antike,* vol. 1 (Tübingen: Ernst Wasmuth, 1963). This important essay was first published in 1948. The following account of the relation between the two different versions of *Sculpture* is indebted to Schweitzer's work.

43. Ibid., 224.

cannot be judged in terms derived from any other, humanity as a whole is carried forward to higher levels of development.[44]

When Herder returned to the text of *Sculpture* after his move to Weimar in 1776, his ideas were no longer the same as when he had drafted his thoughts so rapidly in Paris and Eutin. He had somehow to reconcile his earlier project of a "metaphysics of the beautiful" with his deepened understanding of the thoroughgoing historicity of human existence. His solution, rather than to begin the project all over again, was to extend and enrich his argument by adding two chapters to the version completed in Eutin. It seems that he originally intended the book to consist of just three chapters: part 1 providing the theoretical framework; part 2 applying this framework to specific questions and problems; and part 3 deriving general rules and considering the individual parts of the human body from the perspective of the sculptor. The published version of 1778 retains this structure virtually unaltered. The new starting point is achieved by taking out of part 3 everything that is concerned with "expression." This material is then put into part 4, which begins with an interpretation of plastic beauty in terms of "inner perfection," adding posture, movement, gesture, and action to the static physiognomy of the human body detailed in the previous section. The new material is presented as a theory of expression that extends and modifies the theory of form elaborated in the first half of the book. It is structured on the same basic model, with part 4 providing the new theoretical framework and part 5 considering the application of this framework to specific questions and issues.

Schweitzer persuasively concludes that Herder did everything he could to cover over the chasm that had been "torn open" by the eight years separating the first version of *Sculpture* from the published version.[45] Herder's efforts have left clear traces in the construction of the text, the long gestation of which remains visible in the relation between its different parts. Not only does Herder not make use of the historical insights of parts 4 and 5 in the first half of the book, but the theoretical framework laid out in part 1 no longer suffices for the work as a whole. The resulting conflict gives rise to a highly productive tension that runs throughout the finished work. In the published version of *Sculpture* we see the ideas for which Herder is best known—his recognition of the cultural and historical specificity of the values and ideals of the

44. For an analysis of the contradictions contained in Herder's concept of history, see Arthur O. Lovejoy, "Herder and the Enlightenment Philosophy of History," in *Essays in the History of Ideas* (Baltimore, Md.: Johns Hopkins Press, 1948), 166–82.

45. Bernhard Schweitzer, "J. G. Herders 'Plastik,'" 225.

Enlightenment—emerge in the context of a fundamental revision of his own views concerning the relation between the visual and the plastic arts. As we have seen, Herder set out to arrive at an understanding of sculptural form through an analysis of our most fundamental sensory capacities. This gives rise to what might be termed a phenomenology of the visual arts that is based on an anthropological account of our sensory and embodied character as human beings. In the first half of *Sculpture* Herder is still insistent that the limits or boundaries separating the different forms of art are not a matter of "convention or agreement" but are instead limits "imposed by *Nature* herself."[46] In the second half of the book, however, this naturalist account of what would appear to hold true for all peoples and cultures gives way to a historically mediated account that acknowledges fundamental differences between the art and culture of earlier peoples (the Greeks above all) and that of the "moderns." Indeed, the latter part of the text offers a striking anticipation of ideas subsequently put forward by figures such as Schiller and Hegel.[47] Herder argues that not only certain subjects, but also certain forms of expression, are no longer possible in the modern age. Ours has *become* a predominantly visual culture, and we have lost the primacy of touch that the Greeks still enjoyed.

The process of analysis as anamnesis that should enable the recovery of the neglected sense of touch is thereby shifted from the ontogenetic level of the particular individual to the phylogenetic level of the development of humanity as a whole. Significantly, however, this means that Herder is not in a position to urge a renewal of sculpture on the model of the Greeks. The differences in the social, political, and cultural lives of the ancients and the moderns are such that the same forms of expression are no longer viable: "Nature has departed from us and is hidden from us; in its place we find art and social rank, mechanisms and patchwork. But such things, it seems to me, cannot be formed out of wax or clay. Let someone go into our markets, our churches and our courtrooms, our houses and our salons, with the intention of giving form to what he sees. What would he begin to sculpt? Chairs or human beings? Hooped skirts or gloves? Plumed hats or ceremonies? Give these form? *How?* By means of which sense? With the eye or with the sense of smell?"[48]

46. *Plastik,* SW 8:16; this translation, p. 43.

47. See Friedrich Schiller, *On the Naive and Sentimental in Literature,* trans. Helen Watanabe-O'Kelly (Manchester: Carcanet New Press, 1981), and Hegel, *Lectures on Aesthetics.*

48. *Plastik, SW* 8:62; this translation, p. 82.

Herder's insight into the historically conditioned character of art is directly opposed to Winckelmann's celebrated claim in his *Reflections on the Imitation of Greek Works in Painting and Sculpture* that "[t]he only way for us to become great or, if this be possible, inimitable, is to imitate the ancients."[49] Indeed, his insistence on the relativity of art to the social practices and customs of the society in which it originated ultimately serves to undermine the normative basis of Winckelmann's classicism.[50] Some commentators have suggested that the almost universal admiration in which antique sculpture was held, conjoined with Herder's own deeply felt attachment to the works he had seen in Paris and Mannheim, prevented him from carrying through the historicist project that he had undertaken so effectively in his writings on literature.[51] The issue is more complex than this would suggest, however. While Herder does, indeed, consider the sculptural achievements of antiquity unsurpassed, this claim forms part of a larger historical narrative in which he identifies a shift or transition from the primacy of touch to the dominance of vision. Although Herder's elucidation of the essence of sculptural form is carried out exclusively through an analysis of works of antique sculpture, he is insistent that imitation of the art of the ancients can result only in bloodless copies or the imposition of models that are inappropriate to the present age. He is fiercely critical of eighteenth-century neoclassicism, not only for imposing strictures on painting that are derived from a different medium, but for sustaining the illusion "that we should live in *another* time, among a *different* people under a *different* sky."[52]

Herder's writing on sculpture resides on the fault line that would subsequently open up between classicism and romanticism. In his choice of examples and his treatment of certain issues, such as the significance of allegory or the representation of ugliness, he conforms

49. Johann Joachim Winckelmann, *Reflections on the Imitation of Greek Works in Painting and Sculpture,* trans. Elfriede Heyer and Roger C. Norton (La Salle, Ill.: Open Court, 1987), 5.

50. It is worth remarking that this tension is *already* present in Winckelmann's attempt to explain the excellence of Greek art on the basis of the specific social and climatic conditions of ancient Greece. Alex Potts has drawn attention to the conflict between Winckelmann's normative classical aesthetic and his whole conception of a history of ancient art. Potts suggests that Herder and later, more historicizing thinkers did not challenge Winckelmann so much as draw out the consequences of key aspects of the schema and mode of analysis he proposed. See Potts, *Flesh and the Ideal: Winckelmann and the Origins of Art History* (New Haven, Conn.: Yale University Press, 1994).

51. See Mülder-Bach, "Eine 'neue Logik für den Liebhaber,'" 365, and Michael Podro, "Herder's *Plastik,*" in *Sight and Insight: Essays on Art and Culture in Honour of E. H. Gombrich at 85,* ed. John Onians (Oxford: Phaidon, 1984), 346ff.

52. *Plastik, SW* 8:34; this translation, p. 60.

closely to classical canons of propriety. His insight into the thoroughgoing historicity of art and his recognition of the need to find new and more vital forms of expression that are appropriate to the modern age, however, are important precursors of romanticism. The philosopher whose name is most closely associated with awakening the historical consciousness of his age is obliged to abandon the search for extracultural and supratemporal principles that can be grounded in the physical a priori of the human body. Although his aesthetics is grounded in a theory of the senses, he subsequently comes to recognize that the senses themselves, and the contribution they make to human knowledge and experience, are subject to historical change. The normative foundations laid out in the first part of *Sculpture* are not sufficient to establish a set of aesthetic criteria that remain valid independent of time and place. Herder's sense of the *loss* entailed by the shift from touch to vision impels him to recover the tactile experience that lies at the basis of antique sculpture, but he no longer identifies the imitation of the ancients as the path to perfection in the arts. He is confronted, rather, with a task of *historical* understanding, and this requires that he draw upon resources beyond those that are made available in the surviving artworks themselves.

The reference to Pygmalion in the subtitle of *Sculpture* should also be read as a description of Herder's own attempt to enter into a more vital and immediate relation to works of sculpture. At the start of the longest and most substantial of the Paris fragments he declares: "A statue must *live:* its flesh must come to life, its face and expression must speak. We must believe that we touch it and feel that it warms under our hands. We must see it stand before us and feel that it speaks to us."[53] In order to overcome the historical and cultural distance that separates his own age from that of the ancients, Herder draws on a vast range of literary, philosophical, and religious sources. *Sculpture* is suffused with references to classical authors, including Diodorus, Pausanias, Strabo, Pliny, Virgil, Ovid, and, above all, Homer. Herder refers to other sources, however, such as Norse legend and the writings of Shakespeare and Milton, where these can help him to grasp the affective power of sculpture. Herder also makes constant reference to the Bible, interpreting it not as a direct revelation of the word of God but as a poetic expression of early human religious experience. His description of the human body in part 3 is deeply colored by the language of the Song of Solomon, which he translated from the Hebrew and published

53. "Von der Bildhauerkunst fürs Gefühl (Gedanken aus dem Garten zu Versailles)," *SW* 8:88.

with a commentary in the same year as *Sculpture*.[54] He identifies the God of Genesis as the "first sculptor," deliberately confusing the boundaries between the actual human body as something divinely created and its sculpted representation. His interpretation of ancient sculpture is also informed by the Greek concept of "kalokagathia," used to suggest the unity of beauty and morality, that is, of inner and outer perfection. For Herder, the body is not a mere assemblage of parts, but a bearer of meaning and an expression of the subject's inner life. The soul speaks through the body and we must learn its language if we are to understand and appreciate the deeper significance of sculptural form.

Underpinning Herder's analysis of sculpture and his assessment of the possibilities for its revival as an ambitious art form in his own day is the unexamined assumption that its proper subject is the human or animal body. Throughout much of the eighteenth century it was widely accepted that the principle of the "imitation of beautiful nature" lay at the basis of both the visual and the plastic arts. This mimetic conception of art first came under pressure with the emergence of romanticism, which offered a rival theory of expression as the ultimate end or purpose of art. It was not until the crisis of representation that took place in the late nineteenth and early twentieth century, however, that the traditional concepts of unity and completeness based on the human form were finally abandoned. Once sculpture had been liberated from the demands of mimesis and figuration, artists could begin to make sculpture's own means—that is to say, the medium in which sculpture operates—the subject of representation. This encouraged artists to focus on the very problems of mass, volume, weight, substance, and materiality that Herder had foregrounded in his attempt to distinguish sculpture from painting. Artists such as Constantin Brancusi, Jacques Lipchitz, and Jean Arp not only sought to evoke the human body while eschewing literal representation, they also explored the expressive and sculptural possibilities of three-dimensional form without reference to any determinate subject. By 1954, Herbert Read could confidently argue that "[s]ince Rodin's time there has arisen what is virtually a new art—a concept of a piece of sculpture as a three-dimensional mass occupying space and only to be apprehended by senses that are alive to its volume and ponderability, as well as to its visual appearance."[55]

54. *Lieder der Liebe: Die ältesten und schönsten aus Morgenlande* (Leipzig, 1778); reprinted in *SW* (8:485–588).

55. Herbert Read, *The Art of Sculpture* (London: Faber and Faber, 1954), ix. Drawing on the work of Piaget and William James, Read characterizes painting as an art of "sight-space" and sculpture as an art of "touch-space." He defines sculpture as "an art of *palpitation*—an art that gives satisfaction in the touching and handling of objects" (49). Whereas

Whereas modernist sculptors were still primarily concerned with the integrity of the sculptural form and the complexity of its *internal* relations, the generation of Minimalist and post-Minimalist artists working in the 1960s and 1970s turned their attention to the physical space occupied by three-dimensional objects and to the staging of the viewer's encounter with the object. Artists such as Carl Andre, Eva Hesse, Robert Morris, and Richard Serra explored the way in which the body is implicated in processes of viewing through phenomena such as scale, texture, and location. This involved a shift away from a preoccupation with the "syntax" of sculpture and toward a new concern with the relations that pertain between the physical object, the space it occupies, and the viewer.[56] While Herder was exclusively concerned with figurative sculpture, his analysis of the role of the *perceiving body* in our engagement with freestanding sculpture offers a rich set of resources for investigating our affective responses to three-dimensional objects. Indeed, his insistence on the mediation of visual perception through bodily experience offers a remarkable anticipation of some of the ideas that helped to generate these new forms of sculptural practice.[57]

Herder is primarily concerned with our imaginative engagement with objects in the round and the particular conditions of *viewing* that the appreciation of sculpture requires, however, Read insists upon the literal handling of sculpture. He maintains that the request "not to touch" the exhibits deprives visitors of one of the essential modes of appreciating sculpture and claims that circumambulating a work can only give us "a ghostlike version of the solid object" (50).

56. In his "Notes on Sculpture," Robert Morris observes: "Some of the new work has expanded the terms of sculpture by a more emphatic focusing on the very conditions under which certain kinds of objects are seen. The object itself is carefully placed in these new conditions to be but one of the terms. The sensuous object, resplendent with compressed internal relations, has had to be rejected." "Notes on Sculpture II," *Artforum* 5, no. 2 (Oct. 1966): 20–23; reprinted in Gregory Battock, ed., *Minimal Art: A Critical Anthology* (Berkeley and Los Angeles: University of California Press, 1995), 228–35. In the same essay, Morris argues, "The better new work takes relationships out of the work and makes them a function of space, light, and the viewer's field of vision. The object is but one of the terms in the newer aesthetic. It is in some way more reflexive because one's awareness of oneself existing in the same space as the work is stronger than in previous work, with its many internal relationships. One is more aware than before that he himself is establishing relationships as he apprehends the object from various positions and under varying conditions of light and spatial context."

57. The extent to which visual perception is embedded in prior experience and forms part of our embodied engagement with the world was investigated by Maurice Merleau-Ponty in his *Phénomenologie de la perception* (Paris: Gallimard, 1945). The translation of this work in the early 1960s made Merleau-Ponty's ideas accessible to a wider English-speaking audience, which included many of the early Minimalist artists. For a comprehensive discussion of these developments, see Rosalind Krauss, *Passages in Modern Sculpture* (London: Thames and Hudson, 1977), and Alex Potts, *The Sculptural Imagination: Figurative, Modernist, Minimalist* (New Haven, Conn.: Yale University Press, 2000).

Although attempts to develop an independent aesthetics of sculpture have been rare, even in the twentieth century, the importance of *Sculpture* does not reside in its demarcation of the limits or boundaries between the arts, which are no longer productively constrained by the idea of medium specificity. If Herder's reflections on the experiential basis of our appreciation of three-dimensional art are to speak to us today, we must go beyond the opposition between painting and sculpture and refer Herder's ideas to a range of different artistic practices. Produced during one of the richest periods of German thought and ideas, *Sculpture* is at once an important document of eighteenth-century aesthetics and a timely contribution to later debates. Herder succeeded in bringing together an extraordinary confluence of sources, including rationalist and empiricist philosophy, literature, history, and the psychology of sense perception, in order to comprehend and disclose his own powerful responses to plastic art. To appreciate the full range and complexity of Herder's views, we must commence our own task of historical understanding. The moments of incompletion and contradiction in *Sculpture* are as richly informative as the text itself. Renewed engagement with Herder's ideas, however, should allow us to identify a continuity of problems and issues that reach beyond his own time and connect directly with our own.

NOTE ON THE TRANSLATION

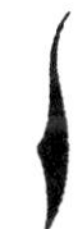

This text is translated from the original, 1778 edition of Johann Gottfried Herder's *Plastik*, published by Johann Hartknoch in Riga. Since the Riga edition is vitiated by numerous typesetting errors, careful comparison has been made with the version of the text edited by Bernard Suphan and Carl Redlich (Herder, *Sämtliche Werke*, ed. Bernard Suphan [Berlin: Weidmannsche Buchhandlung, 1892], vol. 8). Suphan and Redlich were able to check the Riga edition against Herder's original manuscript and incorporate Herder's own corrections to the proofs.

In preparing the explanatory notes, I drew on the extensive annotations provided by previous editors of the text. The most important recent editions of *Plastik* are:

Lambert A. Schneider, ed., *Plastik: Einige Warhnehmungen über Form und Gestalt aus Pygmalions Bildendem Traume*, by Johann Gottfried Herder (Cologne: Jakob Hegner, 1969);
Wolfgang Pross, ed., *Plastik*, by Johann Gottfried Herder, in vol. 2 of *Werke* (Munich: Carl Hanser, 1987);
Giorgio Maragliano, ed., *Plastica: Alcune osservazioni su forma e figura a partire dal sogno formativo di Pigmalione* (Palermo: Aesthetica edizioni Palermo, 1994);
Jürgen Brummack, ed., *Plastik*, by Johann Gottfried Herder, in *Schriften zu Philosophie, Literatur, Kunst, und Altertum*,

1774–87, ed. Jürgen Brummack and Martin Bollacher, vol. 4 of Johann Gottfried Herder, *Werke*, ed. Günter Arnold et al. (Frankfurt am Main: Deutscher Klassiker Verlag, 1994); and

Helmut Pfotenhauer, ed., *Plastik*, by Johann Gottfried Herder, in *Klassik und Klassizismus*, Bibliothek der Kunstliteratur, vol. 3, ed. Helmut Pfotenhauer and Peter Sprengel (Frankfurt am Main: Deutscher Klassiker Verlag, 1995).

References to these sources are indicated in the explanatory notes by the name of the editor followed by the year of publication.

Where relevant, I have cross-referenced the works of ancient sculpture to which Herder refers to the catalog of sculptures in Francis Haskell and Nicholas Penny, *Taste and the Antique: The Lure of Classical Sculpture, 1500–1900* (New Haven, Conn.: Yale University Press, 1981).

All references to the Bible in the explanatory notes are to the Revised Standard Version.

S C U L P T U R E

Some Observations on Shape and Form from Pygmalion's Creative Dream

Τί καλλος; ἐρώτημα τυφλοῦ

Johann Gottfried Herder

Largely written in the years 1768–70

An incomplete beginning to similar attempts at an anaglyphics, optics, acoustics, and so forth

—en! ille in nubibus arcus
mille trahit varios adverso sole colores

Virgil

PART ONE

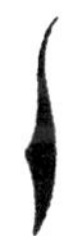

1

The person blind from birth whom *Diderot* observed[1] imagined the sense of sight to be like an organ upon which the air makes an impression, just as the hand feels the impression of a stick. A mirror he conceived as a device for projecting bodies in relief, but he could not understand how the relief could be felt, and he believed that there would have to be a second device that could uncover the deception caused by the first.[2] He held his keen and accurate sense of touch to be a fully adequate replacement for the sense of sight. He could distinguish the hardness or smoothness of a body no less subtly than a voice by its tone, or than we who can see distinguish colors. He did not therefore envy us our sense of sight, which he could not imagine to himself. If he wished for an increase of his senses, then it would be for longer arms to be able to feel the moon's surface with greater clarity and certainty, and not for eyes to be able to look upon it.

As romantic and overly philosophical as this account may seem, it has been confirmed by others who did not look through Diderot's eyes. The blind *Saunderson,*[3] despite his knowledge of mathematics, could not grasp the idea of images upon a surface, which he could only represent to himself by means of devices. He used these rather than numbers to count, replacing the lines and figures of geometry with tangible bodies. Even the rays of the sun became in his optics fine tangible rods. The image which they produced upon a visible surface meant nothing to him; he considered it an ancillary concept derived from a foreign sense, from another world. The most difficult problem in geometry, the construction of bodies as a whole, was easy for him to demonstrate; but the easiest and most intuitive task for the sighted, the representation of figures upon a surface, was for him the most difficult. Here he had to build upon concepts that were foreign and intangible for him, and he had to speak to the sighted as if they were blind. It was easy for him to conceive a die as composed of six pyramids, but he could represent to himself an octagon upon a surface only by means of a physical octahedron.

The distinction between the sense of sight and the sense of touch—between concepts belonging to surfaces and concepts belonging to physical bodies—is clearest in the case of the blind man to whom *Cheselden*[4] gave back his sight. Even when the man's cataracts were at their worst, he could still distinguish light from dark, and, in strong light, black, white, and scarlet.[5] But his sense of sight was still only a sense of touch. What moved upon his closed eyes were bodies rather than properties of surfaces or colors. Accordingly, after his eyes had been operated on, his sense of sight did not allow him to recognize any of the things that he had previously known through touch. He did not see space, nor could he distinguish even the most diverse objects from one other. Before him, or rather, around him, he saw only a vast painted panel. He was taught to distinguish, to recognize visually, what he had previously known through touch, to transform figures into bodies and bodies into figures. He would learn only to forget again. "That is a cat! That is a dog!" he said. "Now I recognize you and you will not elude me again." But often they did elude him until finally his eye was able to see figures in space as the same letters that had earlier constituted his tactile knowledge of bodies. By confronting rapidly the one with the other he was finally able to *read* the objects around him.

> We thought he soon knew what pictures represented, which were shewed to him, but we found afterwards we were mistaken: for about two months after he was couched, he discovered at once, they represented solid bodies; when to that time he considered them only as party-coloured planes, or surfaces diversified with variety of paint; but even then he was no less surprized, expecting the pictures would feel like the things they represented, and was amazed when he found those parts, which by their light and shadow appeared now round and

> uneven, felt only flat like the rest: and asked which was the lying sense, feeling or seeing? Being shewn his father's picture in a locket at his mother's watch, and told what it was, he acknowledged a likeness, but was vastly surprized; asking, how it could be, that a large face could be expressed in so little room; saying it should have seemed as impossible to him, as to put a bushel of anything into a pint. At first, he could bear but very little light, and the things he saw, he thought extreamly large; but upon seeing things larger, those first seen he conceived less, never being able to imagine any lines beyond the bounds he saw: the room he was in, he said, he knew to be but part of the house, yet he could not conceive that the whole house could look bigger. He knew not the shape of any thing, nor any one thing from another, however different in shape, or magnitude, but upon being told what things were, whose form he before knew from feeling, he would carefully observe, that he might know them again; but having too many to learn at once, he forgot many of them: and (as he said) at first he learned to know, and again forgot a thousand things a day.*

2

What do these strange experiences teach us? Something that we ourselves could experience daily if we were to acknowledge that *sight reveals merely shapes,* but *touch alone reveals bodies:* that *everything that has form is known only through the sense of touch* and that *sight reveals only visible surfaces*—moreover, not the surfaces of bodies but solely *surfaces exposed to light.* This will appear paradoxical to some, a mere commonplace to others. Howsoever it is received, it is nonetheless true, and important consequences can be shown to follow from it.

What is light able to paint upon our eyes? That which can be painted: *pictures.* As upon the white wall of a camera obscura, pencils of light fall upon the retina of the eye from everything that stands in front of it. But they can only draw what is there—a surface, the most diverse visible objects ranged *alongside one another.* Things lying *behind* one other, solid, heavy objects, can no more be given to the eye than the lover concealed behind a hanging or the miller singing away in his windmill can be painted on a canvas.

* Smith's *Opticks.* [See editor's note 6.]

The spacious prospect I see before me, with all its various aspects, what is it other than a picture, a surface? The sky that lowers to the ground and the wood that merges into it, the broad expanse of the field and the water close by, the bank of the river, the motif that dominates the entire picture—these are but an image, a panel, a *continuum of things placed alongside one another.* Every object reveals just so much of itself to me as the mirror before me reveals of myself, that is, the figure, the frontal aspect. In order to know that I am more than this I must employ my other senses, or deduce that there is more by means of ideas.

Why should it be a source of astonishment, then, that blind people whose sight is restored see before them nothing but a house of pictures, a colored surface? For none of us would see any more than this were we not able to use other means. A child sees the sky and his cradle, the moon and his wet nurse, as if they were alongside one another, and he reaches out to grasp the moon just as he reaches out to grasp his nurse. To the child everything is a picture upon a panel. Awakening from sleep in the nocturnal twilight, before we fully come to consciousness, a forest and a tree, like proximity and distance, occupy a single ground: we see them as giants close by or as distant dwarves, as phantoms that move toward us, until finally we awake and come to ourselves. Only then do we understand that we have actually *learned* how to see through force of *habit* and by using our *other* senses, above all, by using our sense of touch. A body that we have never recognized as a body by touching it, or the corporeality of which we have not been able to establish by means of its similarity to other objects, would remain to us forever like the rings of Saturn or Jupiter, that is to say, a mere phenomenon, an *appearance.* An ophthalmite[7] with a thousand eyes but without a hand to touch would remain his entire life in Plato's cave[8] and would never have any *concept* of the properties of a physical body.

For what are properties of bodies if not relations to our own body, to our sense of touch? The light that strikes my eye can no more give me access to concepts such as solidity, hardness, softness, smoothness, form, shape, or volume than my mind can generate embodied, living concepts by independent thinking. Birds, horses, and fish do not possess these concepts. Only human beings have them, because alongside reason we possess a hand that can feel and grasp. If we did not have this, if we had no means by which we could confirm the existence of a body for ourselves through our own bodily feeling, we could only infer and guess and dream and fabricate, and we would know nothing for certain. The more we are able to take hold of a body as a body, rather than staring at it and dreaming of it, the more vital is our feeling for the object, or, as it is expressed in the word itself, our *concept*[9] of the thing.

Go into a nursery and see how the young child who is constantly gathering experience reaches out, grasping, lifting, weighing, touching, and measuring things with both hand and foot, thereby acquiring securely and confidently the most difficult but also the most primary and necessary concepts, such as body, shape, size, space, and distance. These concepts cannot be acquired by teaching or explanation, but only through experience, through exploring and trying things out for oneself. In a few moments the child learns more, and learns it more vividly, more truly and more powerfully, than ten thousand years of mere gaping and verbal explanations could provide. By continually combining his sense of sight with his sense of touch, allowing each to test, extend, enhance, and strengthen the other, he forms his first *judgments.* Mistakes and false conclusions allow him to arrive at the truth, and the more *solidly* he thinks, and learns to think, at this stage, the better foundation he will lay for what perhaps will be the most complex judgments of his life. Here, truly, we have the first school of the mathematical and physical sciences.

It is a tried and tested truth that a blind person who uses his sense of touch to explore the world around him is free of distractions and is able to develop concepts of the properties of bodies that are far more complete than those acquired by the sighted, who must glide across on a beam of light. With his limited, obscure, but infinitely practiced sense of touch and his method of slowly but surely making out concepts, he is able to judge the form and living presence of things far more subtly than the sighted, from whom everything flees like a shadow. There are blind people who model in wax who are far more accomplished than their sighted counterparts,[10] and I have yet to encounter a single example of someone who was deprived of one sense who was not able to replace it by means of another. *Sight* is replaced through *touch,* luminous color by clearly modeled and enduring *forms.* Thus it is true that "the body seen by the eye remains but a surface, whereas the surface that is touched by the hand is grasped as a body."[11]

Since, however, from childhood on we employ our senses in close union and cooperation with one another, they quickly become entwined and fused together. This is particularly true of the most fundamental and the clearest of our senses: *touch* and *sight.* The difficult *concepts,* which at first we make out only gradually and with great effort, begin to be accompanied by *ideas* derived from sight. These ideas then illuminate what previously we had understood only obscurely. We become accustomed to taking in with a single glance what originally we *had to* make out gradually by touch. When our hand encounters a body, its image is at the same time projected onto our eye; our mind connects the two together and the swift idea proper to seeing runs ahead of the slow concept proper to touching. We believe we see something when in fact we touch it and where only touch is appropriate. Eventually, we see so much and with such rapidity that we no longer feel things, even though our sense of touch remains the solid foundation and guarantor of seeing. In all of these cases *sight* is but *an abbreviated form of touch.* The rounded *form* becomes a mere *figure,* the *statue* a flat *engraving.* Sight gives us *dreams,* touch gives us *truth.*

That this is so we can see from cases in which the two senses have been separated from one other and have had to start all over again in a new medium in which they must learn anew how to work together. If a stick appears broken in water and I reach for it in the wrong place, we cannot speak of a deception of the senses. For I cannot seek to *grasp* a *ray of light.* What I saw was true, a real image upon a real surface. It is only that what I sought to grasp was not true, for who would seek to grasp a picture upon a surface? From their earliest youth, our senses of sight and touch have been educated together as sisters, helping each other with their chores and often taking over completely the other's work. The same is the case here except that one of the sisters has led the other into error. Previously they had worked together on land, but now they must operate in water, a different element in which they are not practiced and which alters the refraction of light. A water sprite would have grasped the stick more accurately.

A further example from the case we recounted earlier: "The blind person cured by Cheselden saw a painting at first only as a colored surface; but as the figures separated out and he came to recognize them, he reached out to touch them as if they were bodies." This seems strange, but it is a frequent and wholly natural occurrence. A child, with his unpracticed eye, sees a painting as a mere colored surface more often than one would imagine. As long as the figures remain attached to the surface, he cannot explain the shadow here, the stripe there. He stares intently. Then, however, the figures start to come to life. Is it not as if they *emerge* from the surface and become *shapes?* The child becomes aware of their *presence* and tries to *grasp hold of them:* the dream becomes *truth.* The greatest passion and delight brings about that which ignorance had earlier achieved. Here is the triumph of the painter! Through the painter's magical deception, what is seen can now be touched, just as the painter transforms what is touched into something seen.

3

I do not think it is necessary to amass yet further examples in order to demonstrate something that is so self-evident: "the sense of sight has access only to surfaces, images, and figures on a plane, whereas bodies and the forms of bodies depend upon our sense of touch."[12] Let us see why we have followed this line of speculation for so long. What do we hope to gain from this distinction?

It seems to me we stand to gain a great deal. For the establishment of a *fundamental law* and the *distinction of two separate realms* proper to two different yet confused senses cannot be considered a matter of empty speculation. Were all the concepts we employ in the sciences and the arts to be traced back to their *origin,* or were we able to do so, we would be able to separate what has become fused together and to unify what has become separated, things which, in that great confusion we term *life,* cannot be ordered. Since all our concepts either begin with Man or tend toward him, it is close to this center, and to the way in which Man thinks and acts, that we will discover the source of the greatest errors and the most visible truth. We must find it here or we shall not find it anywhere! I shall restrict my discussion to just two of the senses and to a single concept—the concept of *beauty.*

The term *Schönheit* (beauty) derives from the words *Schauen* (to behold) and *Schein* (appearance). Beauty can most easily be understood and appreciated in terms of *Schauen,* that is, through *schöner Schein* (beautiful appearance).[13] Nothing is faster, clearer, more dazzlingly brilliant than the light of the sun and our eyes carried upon its wing. A world of external things ranged alongside one another is revealed in an instant. Since this world does not disappear as do sounds, but endures and invites *contemplation,* and since the fine rays of the sun color everything so beautifully and reveal it so distinctly, is it any wonder that our doctrine of psychology chooses to borrow many of its terms from this sense? For psychology, to know is to *see,* and its greatest pleasure is *beauty.*

It cannot be denied that we see a great deal from these heights and that many things are rendered clear, luminous, and distinct. Sight is the most artificial, the most philosophical of the senses. Polished and corrected through the most refined exercises, inferences, and comparisons, it cuts with the ray of the sun. If we succeeded in "deriving" from this sense alone a true *phenomenology* of the *beautiful* and the *true,* we should already have achieved a great deal.

Nonetheless, we would not thereby have achieved everything and certainly not what is most fundamental, simple, and primary. The operation of the sense of sight is flat; it plays and glides across the surface of things with images and color. So much is compressed together and arrayed before it that it can never be used to arrive at the ground of things. It borrows from and builds upon the other senses, taking over from them the *ancillary concepts*[14] that provide it with its *foundation* and then simply bathing them in light. If we do not seek to understand the concepts it borrows from the other senses, if we do not seek to grasp shape and form in their originary mode instead of merely *envisaging* them, the theory of the beautiful and the true that we have based on the sense of sight will be left floating in the air and drift off like a soap bubble. A theory of beautiful *forms* derived from a theory of *optics* is like a theory of *music* derived from our sense of *taste*. "Now I understand the color scarlet," declared the blind person. "It is like the sound of a trumpet."[15] In just the same way, many treatises of aesthetics glide from one sense to another, so that in the end the reader loses all sense of orientation.

The fine arts are generally classified in accordance with our two principal senses: *sight* and *hearing*.[16] The first of these protagonists provides everything that is wanted, even if it is not asked for: *surfaces, forms, colors, shapes, statues, paintings, reliefs, apparel, costumes*. That statues can be seen no one doubts. But we are entitled to ask whether the originary determination of the notion of beautiful form can in fact be derived from the sense of sight. Does the concept of form recognize sight as its origin and as its highest judge? This should not merely be doubted, but vehemently denied. A creature that is nothing but an eye, indeed, an Argus with a hundred eyes,[17] may look upon a statue for a hundred years and examine it from every side; but if it is without a hand with which to touch, or at least able to sense its own touching, if it possesses only the eye of a bird and is all beak, gaze, pinion, and claw, it will never have anything more than a bird's-eye view. The living, embodied truth of the three-dimensional space of angles, of form and volume, is not something we can learn through *sight*. This is all the more true of the essence of sculpture, *beautiful* form and *beautiful* shape, for this is not a matter of color, or of the play of proportion and symmetry, or of light and shadow, but of *physically present, tangible truth*. The beautiful line that constantly varies its course is never forcefully broken or contorted, but rolls over the body with beauty and splendor; it is never at rest but always moving forward, creating the flow and fullness of that delightful, gently softened *corporeality* that knows nothing of surfaces, or of angles and corners. This line can no more be made into a mere visible surface than it can be made into a painting or an engraving, for then it loses everything that is proper to it. Sight destroys beautiful sculpture rather than creating it; it transforms it into planes and surfaces, and rarely does it not transform the beautiful fullness, depth, and volume of sculpture into a mere play of mirrors. It is impossible, then, that sight can be the *mother of this art.*

Consider the lover of art sunk deep in contemplation who circles restlessly around a sculpture.[18] What would he not do to transform his sight into touch, to make his *seeing* into a form of *touching* that feels in the dark? He moves from one spot to another, seeking rest but finding none. He cannot locate a single viewpoint from which to view the work, such as a painting provides, for a thousand points of view are not sufficient. As soon as a single rooted *viewpoint* takes precedence, the living work becomes a mere canvas and the beautiful rounded form is dismembered into a pitiful *polygon.* For this reason, he shifts from place to place: his eye becomes his hand and the ray of light his finger, or rather, his soul has a finger that is yet finer than his hand or the ray of light. With his soul he seeks to *grasp* the image that arose from the arm and the soul of the artist. Now he has it! The illusion has worked; the sculpture lives and his soul *feels* that it lives. His soul speaks to it, not as if his soul sees, but as if it touches, as if it feels. A cold description of a statue no more offers us appropriate ideas than would a pictorial representation of music; better to leave it be and pass by.

If there are those whose enthusiasm I forgive, then they are the lover of art and the artist; for without this enthusiasm there would be no art lover and no artist. The wretched fool who sits in front of his model and sees everything smooth and flat, the poor idiot who stands before a living person and is aware of only a colored surface, these are mere daubers, not artists. If the figures are to emerge from the canvas, if they are to grow, to come alive, to speak, and to act, they must first appear as such to the artist and be felt by him to be so. *Phidias* was inspired to paint the God of Thunder by what he read in Homer.[19] From Jupiter's head and from his tumbling locks of hair came the power to approach the gods and to embrace them in love and majesty. The sculptor of Hercules, *Apollonius Nestorides,* felt the conqueror of giants, felt his breast, his flanks, his arms, his entire body.[20] In creating his gladiator *Agasias* likewise felt his every tendon and sinew and abandoned himself to all his force and power.[21] If artists such as these may not speak with enthusiasm, who else can dare to do so? They spoke fully through their work and then withdrew in silence: the lover of art responds and creates after their example. Submerged in the expanse and sea of life, he stammers out what has overcome him. In general, the *closer* we approach an object, the more *alive* our language becomes. The more vital our feeling for an object *from afar,* the more we sense the weight of the space that intervenes and the more everything in us surges forward to meet it. Pity the lover who gazes upon his beloved from a distance as if she were an image on a surface and for whom this suffices! Pity the sculptor of an Apollo or a Hercules who has never embraced the body of an Apollo, who has never touched, even in a dream, the breast or the back of a Hercules. Truly from *nothing,* there can arise only *nothing:* the ray of light, touching nothing, can never become the warm, creative hand.

4

If we are to allow ourselves to speak about *works of art* and to *philosophize about art,* then our philosophy must at least be exact and, where possible, reach to the *simplest concepts.* When it was still fashionable to philosophize about the fine arts, I sought to discover the *specific concept* by which *beautiful forms* and *beautiful colors,* that is to say, *sculpture* and *painting,* could be *distinguished* from one another—but I could not find it.* Sculpture and painting are always confused with one another; they are placed under a *single* sense, under a *single* organ of the soul, which is supposed to respond to and to create the same beauty in both. A *single type* of beauty is recognized, which *operates* through the *same natural signs,*[23] placed alongside one another in the same physical space, the one on surfaces, the other in forms. I confess that I understand but little of this. If two art forms belong to the domain of a *single* sense, they must be bound by the *same subjective laws* of truth and beauty, for they enter through the same portal, just as they both must leave by it, both existing only for a *single sense.* Painting should be able to sculpt, and sculpture to paint, as much as each will, and the result must be *beautiful!* Both are supposed to serve a single sense and to raise a single aspect of our soul! Nothing can be falser than this! I have closely considered both art forms and have found that no *single* law, no observation, no effect of the one fits the other without some difference or delimitation. I have discovered that the more something is *proper* to a particular art form, and the more *native* it is to the

* Falconet's *Reflections on Sculpture* (translated in the Neue Bibliothek der schönen Wissenschaften und der freyen Künste, vol. 1, pt. 1) is an excellent discussion of this problem by an artist whose goal is not at all to draw the boundaries of these two arts in a way that is appropriate to philosophy. [See editor's note 22.]

most powerful effects of that art, the less it can be simply carried over and applied to a different art form without the most dreadful consequences. I have found wretched examples of this in the execution of art works, but it is incomparably worse in the theory and philosophy of the arts in question, which is often written by those who know nothing about either art or science. Here everything is mixed up in a curious way. The two art forms are regarded not as sisters or half-sisters but simply as a *doubled unity,* and no nonsense is said about the one that is not also imposed upon the other. From this arises that miserable criticism, that wretched attempt to impose *censorious* and *restrictive* rules, that bittersweet nonsense about *universal* beauty that corrupts the young and appalls the master craftsman, but which is taken up in the mouths of the discriminating masses as if it were true wisdom. Finally, I arrived at my own idea of the matter, which seemed to me so true and to conform so accurately to the nature of our senses and to these two art forms, and to a hundred other aspects of our experience, that I was able to use it like a subjective boundary stone to distinguish in the most subtle way between these two *arts* and their corresponding *rules* and *effects.* I discovered a point from which I could identify what was proper and what was foreign to each of them, what was a source of potential and what a hindrance, what was a dream and what the truth. It was as if I had acquired a *sense* that could allow me, fearfully and from a distance, to glimpse the nature of beauty, where . . . but I say too much and too soon. Here is the bare outline of how, in my opinion, the different *arts of beauty* are related to one another.

We have one sense that perceives *external* things *alongside one another,* a second that perceives things *in succession,* and a third that perceives things *in depth.* These senses are *sight, hearing, and touch.*[24]

Things *alongside one another* constitute a *surface.* Things *in succession* in their purest and simplest form constitute *sounds.* Things *in depth* are *bodies* or *forms.* Thus we have distinct senses for surfaces, sounds, and forms; and when it comes to beauty, we have three senses relating to three different *genres of beauty* that must be distinguished from one another just as we distinguish *surfaces, sounds, and bodies.* If there exist forms of art for which the proper domain is to be found in one of these species of beauty, then we know both their internal and external fields of application: on the one hand, *surfaces, sounds, and bodies;* on the other, *sight, hearing, and touch.* These limits or boundaries are imposed by *Nature* herself. They are not a matter of convention or agreement, and no decision can be made to alter them without Nature taking her revenge. Music which would paint, painting which would create sound, a sculptor who would employ color, a painter who would carve stone—all these are monstrosities irrespective of whatever effects they produce. All three arts are related to one another as *surface, sound, and body,* or as *space, time, and force,* the three great media of all-embracing Creation itself, through which they encompass and delimit everything there is.

Let us now consider a second consequence, which concerns the way in which *sculpture* and *painting* are related to each other in general.

If painting is the art that is directed to the eye, and if it is true that the eye can only perceive *surfaces,* that it sees *everything* as a plane or a picture, then a painting is indeed a *tabula,* a *tavola,* a *tableau,*[25] an image on a panel on which the artist's creation appears like a dream, in which everything depends upon *appearance,* upon things placed *alongside one another.* It is here that invention and composition, unity and multiplicity begin and here that they return, together with the further litany of artistic terms. No matter how many volumes and chapters may be written on the subject, the artist can see easily that this follows from a *very simple principle,* that is, from the *nature of his art.* Here is the artist's royal command, beyond which he need acknowledge no other, the divine goddess to whom he pays homage. Once engaged in the faithful execution of his work, all philosophy on this subject must appear to him as something so *elementary* and so *simple* that it does not merit so much discussion.

Sculpture creates *in depth.* It creates *one* living thing, an animate *work* that *stands there* and endures. Sculpture cannot imitate shadows or the light of dawn, it cannot imitate lightning or thunder, rivers or flames any more than the feeling hand can grasp them. But why on this account should these subjects be denied to the painter? The painter follows another law, possesses different powers and a different vocation; why should he not be able to paint the *great panel of nature* in all its different *aspects,* in its *vast, beautiful visibility?* And with what magic he does so! Those who hold landscape painting, the depiction of the great *unity* of created nature, in low esteem, belittling its achievements and even, with ludicrous pretensions, forbidding its practice, lack wit. A painter who is forbidden to be a painter? A descriptive artist who is forbidden to describe? The painter is required to turn out sculptures with his brush and to embellish them with color as the true taste for antiquity would have it. It is considered ignoble to depict the panel of Creation, as if the sky and the earth were something worse and of less importance than the cripple who drags himself between them, whose effigy is, by force, to be made the *sole* subject worthy of painting.

Sculpture creates *beautiful forms.* It forms *shapes in depth* and *places* the object *there before us.* Of necessity, it must create that which merits such presentation and which possesses *independent existence.* It cannot gain anything by placing objects *alongside one another,* so that one object assists another and the *whole* profits thereby. For in sculpture the *one object* is the whole and the whole is *one object.* If this object is unworthy, lifeless, ill-chosen, irrelevant, all the worse for the marble and chisel! Nothing is gained from sculpting toads and frogs or rocks and mattresses if they do not serve some higher work as accessories without raising any *claim* to be the principal subject. What sculpture should create, and what it has succeeded in creating, are forms in which the living soul animates the entire body, forms in which art can compete in the task of representing the *embodied soul*—that is to say, gods, human beings, and noble animals. But whoever, driven by the high idealistic rigor of this law, seeks to impose it on *depiction,* on the *painter of the great panel of nature,* such a person is obliged to ask himself how he would go about fulfilling his own command.

Finally, we may say that sculpture is *truth,* whereas painting is a *dream.* The former is all *presentation,* the latter, storytelling *magic.* What a difference! How little the two stand upon a common ground! A sculpture before which I kneel can embrace me, it can become my friend and companion: it is *present, it is there.* The most beautiful painting is a magnificent story, the dream of a dream. It can transport me, making other moments present, and, like an angel robed in light, lead me away with it. But the impression made by the one is quite different from that made by the other. The ray of light wanes; it is *brilliance, image, thought, color.* I can think of no theorist, no humanly responsive one, who can believe that these two things derive from a *single ground.*

Let us now consider some other questions that are often presented as a form of altercation between these two arts. They have in general been poorly answered, but from the viewpoint we have established they become as clear as the light of day.

PART TWO

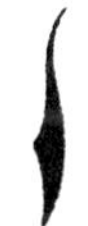

1

Why does the representation of apparel produce such different effects in painting and in sculpture?

Answer: Because, properly speaking, sculpture does not allow bodies to be clothed, whereas painting always clothes them.

Sculpture does not allow bodies to be clothed; for if the human body is fully covered it becomes nothing more than a draped block. Sculpture cannot depict clothing as such, for clothing is not solid, rounded, three-dimensional. It is only something with which we cover our bodies for reasons of necessity, a cloud, as it were, that envelops us, a shadow, a veil. The heavier clothing is in reality, the more it hides the build, the shape, the movement, and the strength of the body, then the more it is felt as a foreign and inessential burden. In sculpture a garment made of stone, bronze, or wood is to an extreme degree *oppressive.* It is no longer a shadow or a veil, no longer an item of clothing: it is a rock with cavities and protuberances, a hanging clump of stone. Close your eyes and touch it, and you will *feel* its absurdity.

Sculpture could not flourish in any country where such clumps of stone were *necessary,* where artists were *obliged* to depict woolsacks rather than beautiful and noble bodies. In the Orient, where for good reasons they prefer to cover the body and treat it as something mysterious, allowing only the face and its messengers, the hands and the feet, to be visible, no sculpture is possible, and in the land of the Jews it was not even permitted. In Egypt, despite the high level of technical skill that the people of this country attained in their art, sculpture developed along a completely different path, at a tangent from beauty. Because of their togas and tunics, their breast armor and their paludaments, the Romans were never able to make sculpture their own or raise it to a higher level: either it remained Greek or it declined. Nor during the period of monks and saints could it make any progress; for monks and nuns covered themselves entirely, and artists were thus obliged to depict folded cloaks of stone rather than bodies. Our own clothing and that of the Spanish may delight painters, but not sculptors. We have made the Spanish costume into the uniform of knights, priests, and fools; our own, when rendered in marble with its flaps and trimming, its spits, tucks, slashes, and pockets, must become the true *apparel of the gods.* Imagine a hero in his uniform, still holding the flag in his hand and with his hat pressed over one ear. Formed out of stone what a hero he would make! The artist who produced this work would need to be a good army tailor. Touch such a statue in the dark of night and you will feel marvels of form and beauty.

How different were the Greeks! These born artists of beauty cast aside bronze plates and mantles of stone and gave form to what could be sculpted—beautiful *bodies.* Did Apollo really return from his victory over the python unclothed?[1] Yet did the artist trouble himself with remaining faithful to the poverty of customary apparel? Not at all! He presented the god, the youth, the conqueror with his beautiful thighs, his free breast and youthful trunk, quite naked; the burdening cloak is pushed back to where it conceals the least and where it cannot hinder his noble step, serving rather to accentuate his proud posture as if it were simply the easy spoils of the victor. Was Laocoön, a grown man, a priest, and the son of a king, really naked when he carried out sacrificial rites before a gathering of the people? Was he really naked when the serpents fell upon him? But who thinks upon this when he sees the sculpture of Laocoön?[2] And who should think upon it? Who thinks of the *"vittas, sanie, atroque cruore madentes"*[3] that here would only reduce his suffering brow, rent by sighs and the agony of death, to the stone fillet of a priest? Who thinks of the sacrificial robes that would turn this laboring breast, these veins swollen with poison, the struggling and already exhausted hands of the father to mortified stone? The pedants who concern themselves with exactitude of apparel, with decency, and with the beautiful description in Virgil desire only to see a priestly figure dressed in a wooden cloak—and that is all they should see!

It is traditionally said of the Greeks that inner fullness mattered more to them than outer covering, provided only that the fullness were *beautiful,* for otherwise it too should be veiled. A philosopher, a Cybele,[4] or a hundred-year-old matron should be presented fully clothed. This is also the case when clothing is tolerated or required by religious ceremony or by the goal or purpose of the sculpture. A philosopher is always presented as a *head* or a *bust,* even if, like Zeno,[5] he only shows his head above the stone covering. It is not *necessary* for him to stand before us like a youth or a warrior. *Niobe,*[6] this unfortunate mother surrounded by her unfortunate children, all of whom wail helplessly and would like to flee into her lap as the youngest succeeds in doing—she kneels before us fully and abundantly clothed, for she is a *mother.* The artist's purpose is expressed sufficiently through the death-like rigidity of Niobe's gaze, which is directed toward the heavens, and the daughter in her lap. He is not concerned with the cold beauty of the naked body. Juno matrona unclothed would contradict her nature, the image she presented even to Paris[7]: she should awaken reverence in us, not love. The protector of nymphs and vestal virgins, the immortally beautiful Diana, must be clothed as is appropriate to her status and character, and art allows this. But figures of *beauty, love, grace,* and *youth,* such as Bacchus or Apollo, Charis or Aphrodite, hidden under a mantle of stone would lose everything that makes them what they are and what, through the artist, they ought to become. We can establish the following as a principle: "When the goal of the Greek artist was to form and present a beautiful body, when there were no religious obstacles or constraints imposed by the character of the subject, and when the figure was a free creation of the Muse—that is to say, a substantial work of the artistic imagination, not an emblem or a historical group but an image of beauty—the artist never clothed his subject, but revealed all that he could despite the conventional claims of apparel."

Here we are not concerned with the effect that such nudity had on the morals of the Greeks, for leaps of this sort from one field to another do not take us very far. Nothing is more delicate than questions of decorum or of what is pleasing or disturbing to the eye. This depends to such an extent on climate, dress, games, early habits, and education, on the relation between the two sexes, and, above all, on the bottomless fund of particularities that is termed the *character of the nation,*[8] that its investigation would require a book of its own. To the Goths, who came from the north, who were stricter and more accustomed to wearing thicker clothing, and for whom the relation between men and women was quite different from that among the Greeks, it may have seemed that the statues they discovered among a *corrupt* people had contributed to their decline. I say that the Goths may with good reason have found the appearance of the statues repellent, even without taking into account their new religion. This was the reason so many of the statues met an unfortunate end. We should not, however, make any inferences about the Greeks from what we know about the Goths. If a whole realm of naked statues were to be placed alongside our roads and bridges, as some free-thinking spirits have quite recently proposed, we should not conclude anything from the effect they would have *at first* upon the multitude, including those *with* standing and those *without* standing, as regards a foreign people who possessed quite different morals and education. *Being prudish* and *being scandalized* are quite distinct from *spreading virtue* and *hating art,* as the following will clearly show. But this digression is already too lengthy; our subject here is *art* and the *Greeks,* not *morals* and the *Germans.* Let us therefore continue.

In those cases in which the Greek artist, too, was obliged to clothe the beautiful body, which sculpture alone *can* and *should* form, when a law commanded that he hide it under weeds, did he dispose of any means by which he could escape this foreign burden or help to accommodate it? Could he *clothe* in such a way that nothing is *hidden?* Could he drape a body and yet allow it to retain its stature and its beautiful rounded fullness? What if the body were to *show through?* In sculpture, in something that is solid, nothing can show through: sculpture is created for the hand, not for the eye. Yet look! The discriminating Greeks found an answer precisely *for the hand.* If the hand that feels is deceived, believing that it touches both clothing and the body at once, the *foreign* judge, the eye, must follow. In short, the Greeks depicted *wet drapery.*

So much has been said on this subject, and so much that is false, that I am reluctant to add anything further. Everyone is surprised that something so effective in sculpture has no effect whatsoever in painting. And yet it seems so unnatural! So unnatural and yet so effective? In art so true and beautiful, yet in nature so ugly? Beautiful and ugly, true and false! Who is to resolve this dilemma? *Winckelmann* explains the effect simply as the imitation of ancient Greek clothing that was made of linen fabric.[9] I do not know if the Greeks ever wore wet linen that clung to the skin. If so, the question arises as to why the artist let it cling in this way rather than waiting for it to dry. But if we trace the artist's work, his art, back to its proper sensory organ, the problem answers itself. Wet drapery offered the *only way* of deceiving the hand that touches, and the eye that now touches in the same way as the hand. Only in this way can the hand be presented with drapery that is only *so to speak* drapery, a cloud, a veil, a mist. But no, not cloud and mist, for the eye must not obscure what it sees. The essence of sculpture remains the *slender body*, the rounded knee, the smooth hip, the swelling grape of the youthful breast. It is these demands to which a solution had to be found. Wet drapery was only drapery *so to speak*, just as Homer's gods possess blood only so to speak;[10] but the fullness of the body was and remains the most important thing, the very essence of sculpture, and not merely *so to speak*.

The situation is quite different with painting. As we have said, a painting is nothing other than a guise, a beautiful covering, a *magical use of light and color to create a beautiful appearance*. Since painting operates upon a flat ground, it can provide nothing other than a *surface;* and this is exactly what clothing is. Clothing gives to our eye the daily *appearance* of truth, decorum, splendor, and adornment. It is scrutinized and chosen for its *look*, its color, its elegance. However, since to the beautiful world that *looks* it offers more than the mere satisfaction of a need, why should it not also be something more for the beautiful *art* of vision? Painting can refashion the most precious aspects of fabrics; it transforms them into broken light, an enchanted vapor for the eye, elevating everything into a haze of beautiful colors. Why *should* it refrain from doing so? Must it sacrifice the advantage it derives from its own proper sense to the deficiency that characterizes another sense? If in the hands of the sculptor drapery could become what it is under the enchanted fingers of light, he would be a fool not to make use of it.

It surely required minds of great refinement to suggest that painting should imitate vast masses of naked flesh, and even wet drapery, so as to come closer to its elder and beloved sister, sculpture, and become *antique*. As a result, painting is made naked and stiff and ugly rather than attaining what its sister achieves with nudity and wet drapery. The passion for imitation and comparison has led some to make the needs of one form of art into the essence of another, thereby losing the very features that make the latter successful. We see depictions of the Last Judgment with flesh heaped up like hay, the Bathing Diana presented as if it were a flesh market! Nothing is more risible than mounting statues onto a canvas and rendering clothing *wet* where everything should rather blossom and dissolve into a haze.

"But the great old masters imitated statues; there are so many stories of Raphael which tell that he . . ."—but Raphael did not imitate what was inappropriate to painting without making it three times as much painting.[11] Precisely the old masters had an exquisite feeling for the *fall of drapery;* they knew that here painting is in an enchanted realm of beautiful illusion, a sovereign workshop of light and color. One garment rustles while another floats and hovers in the air. We stretch out our hand and believe that we can reach deep into the folds of the material; but it is only a surface. Is it possible that this ground and these colors can make the figures so divine and give them such contours and depth? The fall and alternation of the drapery preserves the charm, grace, and diversity of the whole. Here I express in a general and indeterminate way something every artist and every art lover will have experienced in a thousand individual cases, each corresponding to a thousand individual artistic touches and masterful strokes. Painting is *representation,* a magical world of light and colors for the eye. It must obey *this* sense and must not dispense with its sensitivity to light's fine enchanted rays.

The nude in the two arts does not possess the same power to seduce us. A statue stands in its *entirety,* under the open sky, in paradise, so to speak. It is a likeness of one of God's beautiful creatures, surrounded by innocence. *Winckelmann* rightly observed that the Spaniard must have been a beast who lusted after the statue of virtue in Rome, which is now modestly covered.[12] The pure and beautiful forms of sculpture may well awaken friendship, love, and daily conversation, but only in a beast can they stimulate desire. The magic of painting, however, produces quite different effects. Since it is not the presentation of a body, but only depiction, *imagination, representation,* painting opens to the imagination a wide field and entices us into her colored and perfumed garden of pleasure. Depraved pleasure-seekers of all periods have always preferred to fill their cabinets of delight with licentious paintings rather than sculptures. A sculpture, even of a slumbering hermaphrodite, is never *indecent.*[13] A modern or an ancient Chaerea[14] takes more pleasure in looking at *paintings* of Leda and the Swan[15] than in other, complete presentations of the same subject. The imagination yearns solely for perfume, appearance, enticing color. Its wings are bound before the faithful presentation of nature as it is, which is indeed too true for it. A sculpture always stands there naked, but the beautiful *Danae* by Titian[16] is wisely covered by a curtain: painting is an enchanted panel for a corrupted sense that seduces us, unconstrained by any limits.

Here, too, we can see why the moderns remain further behind the ancients in beautiful *form* than in beautiful *appearance*. Beautiful appearance can present many things that are not owed to beautiful form and that are not the result of a deeply felt, faithful, naked truth. Indisputably, there are far fewer means to attain this now than there once were. *Winckelmann* has expressed, in a fashion that cannot be surpassed, the advantages artists enjoyed under the beautiful Greek sky, where from youth onward, unhindered and joyful, the inhabitants exercised their naked bodies in dancing, games, and competitions.[17] We can only give loyal, complete, truthful, and living expression to those forms that communicate themselves to us and that live on in us through our own *living* senses. It is known that some of the greatest modern painters only ever painted their mistresses, their daughters, or their wives, for these persons alone truly took possession of their senses and their souls. Raphael disposed of a rich abundance of living forms because his character and his passionate heart took hold of him and led him to embrace everyone he knew and delighted in. As a result he strayed from the straight path and suffered an early end to his irreplaceable life.[18] Why is it that certain dullards are incapable of grasping that the divine Raphael loved mortal women? Did he not derive from them his contours and his warm, living figures? These are things that he could not have received from heaven or from cold statues alone. And yet Raphael was not a Praxiteles or a Lysippus,[19] artists who undoubtedly knew these forms in a more originary manner at a time when sculpture did not *depict*, but *created* and *presented*. As long as we await the return of the Greek age with its play and delight and its *innocence of youth* in the love between the sexes, as long as artists gaze upon stiff models in whalebone dresses and corsets, and nothing else, it remains mere folly to *anticipate* or to seek to *bring forth* sculpture like that of the Greeks. The artist's senses fail him. Should he conjure from the air angelic forms, or the figure of an Apollo or a houri?[20] These would be mere soap bubbles that vanish before the hand can grasp them. They are even less amenable to being rendered in stone. Generally speaking, however, this is not the case with painting, though there are paintings that contain beautiful forms and which, like living dreams, seek to approach this vigilant truth.*

* *Falconet*, a modern sculptor who has thought deeply about his art, has presented a number of arguments in favor of the rich and (to put it bluntly) painterly clothing of statues. In our age, in which the majority of people see sculpture itself as nothing but a form of *painting*, these arguments may well be true. To my mind, however, they are valid only as exceptions and additions, for we can never attain the *fullness of the nude* reached by the ancients. We seek to make good this failing by the use of drapery, but in sculpture drapery is no longer drapery. [See editor's note 21.]

2

Why is it that sculpture is made ugly rather than beautiful by being colored after nature and other similar devices, while color is employed in painting to such great effect?

Answer: Because color is not form, because it cannot be detected by the eye that is closed or the hand that touches, or rather, it is detected only where it impedes beautiful form. Color is a grain of sand, a veneer, a foreign growth that gets in the way and that distracts from the pure feeling of what nature ought to be.

This question is often asked, but generally it receives a different answer: "color makes the similarity too great, the similarity too similar, even identical with nature itself, which it is not supposed to be. From a distance one can even mistake a painted statue for a living human being, approach it, and so forth."[22] If someone can make sense of this, or is satisfied with such an answer, I do not envy them their satisfaction.

The same author has asked, "[W]ould Myron's cow please us more if it were covered in hair?"[23] He astutely answers this question in the negative on the grounds that Myron's cow would then look *too much* like a cow. A cow that is too like a cow? That is, a cow, but too much cow? I answer straight away that as far as art is concerned it would no longer be a cow but a stuffed pelt of hair. Close your eyes and feel it: you will no longer encounter a form, let alone a beautiful form, a beautiful shape. Even if a herdsman wished to drive away Myron's iron cow, the cow would not make any impression either on the herdsman or on the artist, for it is "too like a cow and yet not a cow," that is to say, a phantom.

Statues must be kept free of much finer things than varnish and cow skin, for these repel our sense of *touch;* our *sense of feeling* does not experience them as a part of an *unbroken, beautiful form.* The veins in the hands, the cartilage in the fingers, the knee-pan must be softened and veiled in the fullness of the whole. If not, the silent sense of touch that feels things in the dark will register the veins as wriggling worms and the cartilage as protruding growths. Rather than being experienced as belonging to the fullness of a *single* body, they will be perceived as independent, separate entities that prefigure the ultimate demise of the body, from which they should therefore be removed. The blue veins beneath the skin that pulse with life and surge with blood are visible to the eye; as something felt they are nothing but cartilage and bone, devoid of blood or animate life. A living death pervades them. The veins in a statue are alive in a quite different fashion, for under the hands

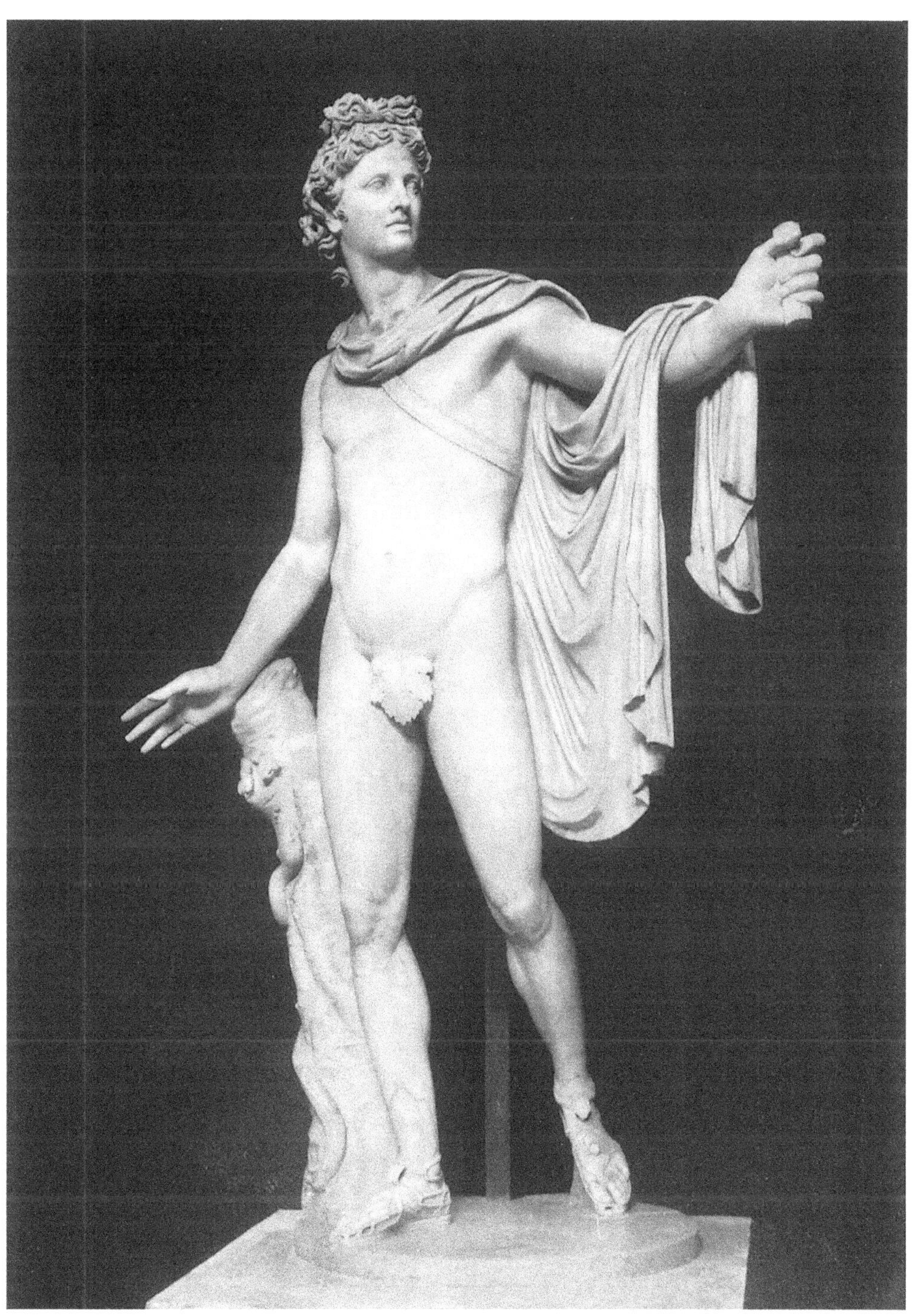

FIGURE 1

Apollo Belvedere, marble, height: 2.24 m. Rome: Musei Vaticani (Belvedere Courtyard). Photo: Vatican Museums.

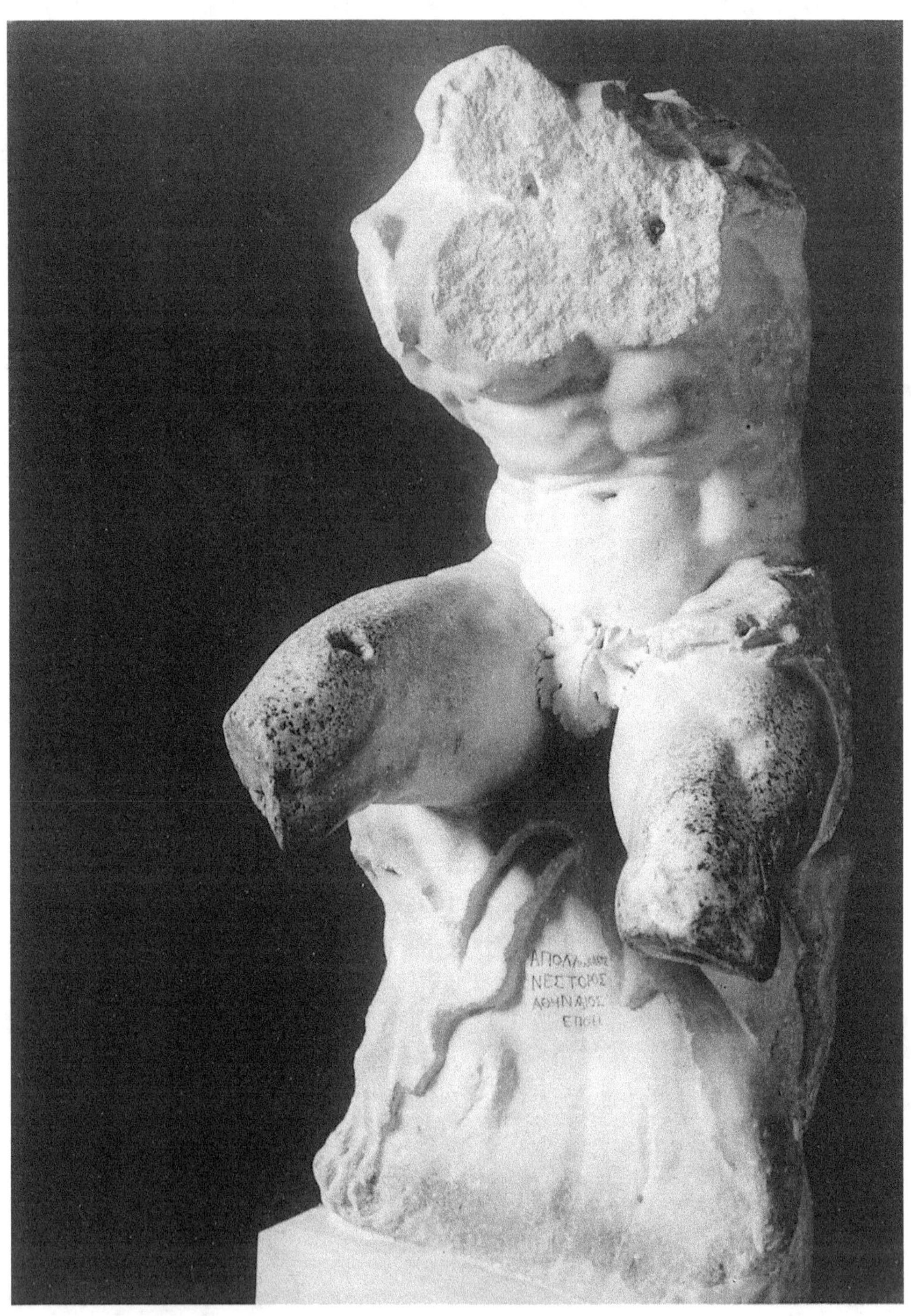

FIGURE 2

Belvedere Torso, marble, height: 1.59 m. Rome: Musei Vaticani (Atrio del Torso). Photo: Vatican Museums.

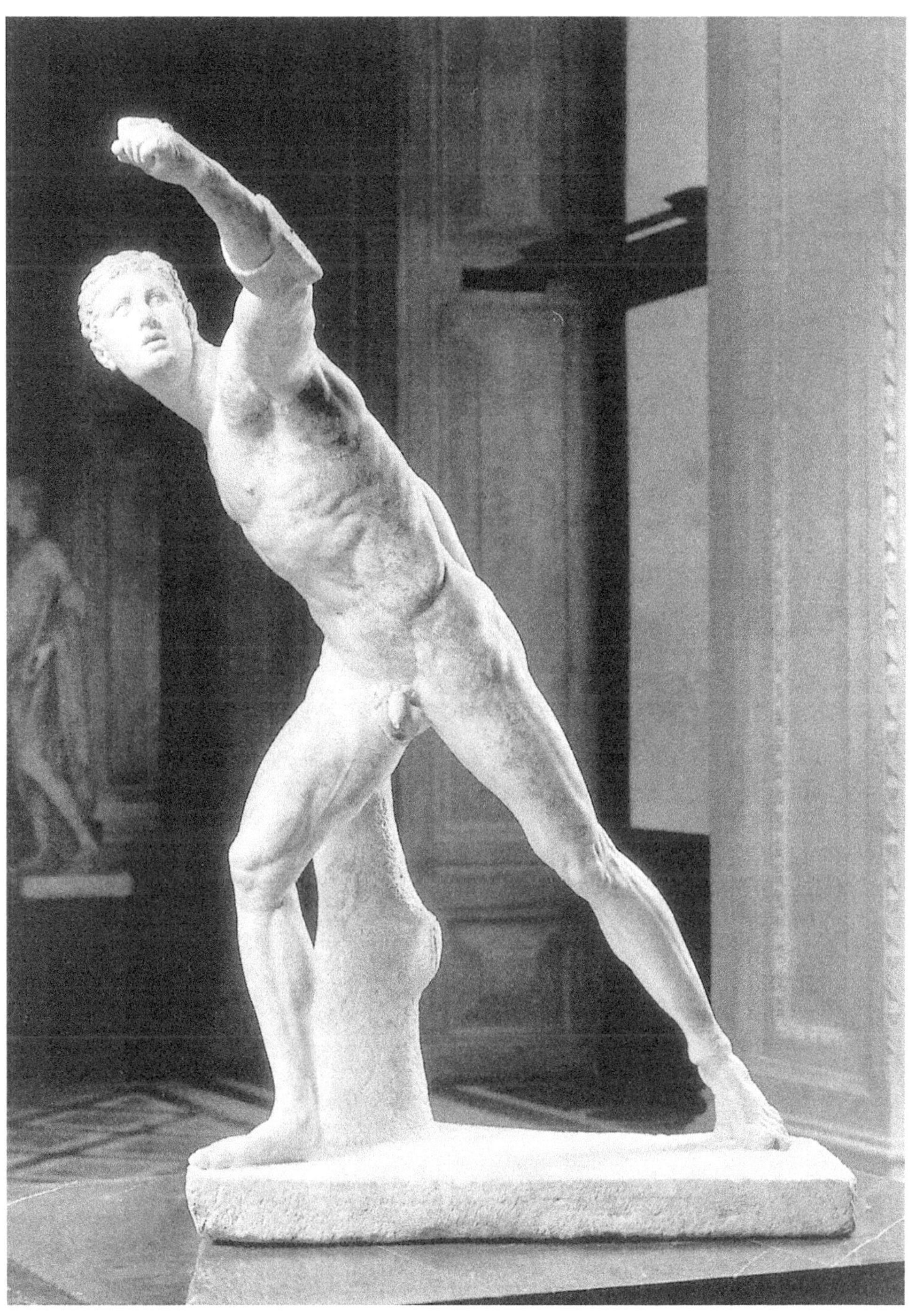

FIGURE 3
Borghese Gladiator, marble, length (from head to left heel): 1.99 m. Paris: Musée du Louvre. Photo: © Photo RMN—Hervé Lewandowski.

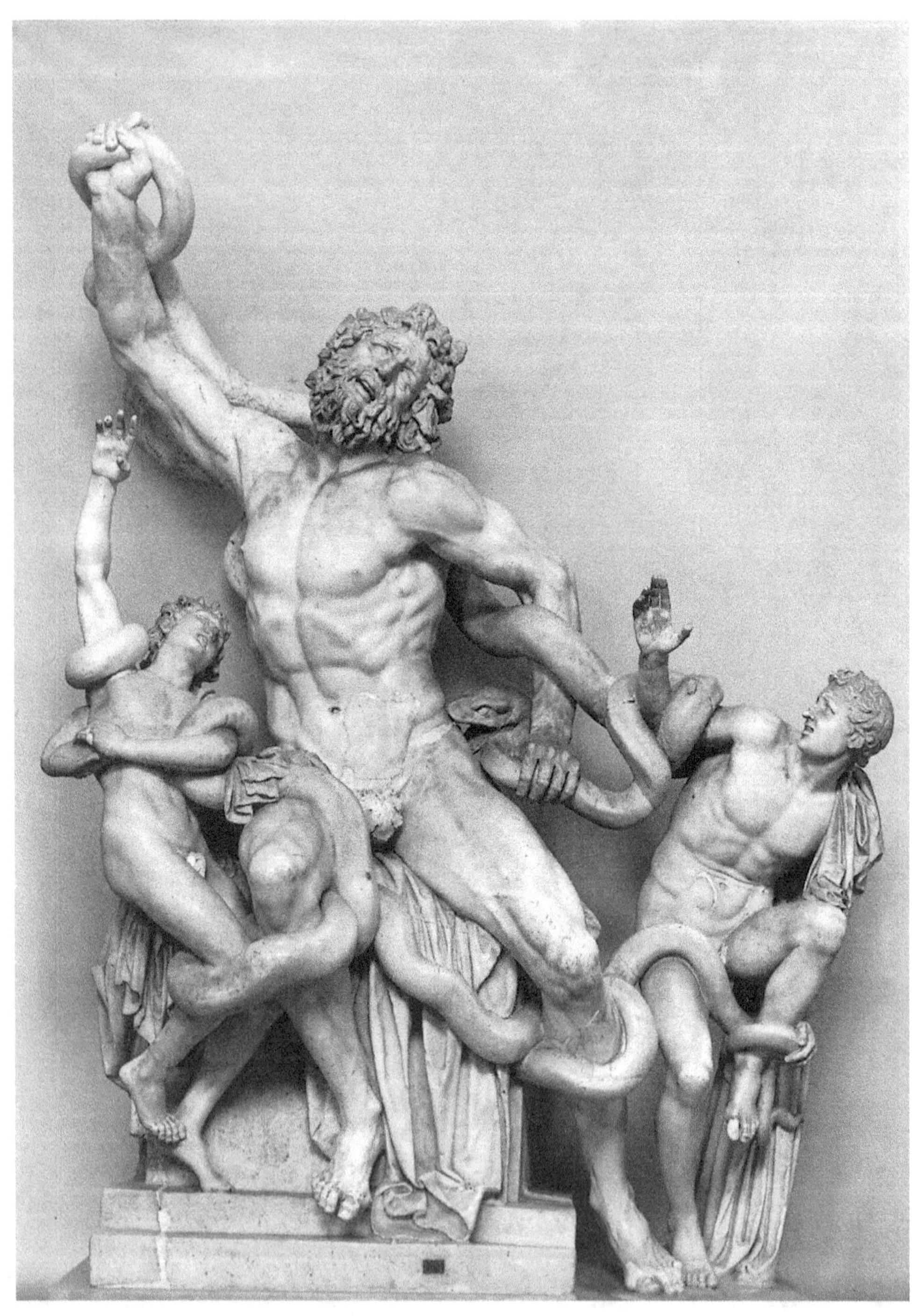

FIGURE 4
Laocoön, marble, height: 2.42 m. Rome: Musei Vaticani (Belvedere Courtyard). Photo: Vatican Museums.

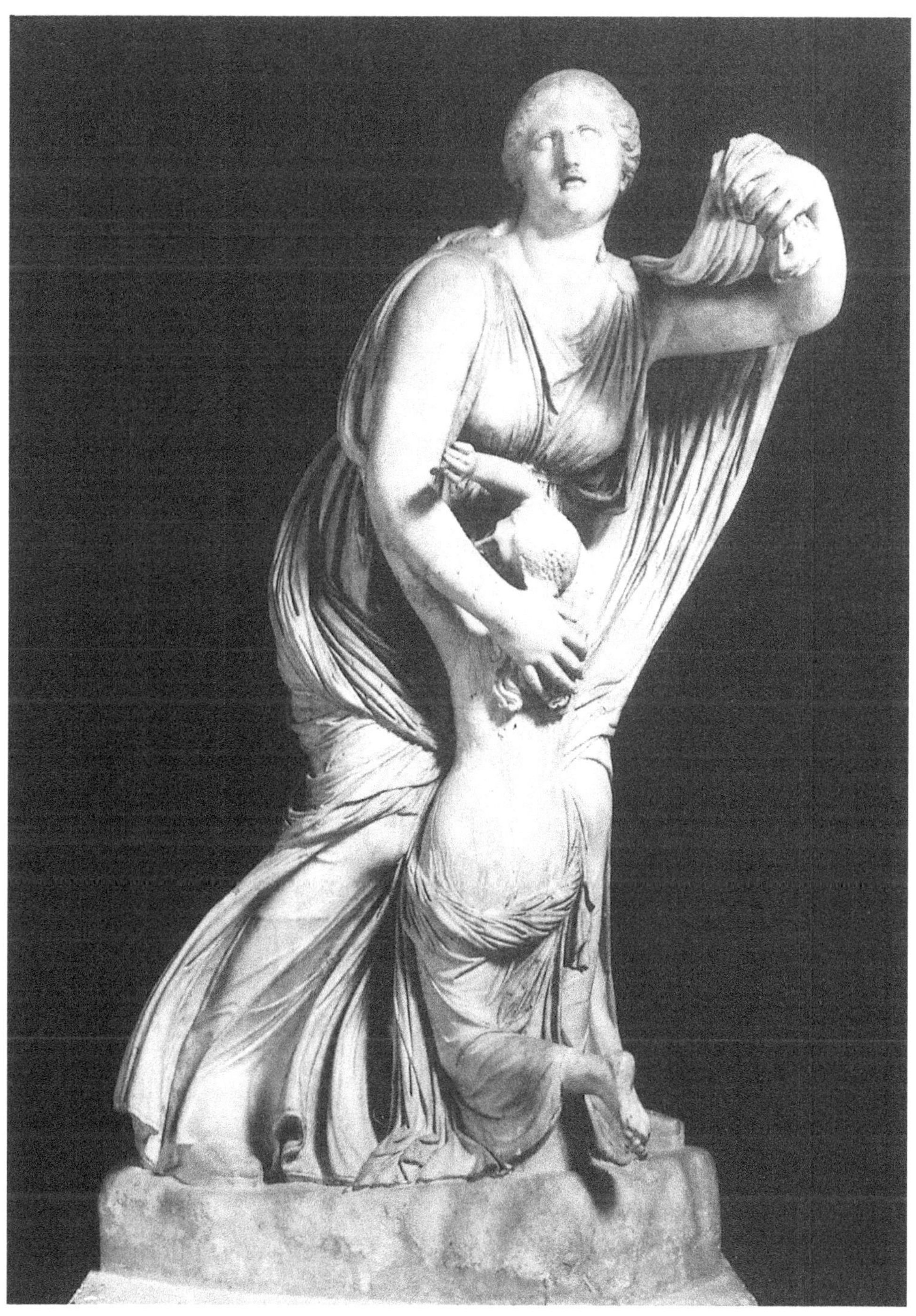

FIGURE 5

Niobe and Her Youngest Daughter, marble, height: 2.28 m. Florence: Galleria degli Uffizi. Photo: © Photo Alinari, Florence.

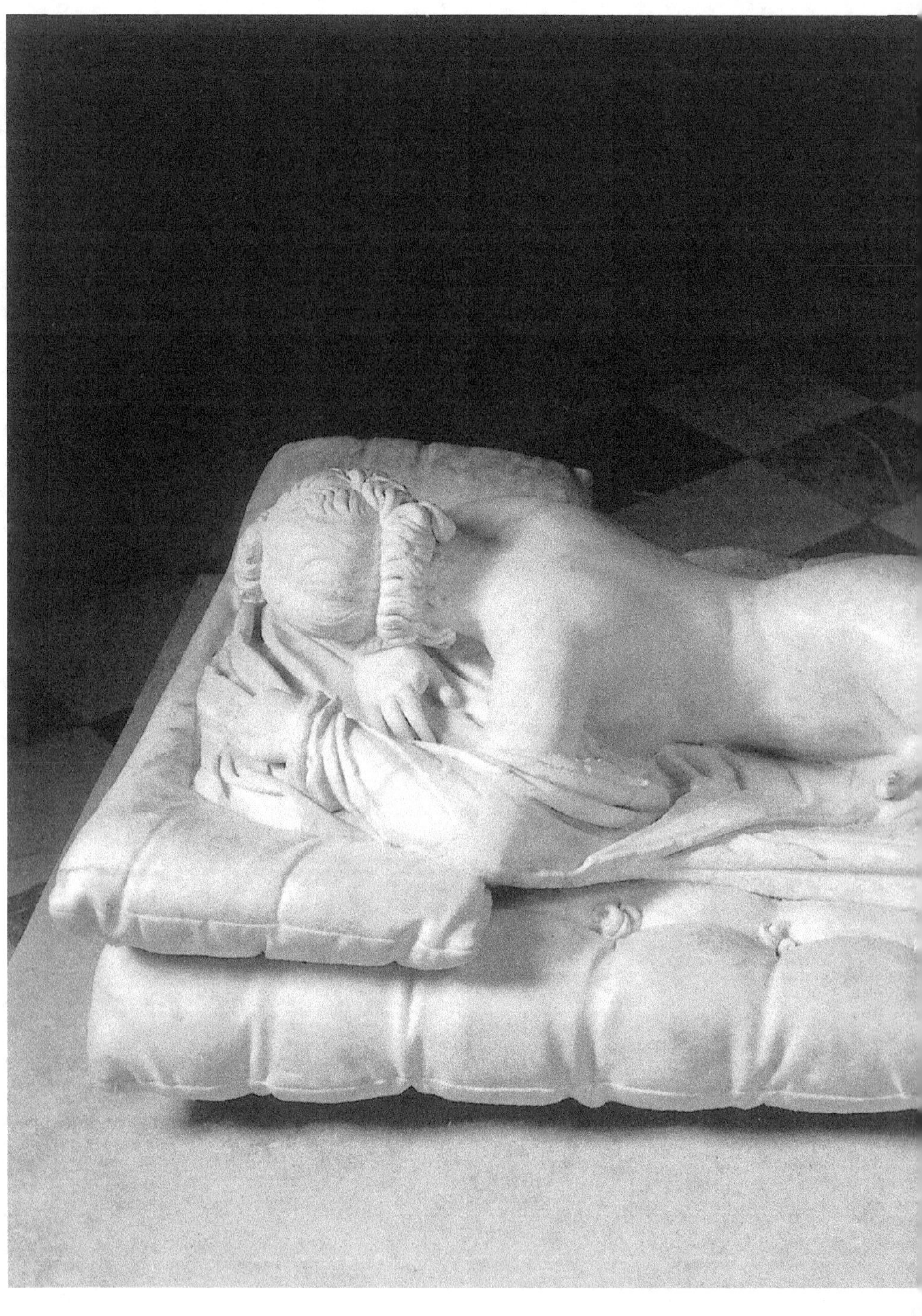

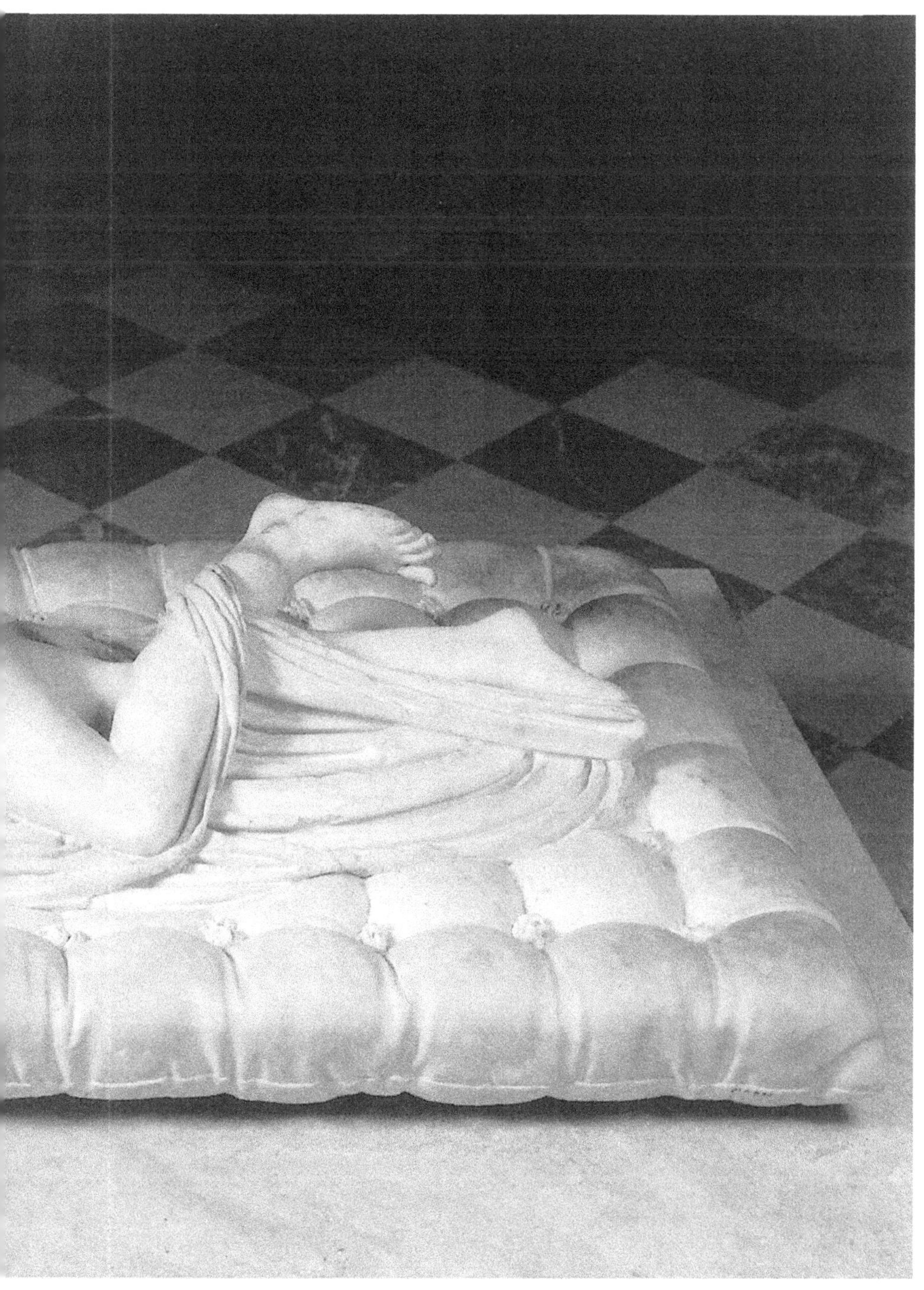

FIGURE 6
Hermaphrodite, marble, length: 1.47 m. Paris: Musée du Louvre.
Photo: © Photo RMN—Hervé Lewandowski.

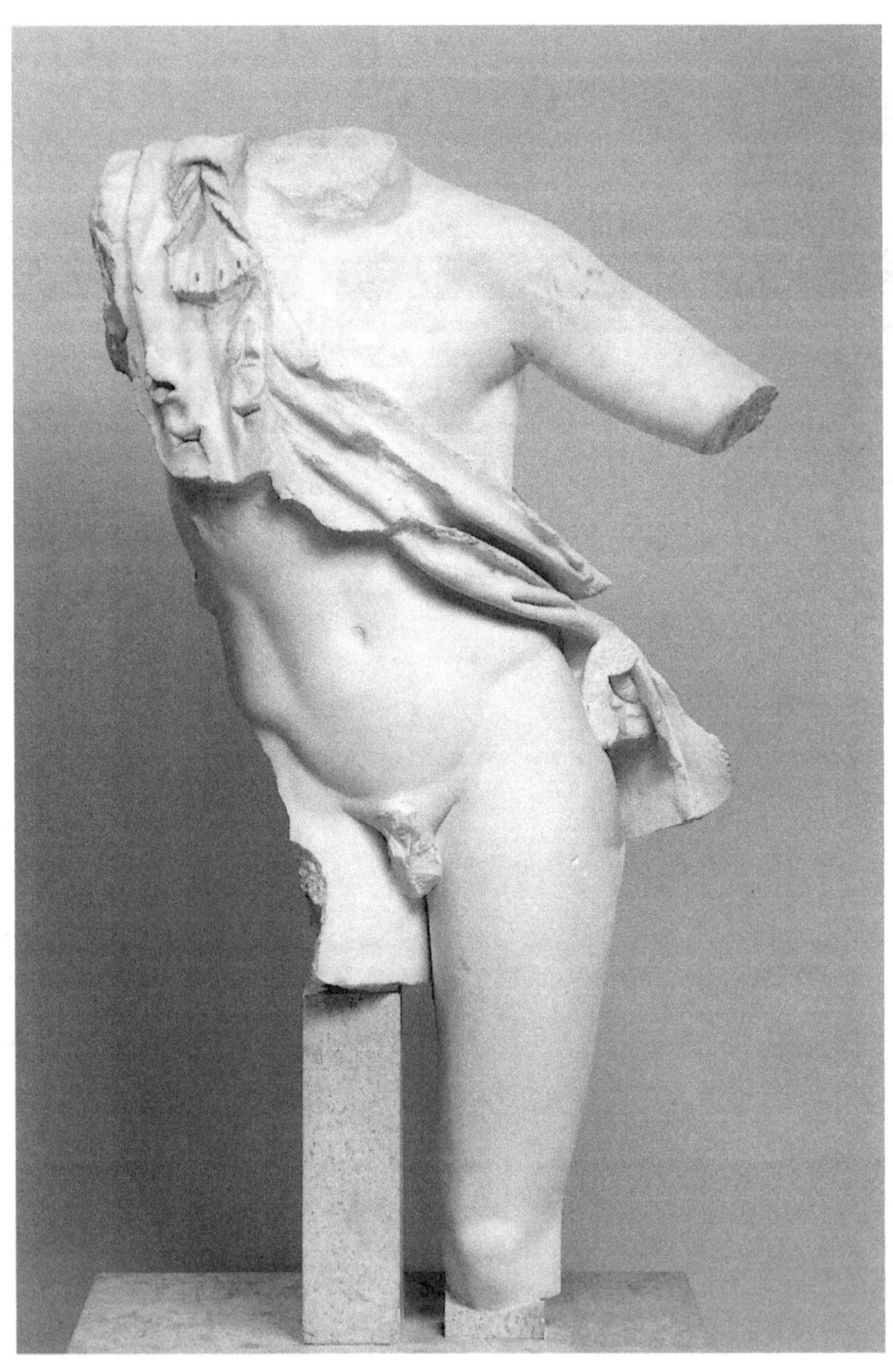

FIGURE 7
Resting Satyr (Bacchus), marble, height: 1.21 m. Paris: Musée du Louvre. Photo: © Photo RMN.

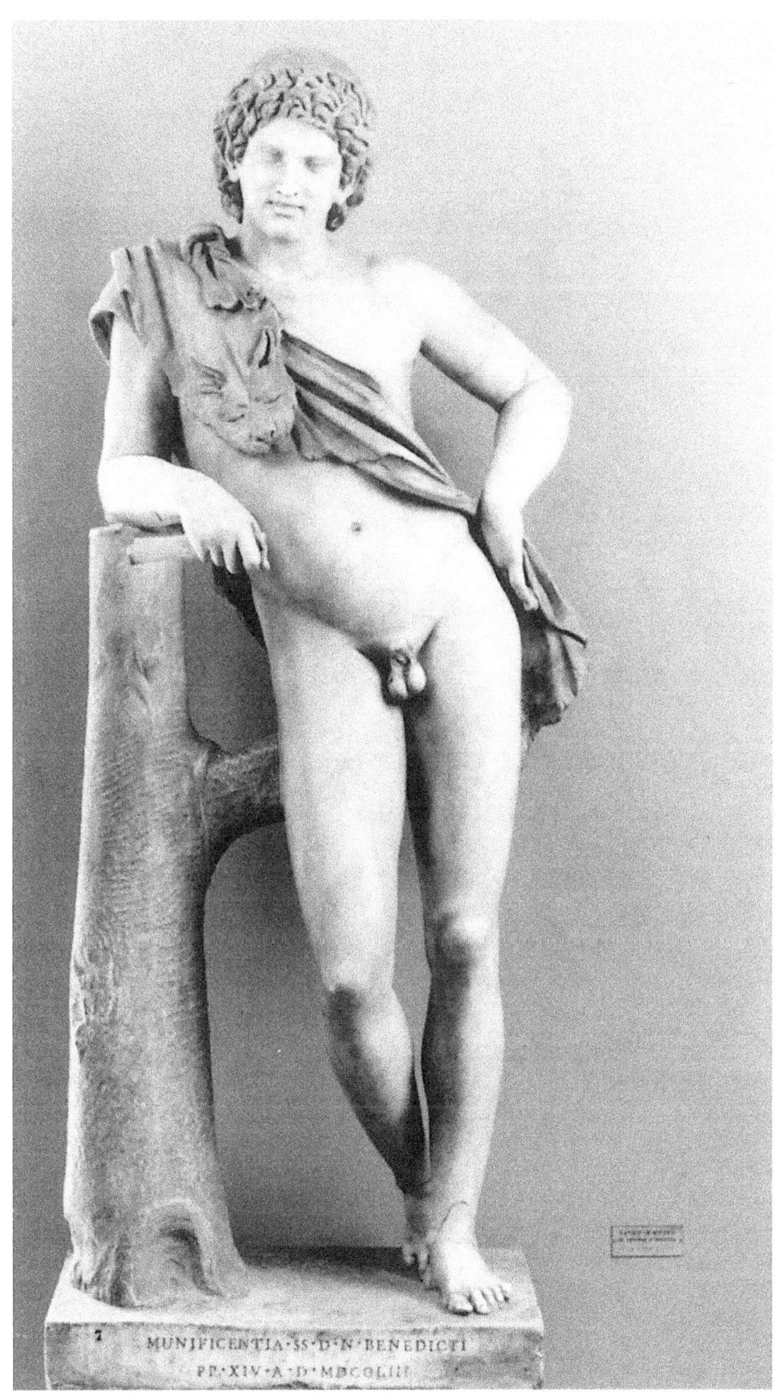

FIGURE 8
Resting Satyr (Bacchus), marble, height: 1.7 m. Rome: Musei Capitolini.
Photo: Archivo Fotografico dei Musei Capitolini.

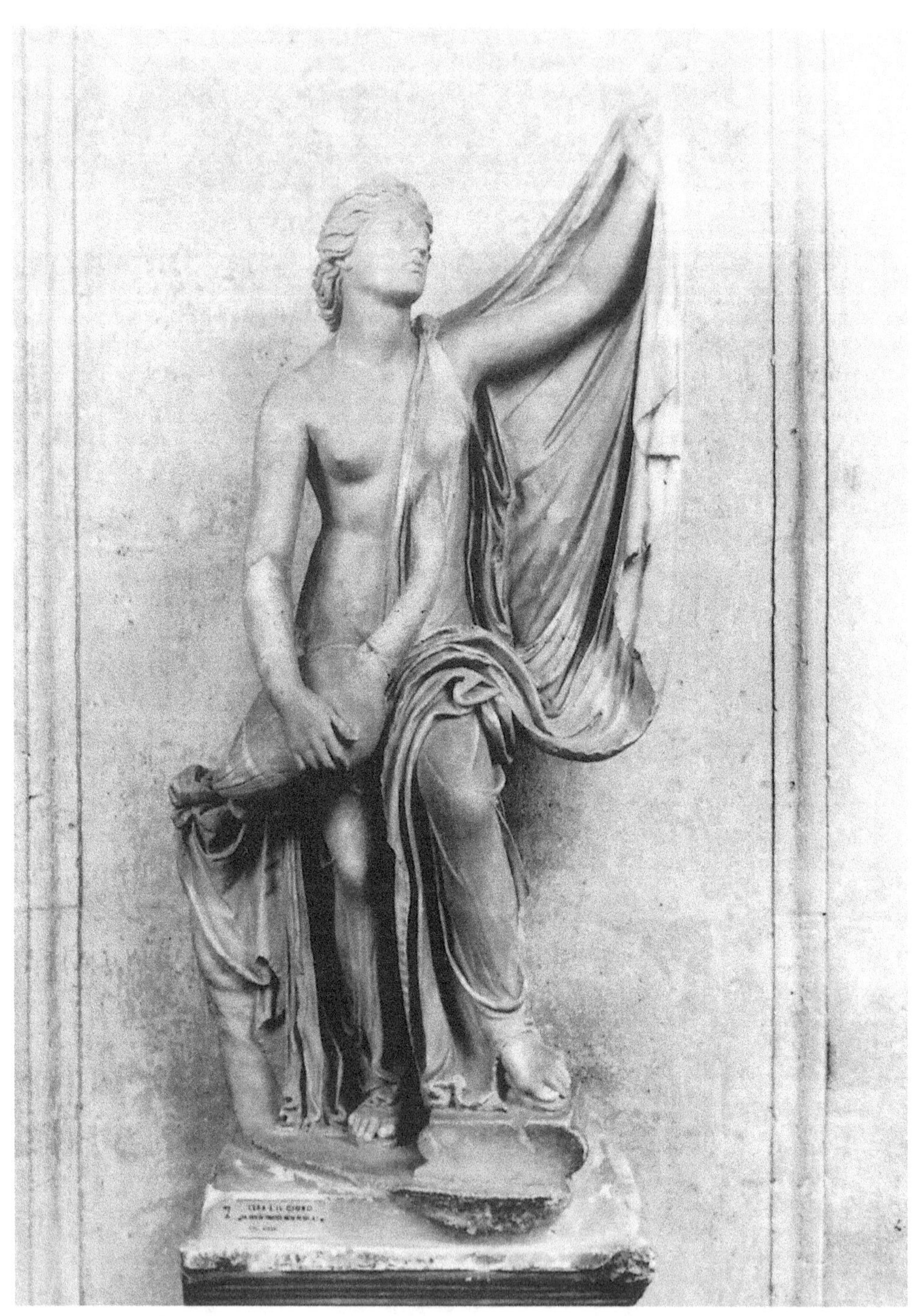

FIGURE 9

Leda and the Swan, marble, height: 1.32m. Rome: Musei Capitolini.
Photo: Archivo Fotografico dei Musei Capitolini.

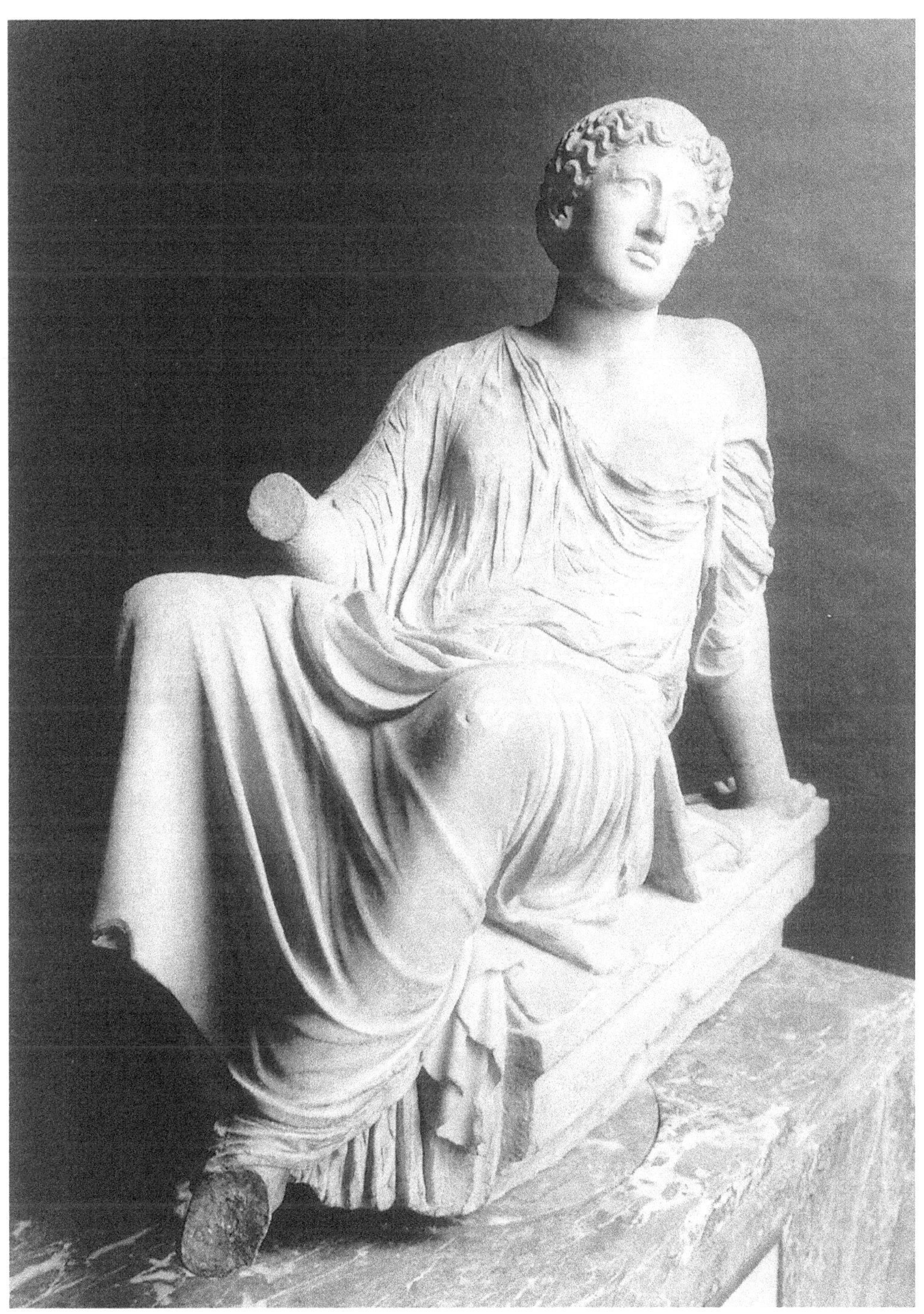

FIGURE 10
Danae (Barberini Suppliant), marble, height: 1.01 m.
Paris: Musée du Louvre. Photo: © Photo RMN—Peter Willi.

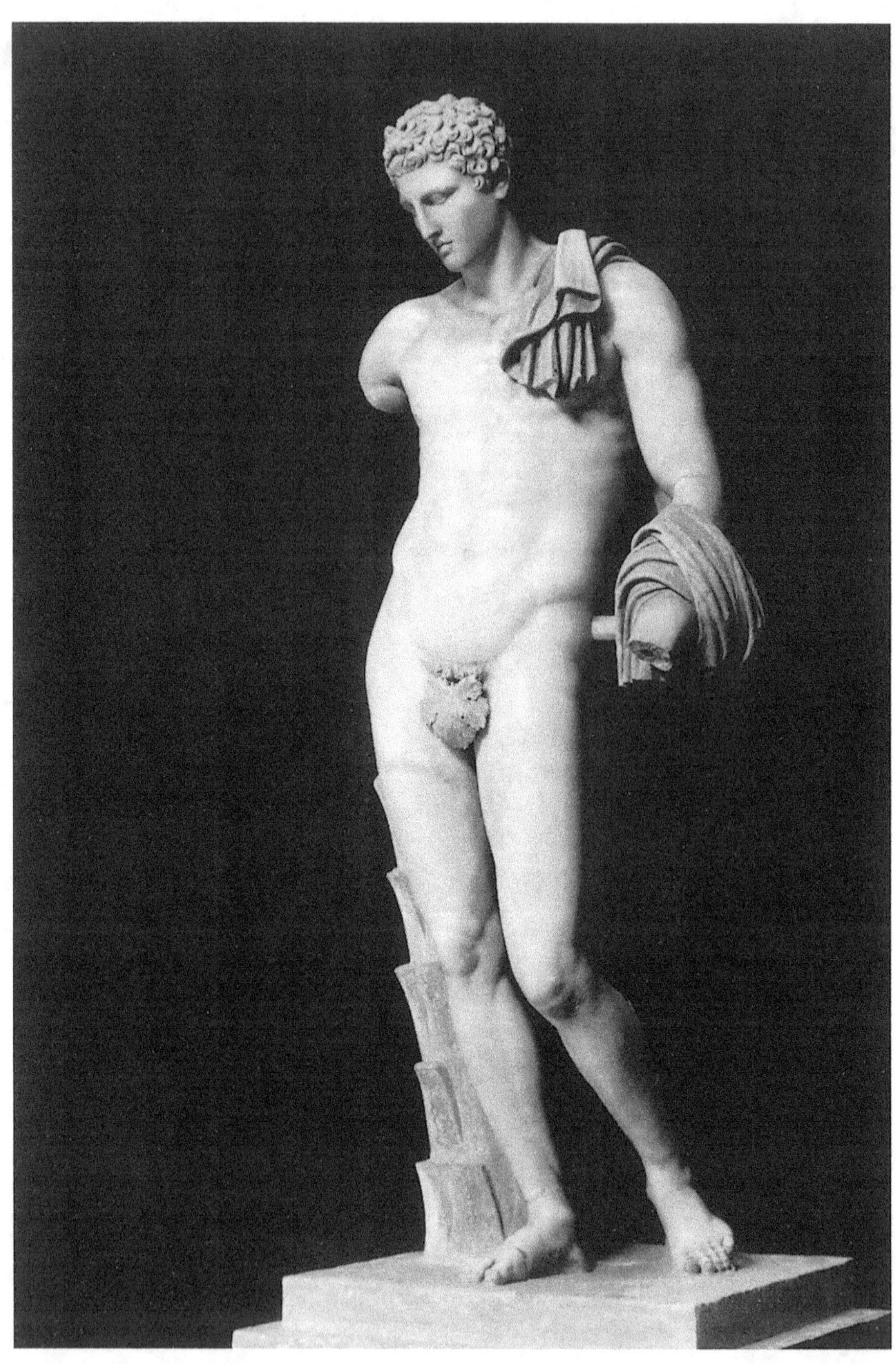

FIGURE 11

Belvedere Antinous (Hermes), marble, height 1.95 m. Rome: Musei Vaticani (Belvedere Courtyard). Photo: Vatican Museums.

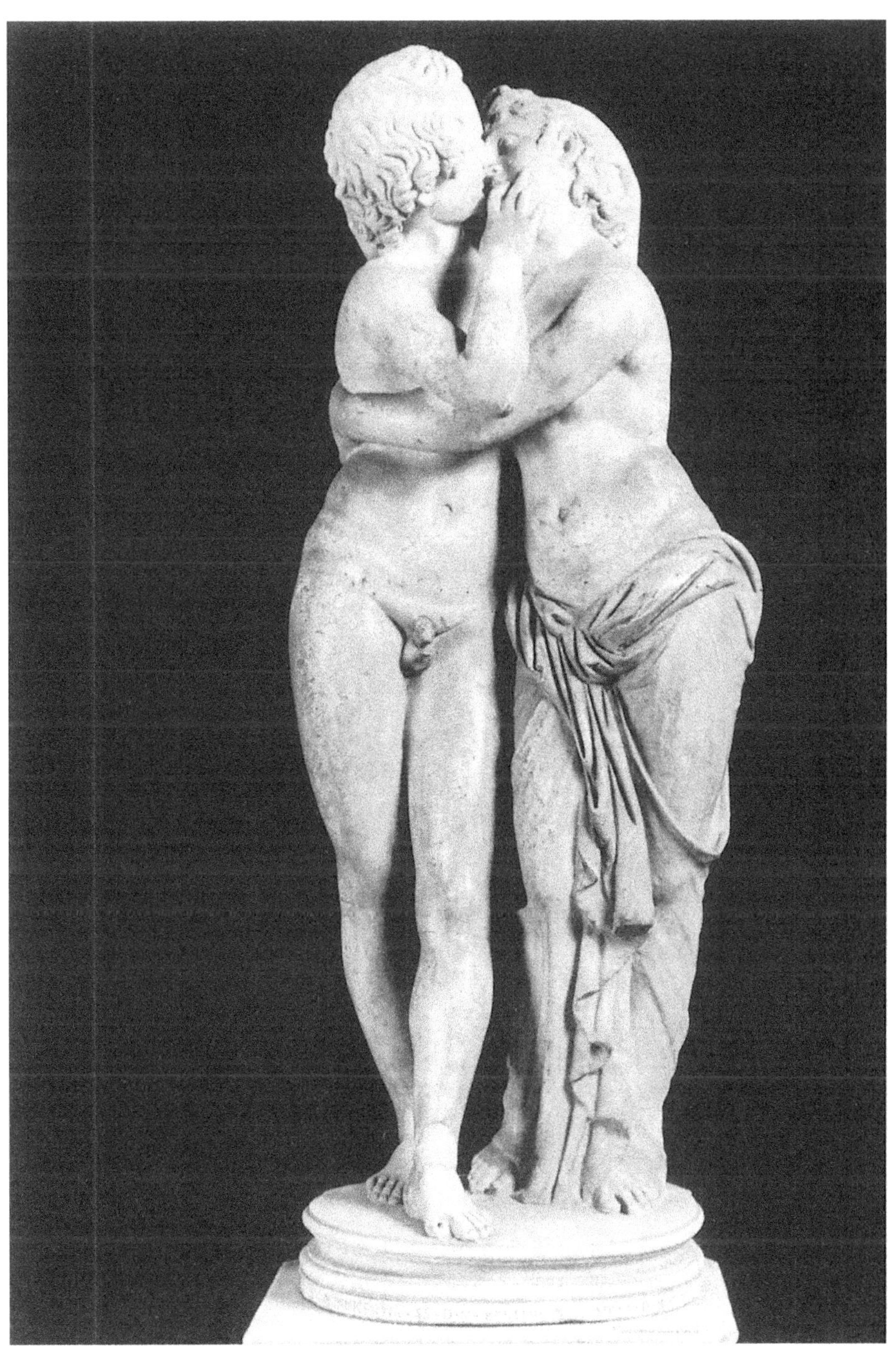

FIGURE 12

Psyche and Cupid, marble, height: 1.25 m. Rome: Musei Capitolini.
Photo: Archivo Fotografico dei Musei Capitolini.

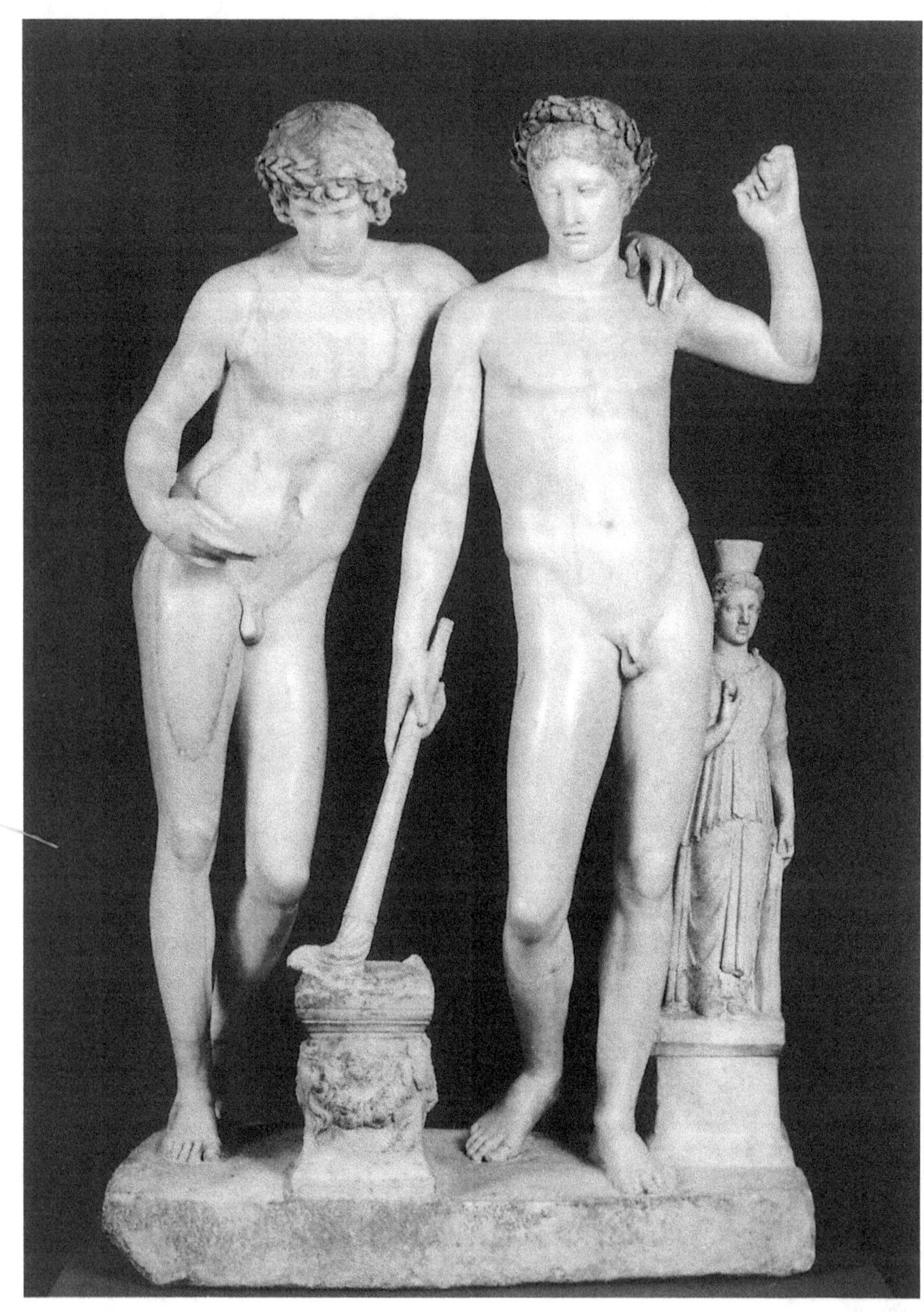

FIGURE 13
Castor and Pollux, marble, height: 1.61 m. Madrid: Museo del Prado.
Photo: Museo del Prado.

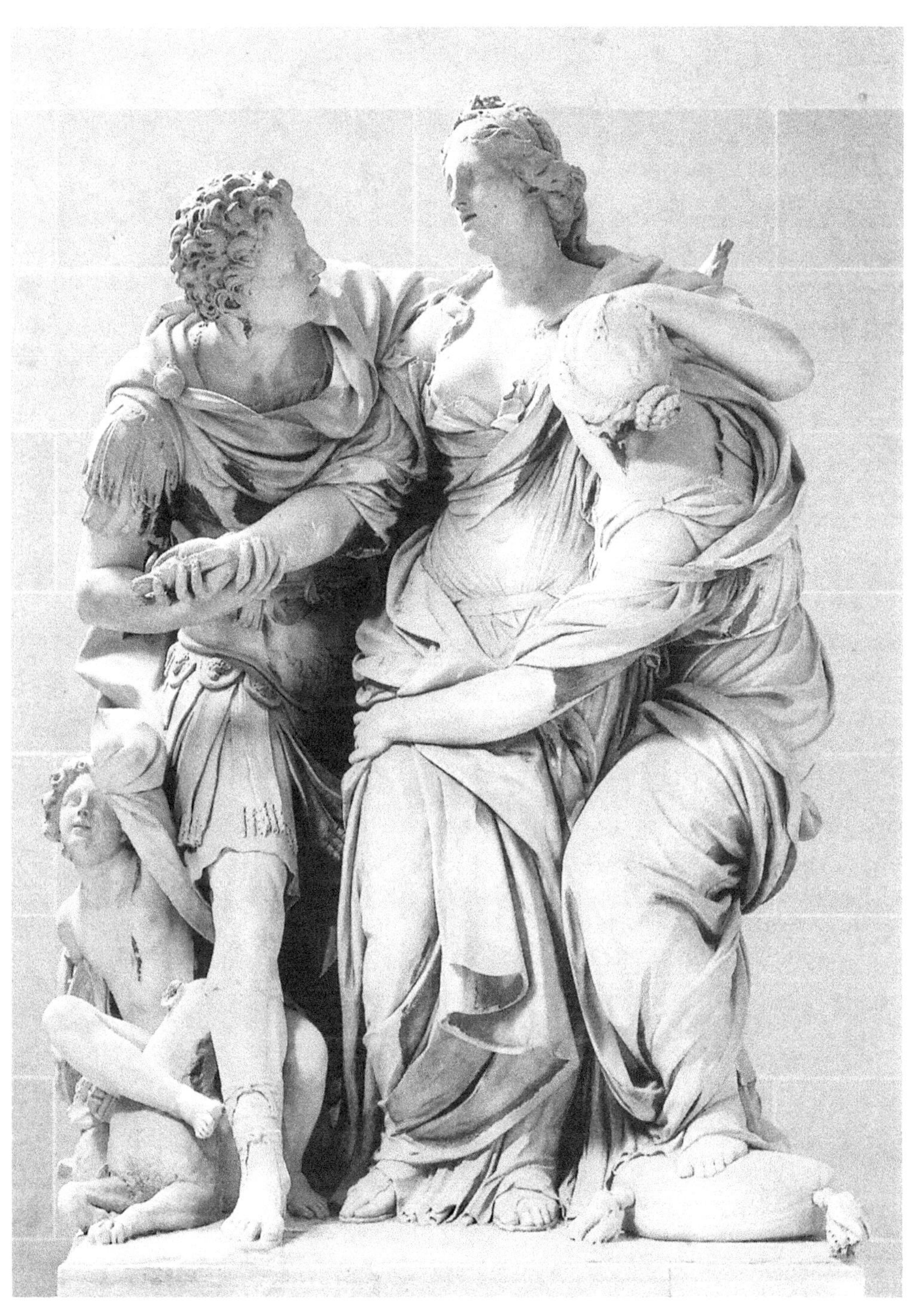

FIGURE 14
Arria and Paetus, marble, height: 2.65 m. Paris: Musée du Louvre.
Photo: © Photo RMN—R.G. Ojeda.

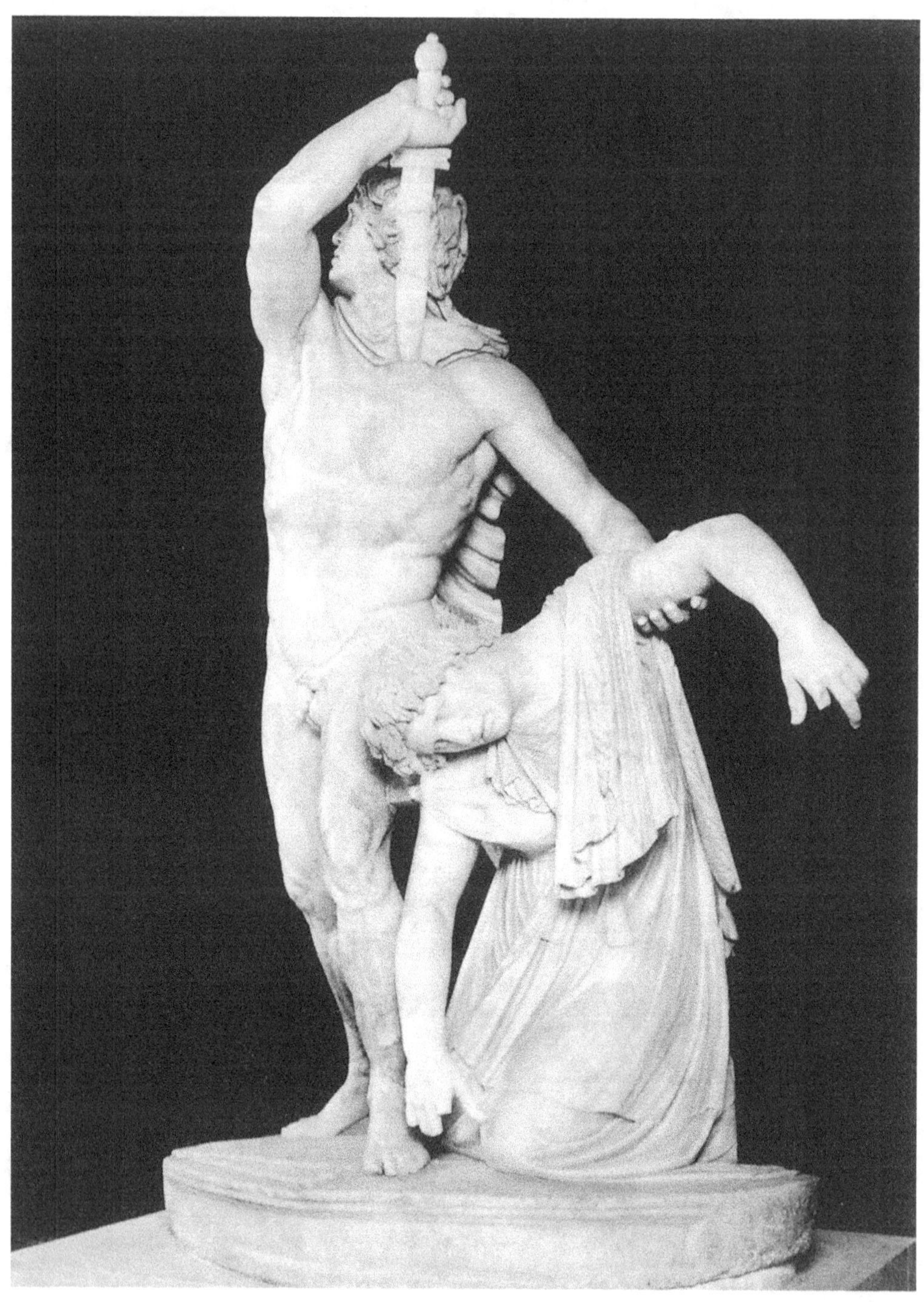

FIGURE 15

Gaul Committing Suicide with His Wife (Arria and Paetus), marble, height: 2.11 m. Rome: Museo Nazionale Romano (Museo delle Terme). Photo: Ministero per i Beni e le Attività Culturali—Soprintendenza Archeologica di Roma.

of the artist and the lover of art they are as soft and animate as clay. It is as if they *move, pulsing* with *life,* but not in thick swollen cords. Winckelmann says that a heavenly essence, diffusing itself like a gentle stream, has filled the contour of the figure.[24] Everything lives, and the less the tranquil sense of touch, in the obscure range that is proper to it, perceives the body as something disjointed and broken, the more it *intimates* what lies within.

The ancient artists were prized and highly famed for their capacity to give *form to hair.* They have been praised for this by lovers of art and literature, but they have not been well understood by the theoreticians. Where and how did they give form to hair? There and in the manner in which it could be given form, such that even a blind person could identify it as a beautifully formed ornament. The decorative head of hair that adorned the gods and goddesses (for a Roman without hair is always presented as needy and aged) made them *into bodies,* without being made to seem a mere mass of stone. The hair falls in beautiful, heavy locks, or in the case of women, whose hair needs to be softer, it is bound up on the head rather than floating free. No bacchant is depicted with fluttering hair, for it is not allowed to flutter. The hair of the swift and raging Apollo "plays around his head as if agitated by a gentle breeze, like the slender, waving tendrils of the noble vine."[25] On some it sits like a beautiful mantle (ἐξουσία),[26] on others it is coiled in rich furrows. It is never allowed, however, to cascade downward so as to hide the form of the back as it does in some paintings of Eve. Even when the subject is Aphrodite born from a shell or bathing, the hair is wet and as if formed into chains; it falls down in an orderly fashion rather than in thick bushes. The sense of touch must never encounter the hair as a bush but always as gentle, pliant masses that infinitely entwine. For painting, however, hair is color, shading, and chiaroscuro, and it can be arranged in a far freer manner.

The delicacy with which Greek artists indicated the *eyebrows* on their statues is well known; they *suggested* them with a fine, sharp *line* rather than *modeling* them out of separate filaments or masses of hair. Winckelmann identified these lines as the "eyebrows of the Graces."[27] I, too, believe that this is the case—in the realm of art. In nature such sharp, naked lines are something quite different. This is also true of the nature of the Greeks, which was not and is not different from our own, as is confirmed by the statements and writings of travelers. Enough! It suffices to observe that in art these "eyebrows of the Graces" are made for the *soft, still sense of touch.* Can one imagine in their place bushes *(stupori)*[28] or arches that rise up? Who has not remarked upon the crude and unpleasant effect made by the trace of any individual hair or by any evenness or protuberance when a plaster cast is removed from the face? Each isolated hair causes us to shudder, like a nick in the blade of a knife; it disturbs the form and does not belong to it. For this reason, Greek artists simply *suggested* the presence of the eyebrows; they marked the *division* between the brow and the eye with a gentle ridge, allowing the sense of touch to glide over it and to *intimate* the rest.

Some statues are given *eyeballs.* If this is to be tolerable, they must be merely *suggested;* the majority of statues, and the best, have none. It was the bad taste of the last few centuries that made things opulent, rather than beautiful, by the addition of glass or silver. But it was in the *youth* of the art, when monuments were still made of *wood,* that statues were *colored.* In the most beautiful ages statues did not require drapery or colors, eyeballs or silver; art stood naked like Venus, and this was all the adornment and riches it needed.[29]

As everyone recognizes, painting is a different matter. Painting is made for the eye and speaks directly to the eye: for color is simply the division of a ray of light, the language of vision. It can allow the hair to entwine and unravel like silk and to float freely in the air. Paintings are not blind; they look and speak. *Omnipresent light* can *give life* to a single luminous point and make it into an eye that penetrates the soul. A painting is *a panel of color, enchantment, and luminosity.*

3

To what extent can sculpture give form to things that are ugly? And to what extent can this be done in painting?[30]

Answer: To the extent that the relevant sense allows it. In the case of painting this is the sense of sight; in the case of sculpture, the sense of touch. Both, however, rest upon the same foundation.

The painter who used his skills to conjure on canvas a decomposing corpse that caused the viewer to hold his nose—rather than have the figures in the painting do so, as in a work by *Poussin*[31]—was (if the story is true) undoubtedly a wretched painter. The sculptor, however, who offers to our sense of touch the revolting form of a corpse, the food of worms, so that we become one with it and are anointed by its repellent and suppurating fluids—for such a hangman of our pleasures I can find no fitting name. I can turn my eyes from a painting and recover by looking at other things. But a sculpture requires that I slowly and blindly feel my way forward, until I register a gnawing at my flesh and bones and the shudder of death along my nerves.

Aristotle justified the representation of ugly or repellent things in art by pointing out that "it is natural for human beings to pursue ideas and to take pleasure in imitation."[32] Where both of these *can* take place and where the pleasure in receiving new ideas *exceeds* the feeling of repulsion, this justification may be valid. Everyone knows that as regards contemplation and the awakening of ideas the sense of *touch* is the obscurest, tardiest, and most sluggish of the senses, but that it has *primacy* and stands as the *judge* when it comes to feeling beautiful form. Forgetful of imitation and ideas, it simply feels what it *feels,* awakening a response of inner sympathy that is all the more profound for being obscure. A ravaged, ugly, or distorted form, *Itys* torn to pieces, *Hippolytus* in Euripides' play, *Medea* contorted with rage, *Philoctetes* in the worst convulsions of his illness,[33] someone in the throes of death, or a decomposing corpse struggling against the worms—all these are repugnant when encountered by the feeling hand as it advances. Instead of encountering ideas, it encounters horror, and instead of the imitation of the things that are, it encounters the terrible degeneration of that which is *no more.* Atrocious art that bestows form upon deformity! When Saint Bartholomew stands before me half flayed, with skin hanging from his torn body, and cries out to me, *non me Praxiteles, sed Marcus finxit Agrati,*[34] I am supposed to touch and feel this monstrous and unnatural nature! Hideous object, speak not, quit my sight! Praxiteles could not have made you, for he would never have *desired* to make you. What Greek would ever have been capable of feeling and carving you from the stone, of conjuring forth your broken form?

Everyone can see that what is valid for sculpture is not necessarily valid for painting and the other fine arts, not even for the art of intaglios and coins. Recently, certain crude people have treated these very different arts as if they were one and the same. Moreover, in their supposed refinement they have categorized as ugly creatures that neither God nor Man would recognize to be so. Are lions and tigers, snakes and lizards, hippopotamuses and crocodiles *ugly* because they are *terrible,* because they awaken our horror and fear? How beautiful is the lion, both in nature and in the art of the sculptor! How gracefully the snake winds itself around the staff of Aesculapius![35] Is the tortoise an unworthy pedestal for gods and goddesses? No, for the very armor of Minerva is decorated with images of fear and terror, with snakes and medusas. It would never occur to anyone to hold such creatures for the *principal subject* of art. Humanity is seated upon the throne and is the sacred subject of sculpture. But what fool would forbid these things as adjuncts, accessories and pedestals, simply because God's creatures appear ugly *to him* and because he is frightened of spiders? How many noble horses have merited the statue more than the rider? Pindar,[36] and even the Lord Himself,[37] have dedicated to the horse the most splendid monuments. The more beautiful and unbroken the form of an animal, the more it nestles and entwines itself around us, the closer it comes to gods and humans by serving at their feet, the greater its *entitlement to be sculpted by human hands.* It goes without saying that a faithful dog or a beautiful horse will be sculpted more often and will be preferred over the heavily armored hippopotamus or the mountain of bones that is an elephant. But by nature, and in its proper environment, a lizard is no more ugly than Leda's swan or a dolphin that nestles at the foot of a sea goddess.

Here, too, the ancients made finer and truer distinctions. Why should a *centaur* or the *Minotaur* not be sculpted? Consider the beautiful epigrams in *The Greek Anthology* that are dedicated to these two creatures.[38] How powerfully and beautifully the human body emerges out of the horse, rearing up in the same way!* We wretched moderns term sirens, fauns, and satyrs ugly and *deformed* because they are so unlike an Apollo. But this was not the case with the ancients. They were not repulsed by tails, horns, or goat's hooves as long as they were appropriate to the circumstances. For us moderns, by contrast, everything has to be an altarpiece in the temple of holy *theoria.* The ancients even held the Calydonian boar worthy of an epigram—so long as it was of the right sort.[40]

The ancients avoided ugliness where it had to be avoided—in *human* and *divine bodies. Lessing*† and *Winckelmann*‡ have both sufficiently argued that when representing powerful emotions, suffering, or discord the ancients avoided showing deformity wherever possible. They chose the most favorable moment, brought the highest pitch into accord with the gentlest, or introduced a foreign element in order to alleviate the tension in the features. Here we need only think of Medea, Niobe, and Laocoön. Philoctetes limped, but he was a hero who deserved to be seen as he was. The sculptor Lysippus tilted the twisted neck of Alexander up toward the heavens, so that he felt himself the lord of

* *Anthol.,* l.IV.c.7. [See editor's note 39.]

† *Laocoön,* 9ff. [See editor's note 41.]

‡ *History of Art,* 142ff. [See editor's note 42.]

the world.[43] Imitation εἰς τὸ χεῖρον[44] was forbidden on threat of punishment. The Olympic victor had thrice to claim the prize before he was granted a portrait statue, although he could expect a noble statue with his first victory.[45] I consider these to have been the best means, to have imposed the right constraints in order to prevent ugliness of *forms*. Ugliness of form *can* easily be avoided. Although it costs a great deal of effort to feel it and to bring it forth, once such ugliness exists it endures forever. Imperceptibly, it is taken for something natural and as a presentation of truth, causing untold damage to later generations. Consider the description of the enchanted palace in Sicily built by a crazed human demon that is to be found in the account of one of the finest travel writers.* Here we can see the effect that even just reading about ugliness of form has upon our brains and our nerves.

It would be harsh to extend a law that was *primarily* and *exclusively* concerned with form, that is to say, with the living form of the human body, to another type of art that knows nothing of such things, but is concerned instead with appearances and with shadows and patches of color. Painting is an enchanted canvas as large as the world and as human history; not all the figures it depicts either can or should be made into statues. I, too, love what is beautiful more than what is ugly, and I take no more pleasure in seeing contorted figures on a canvas than I do in everyday life. At the same time, I recognize that excessive delicacy and too refined a sense of propriety ultimately renders the world we inhabit as narrow as our rooms; the freshest and deepest sources of truth, excitement, and energy dry up into miserable puddles. In a painting no one figure is everything. If all the figures are made equally beautiful, none are beautiful. We are left with the monotony of a uniform parade of long-limbed, straight-nosed, so-called Greek figures, who simply stand there before us as inactively as can be imagined. Within a few days or hours they seem so vacuous that for years afterward we cannot bear to see any other masks of this sort. I gladly admit that I prefer it when God has made the central protagonist beautiful rather than ugly. But must every *ancillary figure* be beautiful, too? Every angel who is hidden in a corner or stuck behind a door? The *lie* of beauty can make a mockery of the whole scene, including the story and the character of the deed or event—the whole is turned into a deception. It generates a *false note,* something *insufferable* in the painting as a *whole.* This may give pleasure to the foolish Grecophile, but

* Brydone. [See editor's note 46.]

it will be a source of anguish to the true admirer of antiquity. Our own age, including the richest subjects of history and the most vital historical figures, together with all feeling for truth and determinacy, are in this way ultimately antiquated out of existence. Those who come after us will look back with astonishment at such attempts to render our theory and our art beautiful and will ask what sort of people we were. What sort of times did we live through? And what brought about the wretched illusion that we should live in *another* time, among a *different* people under a *different* sky, that we should *abandon* the great canvas of nature and of history, or pitifully *corrupt* it. Enough about the great law of *ugly* beauty in an art that is properly the *imaginative representation of appearances* and the *canvas of the world!*

4

To what degree are the forms of sculpture and of painting constant and eternal? Or are they subject to the diversity of ages and peoples, changing as these change?

Answer: The forms of sculpture are as constant and eternal as pure and simple human nature; the forms of painting are an image of their age and vary in accordance with history, peoples, and times.

If an entire people considers corseted bodies and small Chinese feet to be beautiful; if it prostrates itself before them on divans and sofas as if they were altars of grace; if it puts feet into narrow shoes and lifts them up on high heels like statues upon pedestals, such things speak for themselves and all commentary is superfluous. The same is true of tapered corsets, breasts forced upward, hair styled into a tower, and dresses as wide as tents. In everyday life such artifices contribute to improving certain aspects, or if you like, everything, by means of *secondary concepts,* or *customs,* whether they be ancient, modern, or completely novel. A small face under a tall coiffure, breasts protruding from the funnel of a body, tiny feet beneath a mighty tent—all make an unattractive impression. As the great Montesquieu observed, such things stimulate the imagination and encourage it to glide upward or downward, which is no doubt the real purpose of the whole exercise.[47] But now imagine the *entire figure* with its tower, its tent, and its inverted cone *as a statue,* and you will see that the imagination no longer glides at all. We behold then a hideous and unnatural creature of lechery and gothic constrictions; the body is distorted and all good form destroyed. If this figure still possesses any remnant of feeling, how it must wish for the ample form or the ungainly silver foot of a Greek Ceres or a Thetis![48]

A statue, then, is a *model of good form,* and Polykleitos's *Canon*[49] remains the most enduring law of any human legislator. Just as there is one region of the earth in which beautiful proportion is a product of *nature,* so God gave to one people of this region the space, time, and leisure to divine and *give shape* to things that would remain permanent monuments for all subsequent ages and peoples. In the full exuberance of their youth, the Greeks felt their way toward *works* that were complete and pure and beautiful. The monuments they produced are the classical products of their feeling hands, just as their writings are the work of their sensitive human minds. They stand like lighthouses in the tempestuous ocean of time, and the sailor who steers by them will never lose his way. It is a tragic and irreplaceable loss that the barbarians destroyed so many of them. And yet it is perhaps for the best. The preservation of too many could have oppressed us and led us astray, just as the city that today possesses the greatest number lacks the spirit to comprehend or renew them properly. We should treat them as friends, not idols. Instead of subjugating ourselves to them, we should treat them, as the name itself suggests, as *exemplars* that present to us in bodily form the truth of ancient times, making us aware of the proximity and distance between their form of life and our own.

We are forced to admire the great *simplicity* with which the statues of the Greeks stand there and bear witness even to the obscurest sense. This sense does not encounter anything uncertain, confused, or mutilated. It does not meet with any repellent attributes, such as a gag silencing the mouth, for the sense of touch would encounter only a strip of cloth instead of a mouth. There are no heads of dogs or stags that serve as allegories or emblems. Even the most necessary attributes are kept as distinct and separate as possible. Hercules does not wear his lion skin wrapped around himself, but at most slung over his arm, or he simply stands there *as himself,* without lion skin or lion. The goddess of love is represented without burdensome attributes: *she herself* is the goddess of love, clad only in her naked charms. The serpents coil around Laocoön, but not in the way described by Virgil. For if they were shown thrice encircling his throat, waist, and legs, he would appear to the unseeing sense of touch as a monstrous body of man and serpent.[50] Only his legs and feet are bound in the serpents' grip; his left hand remains free, seizing one of the creatures. The same is true of Laocoön and his children: they are treated as *one* being, unified by the struggle against their opponent. Even in the smaller parts of the body, most of which are broken off or have not survived, the attributes are kept *sepa-*

rate, specific, and *clear.* The forms of the gods and goddesses were so distinct to the ancient artists that they did not *need* any attributes. Other statues were dedicated only to the most ancient heroes of fable and legend, above all those from Homer. The rest had to be accompanied by a legend or an inscription. In short, the ancient artists gave *contour, shape,* and *character* to their statues with such *economy* and such *precision* that they formed a zodiac of gods and men through which the sun runs its course year after year. Praise be to you, O noble ones, who established these human forms in the fixity of the firmament, offering places of refuge and repose. May your ashes rest in peace and your works endure forever!

It would be a mistake to impose the same uniformity on painting, where there is nothing to fix hold of and preserve, for painting is the whole of *God's enchanted world upon a luminous canvas.* It is *light* alone that gives painting unity, a vast, unutterable, *miraculous unity* that brings together everything new and diverse. A statue does not have its own light: it exists constantly in light and is designed for another, more comprehensive sense. By contrast, an *enchanted ocean* flows in every direction from a *single point of light* on a flat canvas, *binding together* every object into a new and unique creation. I do not understand how certain theorists can speak so contemptuously and dismissively of what are termed *modeling* and *chiaroscuro.* These are instruments of genius that are employed by every student and every master. They are the *eyes* through which the artist saw, the *sea and rays of light* in which he bathed everything and from which every contour and every countenance worthy of praise depends. Whoever lacks all feeling for this *luminous divine sea of light* in faces in drawings or paintings should watch a child play with paint and observe. *Modeling,* the divine instrument of light, presents an *enchanted world,* and no matter how varied its interpretation by each new master it remains something *enduring* in painting. *Chiaroscuro,* as long as it is not made to depend on the fixity of sculpture, borrowing from what is dead, creates a magic panel of *transformation,* a sea of waves, stories, and figures, each of which dissolves into the other. This is how it ought to be. May only the spirit of the artist and the instrument of the eternal Creator endure!

PART THREE

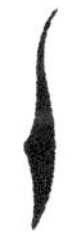

It is an accepted proposition among theorists of the fine arts that only the two *finer* senses afford us ideas of the beautiful and that *fine art* exists only *for these two,* that is, for the eye and for the ear. This proposition has been demonstrated; consequently, it must be true. On this basis a large number of other propositions have been demonstrated, and the house of cards that is the theory of *all* the fine arts and sciences stands there well formed, "measured and arranged by the staff of the writer."* My own staff should come no closer than the space required by the statue I contemplate.

Father Castel's ocular harpsichord has revealed to us sufficiently clearly what a fine art of colors *for the sense of sight* would be like and the sort of effects it would have.[1] So many reasons have been put forward that are false or only partially true as to why this art did not succeed. The real reason, or at least the most natural, is that without the contribution of a more fundamental sense, the sense of sight affords us only a *panel of light and color,* and thus only the flattest and emptiest pleasure. A creature without hands who could see but could not feel forms or what is expressed through forms—in short, the head of a bird—might take pleasure in such an art, but no one else. In painting, too, the *forms* of things

* Judges 5:14; Numbers 21:18.

must provide the *principles* and the *substance* of art, although only as they are shown related to and revealed by light. But since forms are derived from a different sense, this sense, too, must be sensitive to *concepts of the beautiful;* for even the brightest of the other senses cannot do without it. The eye is only the initial guide, the reason of the hand; the hand alone reveals the *forms* of things, their concepts, what they *mean,* what *dwells* therein. A blind sculptor, even a sculptor who was born blind, would be a wretched painter. But in *sculpture* he is not at any disadvantage and would probably even surpass a sighted peer.

"But what of *Hogarth's* line of beauty?"[2] The line of beauty and everything that has been deduced from it tells us nothing if it does not appear on *forms* and is not thereby accessible to the *sense of touch.* Trace ten thousand lines of grace and beauty on a flat surface—if they are not part of a form and do not acquire meaning in this way, they will not give any more pleasure to the eye than the scribbles of a child. Even if they only appear on a corset or on a saucepan, at least they appear on *something* and so are accessible to another sense, that is to say, accessible first to a sense *other* than the eye. I fully understand that a flickering flame of fire or the surge of the sea as it rises in each wave cannot be grasped as something solid.[3] But this does not mean that such things cannot be grasped or touched by the *soul.* In short, just as the plane is only an abstraction from the body and the line an abstraction from the bounded surface, so neither are possible *without bodies.*

It is remarkable that *Hogarth,* who is said to have *discovered* the lines of grace and beauty, put so little grace and beauty into his *paintings.*[4] His figures are generally ugly caricatures, but full of character, passion, life, and truth, for these are the things that made an impression on him and that so vigorously *held* the attention of his genius. He revealed in his practice what sound theory reinforces still further: that all contours and lines in painting depend upon *bodies* and upon *vigorous life.* If this art only gives the appearance of things upon a flat surface, this is because it cannot do otherwise. Its sense and its medium, *sight* and *light,* prohibit it from giving any more. Nonetheless, it struggles with both as best it can; it seeks to raise the figure from the ground and to give wings to the imagination so that it no longer merely *sees,* but *enjoys, touches,* and *feels.* The lines of grace and beauty are not *self-subsistent;* they derive from *living bodies* and seek to return to them.

I shall give just one example. What an act of daring to draw a flat *line* and to use it to construct things that properly speaking can only be derived from the most authentic pleasures, feelings, and experiences that belong to our *embodied* existence. Anyone who has tried knows how difficult it is to reduce a *body* to a *flat surface,* to render something *complete* and *living* into a figure bounded by a *line.* Let us presuppose that this line is *faithful.* Is it not our plastic sense that enables us to *transform* the line back into a *body,* the flat figure back into a *rounded and living form?* How *few* are able to do this only God and physiognomy know![5] Nothing more foolish remains to be said for or against the silhouette, the *sbozzo,*[6] the mere *outline,* the *drawing of nothing.* This would be the case even if all those who can see were to possess the ability to transform this *nothing* into a faithful *something,* and to intimate no more and no less than the mere outline revealed by this delimited *nothing.* The silhouette communicates so *little* in order that it may be *precise, faithful,* and *complete* in what it does communicate. The surest sign that we understand what it says is when we can *conceive it as a body,* that is, when the *silhouette* stands before us like a living *bust.* This is extremely difficult, however, for most silhouettes are characterized by a lack of fidelity and by negligence and ignorance on the part of their maker. Nor are all faces in profile sufficiently eloquent to produce a silhouette in which the relation between the parts can reveal the full living form. The black and white surface of a silhouette gives free rein to the caprice of the imagination: captivated or hostile, it may project onto the silhouette whatever it pleases. After God and money, the last five years of our century have witnessed nothing which has been subject to so much misuse, superstition, slander, deceit, and foolishness as the profile of the human head. The silhouette arose from the very first attempt at painting, carried out by a young girl in love who intended it to remain forever under loving hands and eyes.[7] Now it has been relinquished to the seven sons of Sceva,* who, possessed by an evil spirit, use it to predict the future and to *judge.* This is done, as they say, *after Lavater,* but without his discernment, his spirit or his heart. Give me a moderately faithful statue of a head or a bust, even if it is only a fragment, and no matter how dead it may be (for it is no more than the mask of the dead), my slow and simple feeling will gladly give back in exchange all your glorified ideals, Anubis figures,[9] painted silhouettes, and paintings after silhouettes.

But enough on this subject! Let us approach a statue as if enveloped in holy darkness, as if we shall discover there for the first time the *simplest concept* and the *meaning of form,* the richest, noblest, and

* Acts 19:13–16. [See editor's note 8.]

most beautiful form of the *human body.* The greater the simplicity with which we commence this task, the more the mute image will speak to us. Like Hamlet we must remove from our minds all trivial copies and all scribbled letters and characters.* The hand and fingers of our inner spirit must bring to life the sacred, energy-laden form that has come from the hands of the Creator and is pervaded by His breath. May the breath of He who made it enter into me so that I may remain true to His work in what I feel and write!

No hand can grasp what dwells in the *head,* that is to say, under the *skull* of a human being. No finger of flesh and blood can discover from the external *rind* the tranquil or raging forces that lie concealed in this abyss. Just as He conceals all other sacred places, the Godhead has covered this sacred height, the Olympus or Lebanon of the body's growth, the dwelling place and workshop of its most secret workings, with a sacred grove.† We shudder to comprehend in thought the sphere of Creation. A bolt of lightning issuing from chaos can embellish and illuminate the world, or it can destroy it and render it desolate. The northern peoples termed the sky *the head of Ymir* and imagined that it had come forth from his skull.[11] If it is true that microcosm and macrocosm are in agreement and that Man must be conceived as a part of the greater compass of Creation, we should not look elsewhere to draw comparison with the summit that forms the crown of our existence than to the sky, where an infinite blue recedes in immeasurable distance above the haze and the clouds, encompassed only by *His* hand and inspired by *His* spirit. Here we encounter nothing but mystery and profundity. At times of strenuous work, we sometimes feel that the *senses* and the *vital spirits* are close to their portals, the *eyes,* and to their table, the *brow.* The *eternal* forces, however, are felt as closer to the center; it is as if the rear portion of the head offers a barrier to the play of our senses and our thoughts. Although strokes and other illnesses appear to confirm much of this, the inner fabric of the mind is of too fine a nature to allow us to identify a conclave of cardinal forces, such as was attempted by Huarte.‡ It is as if we were to seek to describe the inner structure and juices of a pomegranate from its outer skin. Much can be intimated, however. When we see a head cut open by an axe, made into a watery pumpkin by a rifle shot, or reduced to an empty

* all trivial fond records / all saws of books. [See editor's note 10.]

† The hair.

‡ *Exam. de ingenios,* chap. 3. [See editor's note 12.]

sphere of vapor, or when it rises up to a pointed hummock like the head of Thersites,* or, finally, if it is made into a burning volcano like the head of the cyclops,[14] we cannot think on such things without a shudder. It seems to me that our *feeling for the whole goes beyond the contour.* Except in certain extreme cases, the smallest movement or the slightest change in what we feel can make the mere individual into a god, or an angel into a devil. *What person knows a man's thoughts except the spirit of the man which is in him?*[15] Through the small cave of the *ear,* and through that which only appears to be a portal, the *eye,* come two wondrous worlds of light and sound, of images and words. These enter into the vault of the mind, combining, lifting up, separating, and dividing the waiting sea of our thoughts and powers. Were the outer covering of this treasure as diaphanous as a soap bubble, still it could never be subject to a certain and *exhaustive interpretation.* What palace or casket of mysteries has written without what it contains within? And if the inner life is of such a character that it never *could* be written down or revealed from the outside? For what is the head other than the dwelling place and workshop of the most secret divine forces? The *face* is a table and reveals what it is able. But that which lies buried deeper, what the divine power has hidden beneath the shades of night—*scrutari, scire nefas.*[16]

The significance that is attached to the sacred grove of this Olympus, to the *hair of the head,* is revealed to us by the variety of different forms of hair that the ancient artists bestowed upon their gods and heroes. On reading in Homer that heaven and earth shook when *Jupiter* let down his ambrosial locks, Phidias was seized by his heavenly spirit.[17] Apollo descended in rage from the summit of Olympus:

χωόμενος κῆρ,
τόξ' ὤμοισιν ἔχων, ἀμφηρεφέα τε φαρέτρην
ἔκλαγξαν δ' ἄρ' οιστοὶ ἐπ' ὤμων χωομένοιο
αὐτοῦ κινηθέντος.[18]

This would have been impossible for the hair of Alcides, even if he had stridden with his club in a similar state of rage.[19] In the same way, a *Diana* can never have the hair of a *Venus* or a *Rhea.*[20] Familiarity with the rich texts of these ancient authors would explain a great deal if modish taste and debased art had not deprived them of every appearance of naturalness. I have yet to see a powerful man with soft hair,

* *Iliad,* B.v.219. [See editor's note 13.]

or a woolly sheep with the courage of a lion. The "knotty soul" of the young Hamlet, suggested in his name,[21] rises up to his hair to form "combined locks":

> As the sleeping soldiers in th' alarm
> His bedded hairs, like life in excrements
> Start up and stand on end—.[22]

The natural *growth* of hair, the way it *falls, parts,* or *curls,* is of particular significance. As Mohammed entered paradise he saw Moses with hair like flames of fire, but the mild Jesus appeared as if his shoulders flowed over with the milk and water of life. The father of all gods and all men[23] would be risible rather than venerable if his head were bald, for Olympus could not then be shaken by the splendid, heavy locks that descend from his sublime brow. Were Samson to have been given soft flowing hair when he tore out the pins of the Philistines, the pins would have remained where they were.[24] I do not know which philosopher observed that men whose hair grows in numerous thick curls are also confused in their thinking and that their thoughts cannot be made orderly or brought to rest until both their hair and their minds are straightened by old age. The ancient saying, *long of hair, short of sense,* is well known, and it is true in the way such sayings can be. On the other hand, we know how powerful an impression it makes both on those to whom it happens and on those who see it when the hair of someone who is still young *falls out* or *turns white.* When an almond tree blossoms early and its upper branches shun the rest and lose their leaves, it acquires a crown, but one that is gained through sorrow.[25] Sometimes the heat of the sun burns the hair away and the head is like a mountain in the clouds; it is higher than the others and looks over them, but it is naked and sad. Think only of the horrid shine on Swift's bald head. But how pleasing and important is the hair on the head of a child. Just as *Plato* has Socrates play with the hair of Phaedo,[26] so in the *Messiah,* as I remember, an angel plays with the hair of Benoni.[27] For women, the hair is a covering to protect their decency, but it is also a snare and a silken band of love.[28] According to the ancient fancy of the Orientals, the hair was the birth and dwelling place of a myriad of angels.

The head sits upon the *neck,* which is robust and free or soft and pliant as a swan; the summit of Olympus reveals where and what it ought to be. The neck is an *ivory tower* says the oldest and truest song of love.[29] It is the neck that effectively indicates not so much what goes on inside a person's head, but how they carry their thoughts—and how they carry themselves. One person will maintain a free and noble posture, another will lean forward submissively, ready to be a sacrificial lamb, and another will show the strength and firmness of a Hercules. If the neck is deformed, if it is crooked or concealed beneath the shoulders, if it is covered in bear fat or with the wattle of a turkey and grunts like a wild pig, this is highly revealing of a person's true character and actions. Both what the Greeks termed the *beautiful nape* and what non-Greeks term the throat and the Adam's apple are of greatest significance here.

I come to the *human countenance*, to the tablet of God and the soul. Holy mantle, protect me from the glittering splendor and let me glimpse the person within!

It is particularly upon the *brow* that the *light of the face* is revealed. It is the seat of light and joy, but also of dark sorrow and fear, of stupidity, ignorance, and wickedness. In a word, when we refer to a person's *fundamental disposition* in the strictest sense, and not merely to his mind or to what will become his character, the brow acts as a luminous table of bronze.

I lack the guile to distinguish between the brows of philosophers and poets, or of rulers and the ruled, and to range them alongside one another in a cabinet. But I fail to understand how anyone can ever look upon *a brow* with indifference. Behind this partition the Graces sing or the cyclops hammer. The brow has clearly been formed by Nature herself in such a way as to illuminate or to obscure the face. The *upper* part of the brow incontestably reveals different types of character. Firstly there is the thick plank of a brow, or what is often termed an iron wall, that reveals the stupidity of an ox. It is covered in bumps and swellings like those on the shields of Cuchullin or Achilles, with the difference that although likewise inherited from the owner's father it has not been adorned by Vulcan with a host of figures.[30] It is a *biceps Parnassus*,[31] upon which someone who has climbed to the summit may gently sleep. Another type is like a shingle roof that rises up toward the heavens; the bearer of such a brow is someone who never lacks a system. Yet another possesses the deep furrows of Cronion or Cronos;[32] weighted with sorrow, these raise us into the clouds without our knowing what our purpose is or what we should do there. Finally, there is the type of υλη,[33] the *repertorium universale*[34] that most of the time fails to find itself. I delight in the youthful Greek brow that lowers the sky and prevents it from curving into immeasurable distance. In early childhood the hair falls like a veil over the brow in order that the kernel of life may grow in privacy, peace, and blessed tranquillity. It required a *Bernini* to reveal once again the *perfrictam frontem*[35] and to remove from his statue the locks of hair that are better suited to the sacred gods than to us.[36] Since the wise of the world are themselves often short of light, they require a gaze that can penetrate a plank of wood in order to read the brows of others who, precisely for them, lack light: throughout all strata of society it has become the fashion to wear the hair parted and sleek to the head.[37] Whoever has but little to contribute to a decorative display of lights would do best to carry his small candle to the window or even to bring over his hearth fire. The same also holds for the light of the brow. Some shine in such a way that it is impossible either to derive pleasure or to warm oneself. The light of a glowworm would be preferable.

Where the brow sinks downward, the *mind* appears to pass into the *will.* When Juno saw Hercules enter Olympus she must first have been reconciled to him by seeing the knotted brow that she herself had caused through her fateful decrees and the danger, sorrow, and worry that she had lain upon him. It is here that the soul draws itself together in order to offer resistance, revealing the *cornua addita pauperi*[38] that assist it when it goes forth blindly in blessed obscurity and yet carries the victory, or when, like the Indian idol, it succeeds in recovering the laws that lie hidden in the mud of the abyss.[39] Even if it were only Winckelmann's dream that the beautiful torso of Hercules leans upon his club, recalling within his bright brow the dream of a life full of effort upon the earth, it is certainly a beautiful dream.[40] I have yet to see an ox before the plough or a Hercules at the rudder of the state who did not possess such supports at times of rest and such weapons at times of war. They are often to be seen on the forehead of a suckling child, an imprint of his future destiny, although none can read the open book of his smooth, bright, round, and radiant brow.

Beneath the brow lies its beautiful confines, the *eyebrows.* When gentle they are rainbows of peace, but they can also form into taut arcs of discord, sending rage and clouds up to the heavens. In both cases, they are *heralds* of *disposition* and messengers from heaven to earth. What has been said of the hair in general also applies to these slender lines. This remains the case whether they are graces or furies: either angels dwell in every gentle filament of hair or flames shoot forth. No pen can describe the impression they make when they form into hemispheres, porcupine bristles, whirls, and zigzags. On the other hand, how smoothly the hand and the eye trace the line of an eyebrow that is soft and gentle, gliding across it like a barque of life in the beautiful light of dawn or dusk. I do not know of any trait that could be more pleasing and attractive to the person gifted with understanding than a keen angle, decisive yet gentle, between the brow and eye. It gives to the profile an unutterably interesting character. It is the knoll upon which genies and Graces bask in the sun before bathing in the source of the beautiful, shaded eyes.

The *Greek profile* is so famed I fear to speak of it. Every connoisseur knows that the straight line from the brow to the nose is characteristically Greek and that, for this reason, it must be beautiful. But when he sees this feature in a living person and fails to find it beautiful he notes in his copy of *Volkmann* or *Richardson,*[41] just like a tailor in his diary, "beautiful: but only on Greek statues because they are made of stone." With this his expertise reaches its end. If a source of beauty is not to be found in *living nature,* it is not to be found in dead statues. And who can mistake it there? Who does not recognize that a nose whose root is bent deep under the brow possesses, so to speak, a needy beginning, and that the breath of life that should reach the soul is obliged to pass through caverns and tunnels? Who, on the other hand, does not respond to the undistorted form and to the sublimity, volume, definition, and majesty of gaze that is given to the face when the front of the nose fails to give the impression of leaping over a ditch. Who, finally, without such elaborate considerations, has not observed the *regality* of Juno's nose or the infinite *freedom* with which Apollo lifts his nose *forward, inhaling scents and aromas?* Perhaps there is only one part of the earth that can allow large numbers of people to acquire this profile. Perhaps, too, the reproach of the Italians that beauty of form declines beyond the Alps is not so unfounded after all. If true, however, I would trace its cause more to the character of the *people* than to the effect of the *land* or the *climate.*[42] However fine the features presented by his people, the artist could not proceed without ennobling his subject. The nose gives *depth* to the entire face. It is the line of *stability,* forming, so to speak, the ridge between the valleys on either side. The first artists must quickly have realized that the work as a whole depends upon this feature and that here everything is won or lost. From this insight emerged the profile that even now, in the words of the Song of Solomon, looks down like a house of pleasure from the heights of Lebanon over the beautiful region of Damascus.[43] Though *we* scarcely venture to name it, no part of this ignoble member is lacking in significance. The root of the nose, its ridge, its tip, the cartilage and the openings through which life breaths—all these are of great importance for a person's spirit and character! But here, too, the description of the individual parts is too exposed to mistreatment and misunderstanding. Whoever is willing and able should interpret them himself.

The *eyes* I will consider here only insofar as they are windows of the soul and wells of light and life. They lie enclosed and confined between sprays of hair. Even blind feeling soon discovers that their beautifully polished form, like their size and shape, is of great importance. Is it not worthy of note how they either protrude forward or are gently submerged under the ocular bone? The temples are either collapsed sepulchres or quiet places of rest, pulsing with fingers of life and blood. The region in which the eyebrows, the nose, and the eyes meet reveals a *trace* of the soul within the face, that is to say, a trace of the *will* and of *practical life.*

Nature has placed the noble, deep, and hidden sense of *hearing* on the sides of the head, where it is partially hidden from view. The ears are positioned so as to allow us to hear and not so that they might themselves be seen. No matter how well formed, the organs of hearing are *unadorned:* they are ornamented only by their delicacy, complexity, and depth. Pity him who has great elephant flaps hanging down on either side of his head or ears of victory like the wise Midas that rise up like towers.[44] With such large ears it must be possible to hear *well* and to judge. I leave it to the natural historians to decide whether through compression and lack of exercise this sense has lost its keenness, just as the sense of sight has grown weak through the use of glasses and having to squint in dark rooms. If this is the case, what is *harmful* can never be *beautiful.*

Finally, I come to the *lower part* of the face. Nature would often obscure this part of men's faces with a thick cloud, and not without reason. For it is here that the face reveals the features of *neediness,* or, what comes to the same thing, the characteristic letters of *sensuality*—something that men should keep covered. Everyone knows to what degree the *upper lip* reveals a person's *tastes* and *inclinations,* together with the *forms of love* and *pleasure* in which he delights. Pride and anger make the upper lip crooked, refinement makes it pointed, benevolence makes it round, while idle voluptuousness makes it sink downward. With what indescribable traits it reveals love and desire, kisses and ardor! The bottom lip merely closes the two and serves as their support: it forms a cushion of roses on which the crown of lordship may rest. If anything may be termed articulate, it is the upper lip of a human being and the way in which it closes the mouth. If the mouth is perfumed with the ambrosia of love and the nectar of Svade, then the lip is the tip of the scales that apportion the food of the gods.[45]

The formation of the *teeth* and the close of the jaw are of great significance in a person. Does he grind his teeth or wear his grin forever? Does the open mouth reveal the *rictum leonis,*[46] the χάσμ' ὀδόντων,[47] which is such an intolerably genial grimace? Or does it fall limply, so that instead of a perfumed rose exuding love and persuasion the mouth appears decrepit and weak? A pure and gentle mouth is perhaps the most beautiful recommendation for social existence: for the door tells us much about the guests who exit through it, the *words* of the soul and of the heart. The expression *to hang on someone's lips,* the two *scarlet threads* of the *Song of Solomon,* the sweet scent they exude, and the saying concerning the *closed* and *open mouth*—all these are pure expressions of physical existence. Here we find the chalice of life, the cup of love, and the most tender friendship.

The lower lip already begins to form part of the *chin;* it is closed by the *jaw bones,* which descend on either side. If I may speak figuratively, it reveals a great deal whether the *root of sensuality* in man is fixed or loose, whether it is firm or slack, and, so to speak, whether it stands full square upon the ground. The chin completes the ellipse of the face. Among the Greeks it was not pointed or cavernous, but flowed downward, gentle and unbroken, the true keystone of the edifice. Any deformation is fearful to behold. In some it is bent forward, as if nature had used it as a lever to construct the head and then cast it aside in rage; in others it scarcely exists at all or fades from view. I have already said enough, and more than enough, about these parts of the body. Since they express deep *sensuality* they cannot easily be described in words. Nature veils them on the faces of men, and perhaps our description, too, should leave them veiled.

Instead, in speaking of men, we should consider the beard. Today nothing more is said of the beard than to remark how often it makes the razor blunt. But the Jews, in the ancient book called the Zohar, have recorded many of the mysteries of its secret streets, ways, and corners.[48] Behind these words, if it is not a misinterpretation of the letter of the text, is hidden considerable knowledge of the physical world that we do not understand. Fashion and custom require that we remain like women or eternal children and youths; in mature age we display only a field of stubble and our heads remain powdered like old men or kept shorn beneath a wig of false hair. If Nature had wished to give us such things, or to take away the things we do have, she would have done so.

I can be briefer in my discussion of the other parts of the human body, for the face is a *compendium* of the whole. As the brow is governed by a man's *disposition,* so the *breast* is the custodian of the most noble of the *vital organs* and gives witness to them. A man whose breast is free is recognized by everyone as noble and free: we believe him capable of action and he can *breath.* The *pectus hirsutum,*[49] the iron armor that clads the soul, is proverbial in the language of every nation. By contrast, the constricted, wheezing, and sunken breast of

Thersites is a natural omen, revealing a person who is limited, stooping, and cowardly.[50] A noble man can often overcome great obstacles by force of principle; as the Qur'an says, God has *given him room in his breast* and sufficient air to breath in the face of his enemies.[51] Often, however, courage is merely *simulated* and political guile is supposed to replace the irreplaceable merits that are lacking. It is known that nothing makes so great a contribution to this as an idle life and laborious crawling on the breast, not to speak of the belly. Every barbarian, that is to say, every nation that stills lives in the freedom of nature, recognizes the consequences this has upon our bodies and our character. Even more than the mind and the soul, it constricts the voice and weakens the eye. The heart beats timidly in its narrow and oppressive confines and at each moment believes itself about to be crushed, creeping after nourishment and slander. What friend can rest his head upon such a breast and cry, "You are my rock!" What person in a state of misery and oppression can turn and say, "Here I find refuge!" To compensate, we are all the more adroit with our minds and with our mouths and hands.

Nature gave to women not a breast, but *breasts.* As Mother Nature, she has encircled the female sex with a girdle of charm and made what is a source of need and love for the suckling child into a source of pleasure. The breast of a man is stronger and more uniform, more noble and perfect; the breasts of a woman are softer, more rounded, washed with the milk of innocence and crowned with the rose of love. When this bud blooms and the unripe mound advances toward harvest, the graces of virginity wind it with a girdle in which, according to the description of the poet, dwell love and desire.[52] When the drink of innocence is ready, the newborn child approaches the source of the first pleasure of both mother and child; it gropes forward with its tiny hand and nestles closer, and then it is replete and mother and child are made one under the dulcet tree of life. What brute is not moved by such a scene or fails to recognize here the lost paradise of innocence?

Winckelmann already lamented that he did not write for the Greeks and so had to pass in silence over many things.[53] I have even greater need of such caution and can only discuss certain features of the body. Whereas the *breast* is seen as the custodian and expression of the more *noble* parts, philosophers since the most ancient times have regarded the *belly* as the seat of desire. This is what underlies Winckelmann's noble description of the belly of *Bacchus.*[54] Youthful *sobriety* and *measure,* the gentle roundness that emerges as if from a dream, finds its contrary in a form and a condition which repels us even in its description. The swollen belly and the thighs that fall away are a punishment for licentiousness and an effect of bitter water, the most severe punishment for a woman who is unfaithful and lascivious.* In the words of the oldest song of innocence and love, the belly is a heap of wheat and the navel a rounded bowl that never lacks mixed wine; it never thirsts and never overflows with joy.† Wise moderation and fear of God will keep the navel healthy and give refreshment to the bones, as is said in the oldest book of proverbs.‡ Today, for all their truth, we mock at these descriptions of simple existence. Like our first ancestors we make aprons of fig leaves for ourselves, and generally for the same reasons.[55] Therefore I shall remain silent and speak only of the back, the hand, and the foot.

Greeks were as familiar with these parts of the body as with the others, and they formed them in the most beautiful way. The beautiful nape of Bacchus flows downward; Venus steps out of her bath with her beautiful back curved like a dove; the beautiful torso sits there and reflects. How can I describe such things? And what does it help to describe them unless you see them with your own eyes and are able to trace the undulating beauty of the form for yourself? See how the back merges into the soft flesh above the hips! Could Prometheus and Pygmalion[56] have given such a gently flowing character to every part of the form if they had not embraced it in their arms? In the language of the ancient book of innocence, the hips are like two jewels from a master's hand. Apollo's thighs are marble columns, his knees, free of dead cartilage that protrudes, are as if blown from soft clay, and his calves are not heavy and bound or needy in any sense but striving muscles replete with strength and youthful vigor. Finally, the foot, animated through to its smallest parts, is not detached from the rest of the body and pulled on as if it were the shoe of a worm, but is one with the whole, which flows into it and is supported by it. Just as the thighs are formed into columns of marble, so Mother Nature transforms the arms into gentle cylinders and encircles them with the first myrtle leaves of love. She softens the point of the elbow and allows a woman's hand to flow gently downward into the small cylinders of the fingers. She has filled out with flower petals and soft, velvety fur every part of the hand, which awaits the caress of the first touch of love. Every member is as made of wax and rendered agile and sensitive. The finger is like a ray of light, and the back of the hand, washed in milk, is an indivisible and articulate mound of vitality, copious with life. Observe the virility of

* Numbers 5:21–27.

† Song of Solomon 7:2.

‡ Proverbs 3:8.

a man's arm! Muscles are its wreath of victory and nerves its band of love. The arms descend powerful and free from the shoulders, the organs of laboring art and the weapons of virtue. They protect the chest and offer safeguard to lovers, friends, and the fatherland, which they envelop in their embrace. The hand is a form full of sensitive feeling, capable of a thousand different movements. How noble is the entire structure that stands before us, revealing its *face*, its *brow*, and its *chest* as it strides forward upon its legs. We are *made wonderfully great,** our *bones* have been *numbered and ordered* with care, *our nerves woven together*, and our *veins* made into torrents of life. We are *made from clay, poured out like milk and curdled like cheese;* we are clothed with skin and *the breath of God gives us life.*† Our form (πλάσμα) has been modeled and shaped (πεπλασμένοι) and it receives its form from the stirring forces of the bestower of all shape.‡ This is the truth contained in the most ancient oracle concerning our origin:

> Ἔπλασεν ὁ Θεὸς τὸν ἄνθρωπον, χοῦν απὸ τῆς γῆς,
> καὶ ἐνεφύσησεν εἴς τὸ πρόσωπον αὐτοῦ πνοὴν ζωῆς,
> καὶ ἐγένετω ὁ ἄνθρωπος εἰς ψυχὴν ζῶσαν.§

* Psalms 139:14.

† Job 10:9–11.

‡ Job 33:4–6.

§ Genesis 2:7. [See editor's note 57.]

PART FOUR

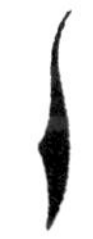

The proceeding discussion is intended neither as a panegyric of beauty nor as a description of antiquity. Even less is it intended as a contribution to physiognomics. I am neither an artist nor an antiquarian nor a physiognomist, and indeterminate and general observations are of no value to any of these disciplines. Rather, my goal was to establish the following elementary principle: "*that the sublimity and beauty of the human body, whatever form it may take, is always an expression of health, life, strength, and well-being in every limb of this artful creature,* whereas everything *ugly* is always *stunted,* an oppression of the spirit, an imperfection of the form in relation to its end." The well-proportioned human being is not an abstraction derived from the clouds or composed from learned rules or arbitrary conventions. It is something that can be *grasped* and *felt* by all who are able to recognize *in themselves* or *in others* the form of life, the expression of force in the human vessel. Beauty is nothing but the *meaning of inner perfection.*

In order to avoid repetition, let us consider the human figure we have described as it is *in action.* We will see that every member *speaks:* the more it corresponds to its end, the more perfect and beautiful it is. Imagine a sculpture of a philosopher with a *brow* that does not *think;* a Hercules without *strength* between his *eyebrows,* or in his *neck* or *chest,* or in his body as a whole; a Venus with a hideous *profile,* hanging *breasts,* and a downturned *mouth;* an antique Bacchus sitting upon one of our wine barrels. Every untrained eye will perceive in the *action* what a subtler sense would register in the *form* alone: that it does not correspond to its *end.* A goddess of love without charm, a Diana without chaste swiftness, an Apollo without the pride and courage of youth, a Jupiter who does not inspire awe and veneration—these would be loathsome creatures. What is true of *individual* characters and actions must, gathered together, be true in *general,* for the general only exists in particulars, and it is only out of the totality of particulars that the general is formed. Beauty, then, is always only the shining through of *form,* the *sensible expression of perfection* in relation to an end, the surge of life, human health. The more a part of the body signifies what it *should* signify, the more beautiful it is; inner *sympathy* alone, *feeling* and the *transposition of our entire human self* into the figure we touch, is the true teacher and instrument of beauty.

Thus we find that where *one* form or part of the body is of greater importance it takes precedence over the others; it is the *first to offer itself to the hand that touches* and is the most pronounced. Imagine before you a figure absorbed in *thought* and *reflection:* the *head leans forward* and the lower parts of the face withdraw as if into the shadows so that the *brow* becomes the *principal feature.* Without needing to hold its finger against its nose, the figure declares: I am thinking. Imagine before you an emperor with a commanding *gaze:* the *gaze* gives *clear and vivid utterance* to the *face,* and the *eyes* become the *principal feature.* For this reason sculptures of Juno always show her eyes to be large and beautiful, for they are the divine sign of her existence: *ast ego regina Deum.*[1] If Apollo is seized by rage and strides forth, those parts of his body are given prominence that reveal his *noble sense of self* and his *movement* in pursuit of his goal: his nose respires vital breath and creates space in front of it; his *breast* becomes a beautiful armor, nobly formed; and his long, valiant legs carry him forward.[2] The other parts of the body modestly retreat, for they do not participate in the action. It is with the mouth that a figure *demands, pleads, wishes, and implores;* this part of the face comes unobtrusively to the fore, and it is *here* that sighs, prayers, requests, wishes, and kisses are seen to dwell. This *movement* and *self-revelation* extends even to the ears when we hearken to something. The *form* of the *part of the body that acts* always declares: I am here, I am active. And if this is true of the delicate features of the *face,* it is even more so of the *body* as a whole. How can the *hand* give an order without being raised in the air and thus revealing its office? How can the breast be *held out* and offer *protection* without becoming conspicuous? It speaks and says: I am vaulted. A beautiful belly is not inflated, but Bacchus adopts a posture that shows it to its best. He leans gracefully on his arm so that the beautiful *femininity* of his *back* and his *chest,* his *belly* and his *hips* speaks a language full of meaning.[3] All this has nothing to do with rules of art or with studied conventions: it is the *natural language of the soul that expresses itself through the entire body,* the basic letters and the alphabet of *posture, action,* and *character* and of all that these can become.

Let us continue! Nature has not made us human beings into a dead sea, a stasis of permanent inactivity, or given us the unmoved tranquillity of the gods; rather, she has *animated* us with an eternally *mobile* current, full of energy and living spirit. Even *from without* her work could not appear as a sculpted mask of beautiful and eternal inactivity; the human form must be animated by the *breeze of life.* Beauty takes on *force* and *meaning* in every part of the body. Even gods and goddesses cannot appear as abstract configurations in the clouds which no eye can see and no ear can hear;[4] they must become *concrete,* each possessing a *character* that belongs to this particular god and no other. The beautiful form of each is determined by *the* living spirit that blows upon and drives forward the barque of *that god* alone. As a consequence, every part of the body becomes *individually* significant to the highest degree. Only insofar as the daemon, the character, of a single divine spirit of life completely and exclusively appears in *this* image is it that of the beautiful *Apollo,* the glorious *Juno* or *Aphrodite.* Here once again it is of no avail to study letters or the clouds. It is necessary to *exist* and to *feel:* one must be human and blindly register the way in which the soul works *in us* in response to every character, every situation, and every passion—and then touch. This is the clear language of nature itself, perceptible to all peoples, even to those who are blind or deaf.

Nireus, the most beautiful of all the Greeks before Troy, does nothing in the entire *Iliad* and only appears in the catalog of the ships.[5] But all those who *act* exist as individual *characters* with firmly drawn and unchanging features that do not fade away; they *are who they are.* Thus the god-like Agamemnon "has eyes and a head like Jupiter, a girth like Mars, and the chest of Neptune; he stands there like an ox pre-eminent amongst his herd."[6] But this is so only in the most tranquil and splendor-filled part of the *Iliad,* before the start of the first attack. Afterward, Homer does not have the time to describe his beauty: Agamemnon *acts.* Priam can look down at him from the tower and marvel at him;[7] Priam can extol Helen, but Homer no longer extols. Of the beautiful Achilles, around whom the entire poem turns, we do not hear a single laudation of his beauty; we are shown him only in his anger, combined in the fairest way with friendship, love, intimacy, and the playing of his lyre. The god-like Ulysses, "broader in the chest and across the shoulders than Agamemnon, goes up and down the ranks of the encamped army like a thick-woolled ram; Menelaos, when he stood up, was larger with his broad shoulders than Ulysses, but when both were seated Ulysses was the more imposing."[8] In these two features, as described from the tower above the fray, Agamemnon and Ulysses stand vividly before us; but afterward we see only the determinate forms of their bodies in *single determinate actions.* Thus Homer! But it was not only the *epic* poets who depicted things in this way because they were gripped by the action. Even Anacreon's *Bathyllus* reveals that the Greeks never conceived beauty other than in *determinate form.*[9] One would think that a song of pleasure such as this would be a collection of fragrances, a floating tissue, a harvest of flowers drawn from a variety of dreams: it is and it is not. Anacreon gathers the honey from many flowers, but only in order to form a highly definite figure. The youth is suddenly transformed into an Apollo, or rather, Apollo into the youth, and the statue stands before us.

It is beyond doubt that the extraordinary *determinateness* and *fidelity* that the Greeks gave to *every* situation, *every* passion, and *every* character helped them to achieve a level of art that has not been seen on the earth since. They perceived as do blind people and through feeling, saw. They did not peer through the glasses of some system or ideal that would conjure the ensouled form of the human body from a cobweb floating in the autumn breeze. No part of the body belonging to any of their gods could represent another god, nor could any aspect of any action belong to any other character than the one who stands there. *One* spirit has flowed into the statue: it guides the hand of the artist who forms the work and makes it into a unity. Whoever (to begin at once with the most difficult) has stood before the celebrated Hermaphrodite[10] and has not felt in every curve and turn of the body, in everything that he touches and does not touch, a Bacchic dream of hermaphroditism; whoever has not been tortured by sweet thoughts and by a pleasure that courses through the entire body like a gentle fire; whoever has not felt or perceived an involuntary resonance and echo of this same music in himself—such a person cannot be made to understand, either by these words or by the words of others. For what is so uncommonly *certain* and *definite* in a sculpture is that, because it presents a *human being,* a fully *animated body,* it speaks to us as an *act;* it seizes hold of us and penetrates our very being, awakening the full range of responsive human feeling.

I do not know if I dare to term *static* and *dynamic* that which streams from the human body into the body of art: it lives in every *curve* and *hollow,* in every mark of *pliancy and firmness,* as if *weighed* upon a balance, and it possesses the power virtually to *transpose* our soul into the same sympathetic *situation.* The rise and fall of the breast and the knee, the way the body rests quietly, revealing the soul—all this passes silently and incomprehensibly over into us: we find ourselves, so to speak, embodied in the nature before us, or the nature in question is enlivened by our own soul. For this reason every new addition is felt as doubly repellent; no matter how beautiful it might be, if it is not animated by the whole of a *single* living spirit, we quite rightly recognize it as an alien travesty. Nothing must be merely *observed* and treated as if it were a surface; it must be touched by the gentle fingers of our inner sense and by our harmonious feeling of sympathy, as if it came from the hands of the Creator.

For this reason, the inscriptions on statues recorded in the *Greek Anthology* praise nothing so highly as the *modeling of the whole,* the capacity to *live through and in us* that they produce.[11] I do not know if this can be replaced by drawing or by depictions that merely reproduce shadows on a flat surface, though these, too, must ultimately derive from the living body. I do know, however, that the more we regard things as shadows, paintings, and fleeting groups, the further the *truth of the physical body* will remain from us. Here, too, our spirit is helped by our sense of touch and by the dark of night; with its sponge it removes all the colors from things and obliges us to attend to the *presence and existence of an object.* The Greeks knew just a few things, but what they did know they knew well: they grasped something completely and were able to render it in such a way that it lives for all times. Just as the profile of the Greek face is *formed* and not *painted,* so too were their works.

How far we stand behind them may be judged by a later age. What is rarer in our day than for someone to grasp a man's *character* as it is, to capture it and to develop it in a way that is faithful and complete? Instead he must always make recourse to reason and morality, as to light and color; the figure will not stand on its own two feet and like a phantom its appearance changes from one side to another. We see so much that we in fact see nothing, and we know so much that we no longer possess anything that is our *own,* that is to say, something we *could* not have learned, something that arises out of the virtues and errors of our own *self*. Holy night, mother of gods and of men, come over us and quicken us and bring us together. *Non multa, sed multum.*[12] With what profound understanding and quiet penetration *Raphael* and *Domenichino* labored on their eternal works. These are not paintings, but statues of Daedalus that walk and live.[13]

It is not sufficient merely to put wax and clay into the hands of our children from an early age, though this would in fact achieve a great deal; and perhaps no one should begin to draw who has not already as a child spent a long time playing and modeling. The first drawings of a child are *forms* set down on paper, imitations of the *entire* living thing, without light or shadow. At first a child cannot understand or comprehend why shadows should be there and why they should be allowed to spoil his beautiful picture. For him they are things that do not exist in nature: his eyes see as his hands feel. Nature proceeds with each individual person in the same way as it does with the race as a whole: it moves from feeling to seeing, from sculpture to painting. With this we have already learned a great deal, but it is not everything. For the question remains: *what* should be formed? Trees, plants, scorpions, our adornments, our clothes? Nature has departed from us and is hidden from us; in its place we find art and social rank, mechanisms and patchwork. But such things, it seems to me, cannot be formed out of wax or clay.

Let someone go into our markets, our churches and our courtrooms, our houses and our salons with the intention of giving form to what he sees. What would he begin to sculpt? Chairs or human beings? Hooped skirts or gloves? Plumed hats or ceremonies? Give these form? *How?* By means of which sense? With the eye or with the sense of smell? No eye recognizes the eye of a friend, nor any cheek a cheek, a mouth a mouth, or a hand a hand. In the age of chivalry it was customary to put on armor before striking at one another; for what reason do we do it now?

Where today are the Greek games, Greek dances, Greek festivals, Greek candor, youth, and joy? Where might they be found? What if a *serenissimus regens,*[14] the founder of a new *Greece* (just as the fifth loge is termed *Paradise*[15]), were most graciously to inaugurate these festivals once again through an edict, printed in black and white and accompanied by a drumroll? Erect Greek statues so that every dog can urinate on them! You will never succeed in making the slave who passes by every day, the donkey that carries its burden, have any feeling to notice that they are there or that he should come to resemble them. You will have planted nothing more than a fence post on which he can lean or rub his itching back! In a famous place in Germany the parade ground is encircled with statues, Greek heroes with newly pointed knees and drums.[16] I do not understand why they have not also been given gaiters, grenadier hats, arms, and a uniform. Otherwise I would consider it an excellent idea to place statues before every sentry: only he would have time to become an Apollo or Jupiter by looking at them.

Oh, the suffocating, wretched vapors that certain new Greeks disperse in exchange for a meager salary! As if it were not palpably obvious that no one can receive the spirit of someone else if they do not possess something in *common,* just as life cannot enter into stone or blood into a plant. The youth who stood before the Greek heroes in the beautiful age of Greece enjoyed the possibility and hope of one day having his own statue. The gods and the heroes belonged to one race; the gods were ancestors to the heroes, and the heroes shared their characteristics. Success in the games or at battle could win the youth a place alongside them. The artist worked for his city, for his people, and for the name of Greece as a whole. So sang Pindar, lifting his song to the praise of statues and of beauty.[17] This is how the Greeks saw the artist and heard the poet. But how do we see; how do *we* hear? It is remarkable how rarely a *person* appears to us, and even more rare that someone *embraces* another person and holds him in such affection that he carries the person with him and gives him eternal existence. In a famous garden are to be found our national products: long wigs together, I believe, with mannequins, formed out of terracotta—here, undoubtedly, is the true image of our country.

But what purpose is there to these ineffectual laments? They will not help to create a new Greece. It is better to return to the beloved *line of beauty,* which appears to be in the process of disappearing from the forms we can feel.[18] It has not completely disappeared, however, for we can find still it here once again, *true* and *corporeal.* Although mathematics is the truest science, only physics can bring it to *life,* just as numbers only exist in things that can be counted. And if there must be some mathematical reason as to *why* the line of beauty is beautiful, it is doubly pleasurably to see this abstract ground confirmed in every one of the *most concrete* forms.

The straight line is the line of *stability*—this is revealed by our sense of touch and our sense of sight. Each part rests upon the other or depends upon the other; it supports and is supported. Wherever stability is necessary, both *vertically* and *horizontally,* nature has chosen this line. Thus the tree develops out of the trunk; it rests upon itself and is perpetually renewed. It is the model of solidity and of the beautiful column. Stone, earth, and even the sea must be level wherever a base is necessary. The same is true of the human body, which has as its base the sole of the foot. Where sublime stability is required we see the *straight position* of the foot, thigh, neck, arms, and hands. Nothing looks worse than a twisted tree or a crooked column: even the hand of a blind person seeks to make it straight, for it is fallen and might break. The greatest obstacle to the impression of *stable posture* and *simple sublimity* in the human form is a crooked neck, or a crooked back or legs. The principal part of the face, the nose, which protrudes forward and shapes the form of the whole, is a *straight* line; if it is crooked it creates a ridiculous impression. One can scarcely speak to someone whose nose is twisted.

The line of *perfection* is the *circle* in which everything radiates out from a central point and returns back to it, in which no point is like another and yet everything forms a single circle. Where it is possible, Nature has entwined the *line* of *stability* with the *circle* of *perfection.* In this way she makes plants and trees grow as they rise; the perfect sun sends out its rays as it makes its path across the vault of the heaven; and the droplet swells into the rounded shape of the earth. In the human body, too, nature has adorned the line of *stability* with *roundness:* arms and legs, the fingers and the neck, together with the heaven it carries, all are rounded. In these parts of the body, any break or sharp angle is unbearable.

The vessels here below, however, are not capable of *perfection* and the line of *real need* always exerts its inexorable force. In the cosmos the conflict between two forces[19] makes the planets move in the form of an ellipse. Here a similar conflict results in the *line of beauty* that encircles the *forms of the body;* it emerges from the straight line and from roundness, just as Plato says that *love* was born from *need* and *superfluity.*[20] The circle is too *full* for us, we cannot take it in at once or *embrace* it, while the straight line is too *needy* to provide the many-faceted organism that our body should be. Thus it *oscillates* and *inclines,* so that *this* or *that* aspect *predominates.* The firm breast and back are not twisted but curved: the latter is a wall and a protector, the former a plate of armor. The lower part of the body, the breasts of a woman, and the organs of weakness are clothed with softness and the appearance of perfection.[21] But it is only an *appearance:* for a belly, a swollen head, or a calf is an overfilled growth that carries within it the seed of its own destruction.

Whence arise these last considerations? I repeat, from the fact that the human vessel is not capable of *perfection,* nor of any sign of such: perfection is rest, and the human body should *act* and *strive.* A round head or a round belly may display an abundance of comfort, repletion, and satisfaction, but they are all the less able to contribute to the motion of the whole; they carry above and before themselves their own Atlas.[22] Just as light flows upward in the flame, the sea produces waves out of its stillness, and the sun itself traces its course through the zodiac and encircles the globe, so the human creature acquires *grace* only through movement: *grace* is nothing but *beauty in movement,* be it in lines, forms, or deeds. Grace distances itself from the line of *need,* though this must nonetheless remain its basis, and it inclines toward *perfection* without ever being able to reach it. The human species, divided into two sexes, hovers between these two extremes: the *bearing* of the male is closer to the line of *stability,* while the female is adorned with the *floating beauty* of *grace.*

There can be no grace without *movement,* which reveals the *dawning of action* even to the sense that feels in the dark. From whence, then, the powerful or moderate passion and action that give rise to *grace*? It exists only in this hovering between two extremes, between night and sun, between rigidity and a fullness that overflows. Touch any part of the body when it is fully tensed, and you will not endure it for long. The corrugated brow or the grinning smile of love that closes the eyes and contorts the mouth, the chin that sinks to the throat, the chest that swells out to a barrel, the pointed and elongated arm, or the foot that is bent double or put under too much pressure—touch any of these parts of the body and you will feel how far they *deviate from all beautiful form and action,* both *mechanically* and *spiritually.* To the hand that feels, the mouth that cries is a cave[23] and laughter turns the cheeks into creases. The eternal laws of human beauty are *metaphysically* and *physically, morally* and *plastically* fully identical. Someone in the dawn of the *year* or in the dawn of *life,* in the spring of *movement* or in the spring of *action,* is always regarded analogically as the beautiful middle between two extremes. The swan that embraces Leda and Leda as she moves toward him, Danae as she awaits the shower and not the state in which they both reveal the fruit of this encounter form lines of grace.[24] Nature keeps in reserve her richest treasures for her most important needs; as the holy writer said, *those parts of the body we think less honorable we invest with the greater honor.*[25]

I have something further to say about the *posture* or *comportment* of the body. Everyone's head is placed upon shoulders, but not all carry it in the same way. Everyone has the center of gravity in the center of the body, but the structure of the body is not always related to it in the same way. Everyone stands upon feet, but there is a great variance in the posture of the body and in the way the feet are placed on the ground. The posture or comportment of the body is of extraordinary importance. It reveals quite naturally those parts of the body that, by nature or arbitrarily, are most pronounced or most hidden, that are the first to speak or the first to fall silent as if they did not exist. It also determines a person's *gait,* which is held to be so characteristic by physiognomists and anti-physiognomists; it influences the way the person appears and shows himself to others, and the manner in which he sits or takes rest. In their depictions of gods, fauns, heroes, and satyrs the ancient artists reveal an infinitely subtle *knowledge of character;* this is something we could demonstrate in detail. In general, nothing deceives less than what speaks of the *body as a whole,* above all, when it speaks to the sense of touch. It is possible to make mistakes concerning individual parts of the body, but here the voice of the *universal* is also the voice of God. It arms us against dreams and sophistry, and especially against a one-sided dependence on a *single* form or a *single* feature that can lead us far from the truth. The modest sense of *touch* feels slowly but without bias; it discovers little, but it discovers what is there. It does not judge until it has grasped the *whole.*

Here, as in other things, it is remarkable the insight that the two sexes have into each other, how deeply men know women and women, men. Each can, and often does, do injustice to his or her own sex, even if only out of envy. But where it is armed by passion rather than blinded by it, the judgment of one sex upon the other is extraordinarily precise. *Love* divines within us the true ideal, the angel, while *hate* discovers the devil in us, often without our being able to see it or find it for ourselves. The reason is obvious: alongside our *universal feeling as human beings* there is also a specific *feeling proper to our sex.* Even in our most elevated judgments concerning what it is *to be human,* this cannot be denied. A man, be he a poet or a ruler, a creator of men or of statues, must always feel *as a man,* and a woman must always feel *as a woman.*

Finally, I cannot avoid dedicating a few words to the praise of symmetry, which reveals itself even to the obscurest sense clearly and powerfully in the human body. Nature always chooses the simplest relationship, that obtaining between one and two: it places them alongside and above one another so that those parts of the body that need to communicate with one another are found together and in intimate proximity. The noble singularity of the head stands between the two shoulders upon the free and solid form of the neck; it forms the beam of the articulated building, which it oversees and dominates. It has the form of a beautiful oval line and at its front is the face. Just as the head rests upon the shoulders, so, in the face, the brow rests upon the two arches of the eyebrows; raised up, it is a solitary sky of thoughts. Between the two eyebrows, the soul and the brow are concentrated in a single point. On either side are the arcs of the noblest of the senses, the eyes, which are once again formed with the beautiful line of the ellipse. The nose and the mouth reside between two flowered meadows, the cheeks, and the ellipse of the head closes with the firm shape of the chin. Nothing could be easier to grasp, arrange, and order than the seven letters of the sacred human face, and yet they offer such multiplicity and diversity. The beautiful radiance and alternation of

the brow
and the eyes,
the nose,
the cheeks, and
the mouth

rest, finally, upon the chin. The one supports, lifts, carries the other until the sense of touch is able to recognize that which light reveals infinitely more to the sense of sight—the *face.* It is clear that the construction of the body and the relation of its parts is based upon exactly *the same* relation: for this reason savages often painted the human face upon their chests or knees. The two nipples of the chest are placed above the navel, the belly above the two feet; the chest resides under the two wings of the arms. These form a single relation; each belongs to the other as one of a pair and communicates with it in the manner it should. This is confirmed by the number and form of the fingers, which are as if cut out of a half circle and cannot be lessened or increased, shortened or replaced. In short, the body reveals a simple and harmonious wisdom, felt, measured and ordered, in us and for us, that circumscribes both contour and volume. The soul has been poured into a measure which is multiple in its organization but which possesses clear limits and is easy to grasp. Wherever and however it can, it has made points of unity in the most delicate places. Thus the eye finds the eye, the mouth presses against the mouth and the chest against the chest; we gaze and drink in the breath of love. If the features of the face are distorted or parts of the body moved or transposed, the least deformation repels us, whether we see it with our eyes or not. Whatever subtle laws of *well-being* and *well-formedness,* of *proportion* and *disproportion,* are discovered in *optics* and the arts of *arrangement,* these all find their great model in the *human form* and in *human beauty:* this noble work is everywhere the favored and most characteristic product of Mother Nature.

PART FIVE

I asked a woman who was born blind,* "What sort of table and what sort of vessel do you prefer? One that is square or one that is round?" She answered: one that is round, for it is easy and pleasant to grasp, and one does not bump into it. Perhaps nothing more straightforward can be said about the *line of beauty* than this. "Why does a round arm or a slender waist please you?"—because it is healthy, lively, and simple. A phantom she imagined as a cold breath that pursued her; she sought attractiveness in a firm, beautiful voice and solicitude in a pleasing scent and gentle warmth, just as with Saunderson and other examples.[2] I passed her a statue: she knew and named every part and found it *good*. But when she came to the clothed parts she faltered and did not know what they were, for it was the first statue she had held. Her timidity at my social standing and the distance at which she lived prevented me from pursuing my inquiries any further. When she spoke, she employed all the expressions deriving from the sense she lacked, but she did not understand any of them: it was pure parrot-speak, just as is a large part of the speech of those of us who do possess all five senses. I hold deficiencies of this sort to be the only certain means of distinguishing and re-identifying the contributions of the

* In the year 1770. [See editor's note 1.]

different senses now that they have become so interwoven in our language and our concepts. Will a practical *doctrine of reason* ever be written, a philosophical lexicon of *language*, the *senses*, and the *fine arts* that traces each word and each concept back to its origin and uncovers the processes whereby a word or concept is carried over from one sense to another, and from the senses to the mind? Without inquiries of this sort to serve as a guide, everything will remain as it currently is, a labyrinth and a chatter of reason.

In this book, I have ventured an initial investigation into one sense in relation to one art and one class of concepts. *Honny soit qui mal y pense.*[3] It is a sincere inquiry into truth, correctness, and simplicity, intended to awaken virtuous feeling for the significant forms of God's Creation and not licentiousness; it is dishonored by the remarks of the dandy or the use that rogues would make of it. The best is exposed to misuse precisely because it offers something that can be misused. Indeed, truths that are not to be found on every street corner *must* sometimes remain remote from the common language. No astronomer has ever thought to alter his theory of the heavens because it does not accord with the way we normally speak. If he is able to explain why he has expressed himself in a certain way, his work will have been done and his reasons shown to be valid. If the principle "forms are only given to us through *bodily feeling*" has been demonstrated both physically and metaphysically, then its consequences must hold true for *every* art and science—assuming, however, that their investigation does not provide new evidence for correction and clarification. (This is something that may well arise from the observations of experienced researchers.) Let the student of art attempt to demonstrate the above principle. If something in the form before him appears obscure, doubtful, or contradictory, or if he starts to vacillate or to worry that he is passing over something important, he should use the fingers of his inner sense in order to discover that which he could not otherwise identify: the shape of the *spirit* within the form. If his soul is pure and tranquil, and if his sense is gentle, he will soon hear the voice of the infallible, silent oracle: his hand, as if of its own accord, will strive to *form for itself* what it has *grasped*.

I could demonstrate this principle by reference to the history of art and metagrabolise[4] exquisitely about the words *plastic* and *toreutic*, ἄγαλμα and *signum*, τόρευμα and *caelaturam*, βαιτύλια, ξόανα, βρέτη, and so forth.[5] I could show that the art of sculpture could not have arisen anywhere except as it arises among our children, in whose hands wax, bread, and clay take on form as if by themselves. I could show that in their use of models the Greeks remained true to the origin of art to the extent that they had to remain true to it and that the method of modeling that *Michelangelo* employed and *Winckelmann* praised so highly* is exactly that of which we speak: "to the eye of the sculptor, the water that gently flows and runs over every form and curve is the subtlest finger." By following these numerous curves, the artist's hand acquires a hovering enchantment and delightfulness. I could point to the *multiformity* that is so natural to Greek sculpture, in which every muscle is *raised:* it is not two-dimensional and no side of the face, nor even any quarter-side, is like any other. Consequently, engravings, drawings, and paintings can never succeed in representing it or standing in for it. Almost without wishing it, our *sense of touch* is *drawn toward* every pliant curve and every delicate form. If the principle I have established is true, however, everyone can and will be able to observe this for themselves.

I conclude with some general observations on a number of misunderstood, and for this reason much disputed, topics in the history of art.

1. The art of sculpture, as soon as it becomes an art and separates itself from *signis,* that is to say, from religious signs and monuments, from blocks and pieces of wood, from piles of stone, and from pilasters and columns, must necessarily first dedicate itself to everything that is *great, sublime,* and *extravagant,* awakening terror and awe rather than love and sympathy. Children, blind people, and those who are in the process of regaining their sight also experience sculpture in this way, and they will continue to do so, no matter what the philosophers might say. The blind man who was healed saw human beings as if they were trees;[7] Cheselden's blind man saw people as if they were a vast panel of images moving densely before his eyes.[8] To a child or to someone who lacks expertise, the very first view of a statue and the impression it makes is exactly like that given in the description of the statue of Daedalus.[9] No matter how linear and foursquare[10] it may appear to the eye of the artist, the first impressions made by art are *awe,* verging on *terror,* and a *shudder,* feelings which make the work appear to *move* and *come to life.* This is particularly the case with half-savage peoples who are completely alive and who respond only to movement and feeling. For this reason, all savages and half-savages recognize statues as

* *Reflections on the Imitation,* 28f. [See editor's note 6.]

animate and *daemonic;* the spirit and the divine are made present, above all, when they pray to a statue in the silence of the sacred twilight and wait to hear it speak in answer.

Even today, we can experience a feeling of this sort in a quiet museum or a coliseum of gods and heroes; if we are alone and approach the statues with devotion, they can, unnoticed, come to life and carry us back to the times in which everything that now exists only as mythology and statues was a living truth. The God of Israel knew the extent to which he had to protect his sensuous people from images and statues: as soon as an image was made, the daemon that animated it was also present to the senses of the people, and idolatry was inevitable. Today, we rational souls read with astonishment and almost with displeasure the impassioned arguments of the prophets against idolatry; but the history of the Jewish people, and indeed of all peoples, shows how necessary such arguments were. Nothing captures sensibility as powerfully as an idol, be it living or dead; it suffices that it exists and that one can go to it in the expectation of learning our fortune or misfortune. "He listens to our prayers and accepts our sacrifices. Why should *he* not be the one who has realized our prayers? We have received satisfaction and it is undoubtedly, he, Baal, who has given this to us." This also explains the improper uses that pagans made of the statues of their gods, which we find no less displeasing. Similar things are still carried out by children and by those who are seized by fury or passion; sensibility will always make them act in the same way. Dolls are beaten and treated as if they were alive. Unfortunate lovers, particularly women, destroy the gifts from the person who was unfaithful or take their revenge on letters and messengers and on the things and places that are held dear in memory. We call the northerners barbarians for having destroyed the statues of Italy, but for just this reason they could not have done otherwise. With their eyes they saw the daemons inside the statues, and they had either to pray to them or to destroy them. As the history of Italy shows, however, if they had lived alongside them for hundreds of years, their extreme and exalted feeling would, with time, have resolved itself into art; art would have resolved itself into taste; and taste into disgust and neglect.

This *history of art* is the same for *all* peoples. Art derives from heaven: reverence, love, or a spark from the gods brings it here below, gives it earthly form and preserves it, albeit for a brief moment, as something *living.* Then it becomes *idolatry,* then *art,* then mere *artisanship,* and finally, a broth in which everything is mixed: *connoisseurship, junk,* and *chatter about art.* Daedalus and Phidias were the first; then came Praxiteles, Myron, and Lysippus; afterward there is an echo or an aftertaste or something yet worse. Time cannot be reversed, and it is mere folly to seek to transform an artist such as Daedalus into an artist such as Lysippus. If the former exists, the latter will follow, for without the former the latter could not *exist.* The first and principal line always remains the straight line; the line of grace merely entwines itself around it.

2. *Colossal figures* are not foreign and unnatural to sculpture, but *proper* to it; they are its *origin* and its *essence.* A statue does not stand in light, it creates its own light; a statue is not placed in space, it creates its own space. Consequently, it should not be *compared* in this respect with painting, which depicts everything from a *single* viewpoint and does so on a *surface,* on a *panel of light,* on something that is given and that can be taken in all at once. Sculpture does not possess a viewpoint: it explores everything in the dark, following the shape of limbs and forms. This is so even if it feels forward longer and more slowly. More than this, the impression sculpture gives of *greatness* and *awe,* of an *immeasurable form* that can be known externally but *cannot be tangibly grasped as a whole,* is the true image of the gods and heroes; it is not the hand but the spirit, the trembling fervor of the imagination, that is here gathered into a unity. We conceive everything *infinite* as *sublime,* and everything sublime must, so to speak, reveal *infinity;* it should reproduce that apparition in which "a spirit passed before him, the hair of his flesh stood up, and an image stood before his eyes; he could not recognize its form and he heard a voice."[11]

Brahma wished to see the head of the tallest of the gods, Ixora, and flew as high as he could. There he encountered three flowers from Ixora's head, and they asked him where he wanted to go. He replied that he was on his way to see the head of Ixora. The flowers answered him: you expend your energy in vain, for even if we were to have flown for three times as long as you from the moment we left Ixora's head, we still would not have reached the point at which we could see his feet. Brahma gave up his attempt and asked the flowers to tell Ixora that he would become dizzy were he to fly any higher. *Vistnum* wished to see the god's feet, but he dug so deep into the earth that he reached the great serpent of the abyss and was forced to turn back in terror. Both divinities declared loud and clear that there was no one who was able to see the god's head or feet.[12] This is a story told in India. But could Greece have represented Jupiter in any other way than as colossal if his very form was supposed to awaken the idea of the infinite? When Phidias lifted himself up to behold Jupiter,[13] what emerged from his soul was the image of a god who, though enthroned in a temple, *could not be contained by any temple.*[14] The joke, that if Jupiter stood up his head would lift the roof off the temple, was a poor one, for Phidias was moved by just this feeling and this obscure intimation. *He above the rest,* says Milton of the hero of his poem,

In shape and gesture proudly eminent,
Stood like a tower.[15]

This is also true of the gods and heroes in Homer and in all the other ancient tales. If the ancient artist did not experience this same feeling and give it expression, he failed to represent the gods. *Lysippus* was able to articulate it in his small and delicate Hercules, even though the statue was only a foot high, causing Statius to cry in enthusiasm:

Deus, ille Deus, seseque videndum
Indulsit, Lysippe, tibi, parvusque videri
Sentirique ingens, et cum mirabilis intra
Stet mensura pedem, tamen exclamare licebit
Si visus per membra feras; hoc pectore pressus
Vastator Nemaees.[16]

Lysippus's statue became in the words and soul of Statius a *colossus;* to become a Hercules, it had to do so. What flower from the head of Ixora would forbid the artist to magnify the proportions of his work if he were thereby to succeed in awakening a more exalted feeling in the eye that comprehends? In general, what we *touch* with our hands appears *larger* than what we *see* with our eyes; the eye is *quick* like lightning, taking in an object in an instant. But the hand never touches the *entire* object. It cannot grasp a form *all at once,* with the exception of the sphere, which is the form of stasis and contains perfection in itself. The hand can rest on the sphere and the sphere in the hand. But with articulated forms, the work of the hand is never complete: it goes on feeling, so to speak, *infinitely*. This is true above all of the form of the human body, even when it appears on the smallest crucifix. The colossus is thus as familiar and natural to the sense of touch as the colored panel with its single viewpoint is foreign. We must be able to take in a painting in a single glance, otherwise it will stand before us as something gigantic and overpowering, an oppressive and horribly distorted wall of masks. To this we should add that to the feeling hand something *lifeless* seems larger than something *living*. Every movement that flows from the breath of the soul delineates connections and differences; a severed hand appears larger to the sense of touch, and even to the eye, than a hand that is part of the body and suffused with life. Further, we should take into consideration the *obscurity* and *night* in which this sense feels, the gradually discovered *unity* and *indeterminacy* that such a form provides, the idea of *power* and *plenitude*, and the gradual and mighty *will* that resides in the structure as a whole: every great and strong god, every goddess of sublimity and awe, not merely *can* but *must* appear colossal to our imagination, as *more than human* in comparison to our own, dwarf-like stature. Sculpture occupies the middle ground between poetry and painting. The poet has no other limits than those dictated by the range of his imagination and the creative powers that dwell within him. His eye, as the inexhaustible Shakespeare says,

> In a fine frenzy rolling
> Doth glance from heav'n to earth, from earth to heav'n,
> And as imagination bodies forth
> The forms of things unknown, the poets pen
> Turns them to shape and gives to aiery nothing
> A local habitation and a name.[17]

It is remarkable that the most uncomplicated of oriental children's stories offer the greatest room for play, even though everything is told in an infinitely simple and undefined manner, without adjectives or coloration. The painter, too, possesses infinity, but only the *infinity of a continuum*, of a *flat panel of light*. He can paint the heavens and the earth for the imagination, and stretches of land that extend for miles, but not colossal figures, for forms belong to a foreign sense. The painter is obliged to represent forms in accordance with the demands dictated by the frame of his picture and by the laws of the diffraction of light and the treatment of colors. In short, he is constrained by the medium in which he works and the sense to which it is bound. The sculptor, however, stands in the darkness of night and seeks out the shapes of the gods with his sense of touch. He has the stories of the poets before him and within him: he feels Homer's Minerva as she grasps the mighty stone that the giants carried in prehistoric times; he feels her mighty head, whose helmet is wrought with as many warriors as a hundred cities could send into battle; he feels the stride of Neptune, the breast of Alcides, and the curve of Jupiter's eyebrows.[18] Could this feeling, which is pregnant with form, allow his hand to produce something small or trivial? The sculptor remains indifferent to the space in which this feeling is to be expressed and given shape. Let Jupiter be the height of one measure or six, as long as his majesty and dignity are grasped by the senses of the artist and by those who look upon him; this will give him his *space* and his *limits*.

It is just this inner feeling that measures each hand-span of the colossus in accordance with the impression it will make and the place in which it is to be confined. The youthful Apollo may be a proud figure of more than human proportions, but he may not be presented as a colossus. For he is not Jupiter and his swift and slender limbs cannot belong to a figure the height of a tower. What is appropriate to Juno, to the mother of all the gods, is not appropriate to the delightful Aphrodite. The Greeks displayed unutterable wisdom in the size they accorded to every creature of the earth and the heavens. This wisdom still speaks to us, though everyone now receives it on the same ground, where it takes the form of threadbare mythology or an academic parade. What must it have been like when every statue stood in its proper place and was raised above the ground or kept at a sacred distance? The wise feeling for such things was lost under the Romans. Flora,[19] a consul, or an emperor could be represented as a colossus if the artist had enough stone at his disposal or the emperor wished to make a great display of metal. Under the Romans, art became merely Greek artisanship.

3. Finally, what results can allegory produce in the art of sculpture? To what extent can sculpture be allegorical?

The question is terribly complicated, for it is generally seen to include all the arts and even *(horribile dictu!)*[20] the sciences on the same basis, without recognizing that no needle and thread will suffice to transform them into one and the same thing. Winckelmann's work on this subject addresses allegory in the *widest* sense, and since it provides the beginnings of an armory for *all* the fine arts, it must necessarily be *general.*[21] Rarely have so many strange and half-true objections been raised against a piece of writing, and neither artists nor scholars seem to tire of doing so. But the central questions remain: What is allegory? and What is it *here?* Through what medium does it operate? and What is its basis? We can see that every art form must have its own proper form of allegory, or there is no allegory at all.

For this reason, that wise ancient[22] made the concept of allegory so broad: it means *one thing through another,* ἄλλο through ἄλλο.[23] The manner in which something signifies and the way in which ἄλλο is ἄλλο cannot be taught by a general theory, but only by the situation, the intention, the art—in short, by the *individual* and *particular* use that is made of it.

I could say that sculpture is a *permanent allegory,* for it represents the *soul* by means of the *body,* and there cannot be any two greater ἄλλα, especially if one follows the philosophy of occasionalism and of pre-established harmony.[24] The artist has the example of *spirit, character,* and *soul* in himself and he gives to it *flesh* and *bone:* thus *he allegorizes through every part of the body.* For him, proportion is the sine qua non, the condition, but not the *essence* of his art or the cause of its effectiveness. The cause is the *soul* that creates for itself *form,* and where the two, form and soul, require a subtle modification in the proportion between them the artist not only can but must modify them, as in the case of Apollo's *lengthened thighs,* the *thicker neck* of Hercules, and so forth. In general, to make proportion the most important thing in a work of art and to impose one and the same proportion on Antinous[25] and Mars, or on Jupiter and the faun, is to prescribe *one* measure to every period and to every part of an allegory, to compose music out of algebra. *Living form* is the temple and *spirit* is the divinity that animates it. But since not every god and every temple are alike, not even the smallest part can possibly possess the same proportion.

Here again it is important to note that the *less* a part of the body *participates in the life of the spirit,* especially as regards movement and action, the *more* its *proportion* is *determined* and the less it can be altered. This is the case, for example, with the abdomen: if it is lengthened or shortened it loses its form. But in treating those parts of the body that are articulate with *energy, life,* and *movement,* and which are *pronounced,* the artist must attend to the floating element of spirit and give these parts the subtlest impulsion of form. He must imbue the stone with a *sculptural allegory* of the *life of the spirit.*

In this sense, then, we may speak of allegory in sculpture. But I am fully aware that the term can only be employed here in an improper sense; for we, who have so little feeling for sculpture, have given the word *allegory* a meaning that does not derive from this art but from other, *less weighty,* arts and sciences. And in this sense, sculpture cannot *allegorize.* To sink into the stone and to rediscover therein a mere conceit, a subtle relation between two concepts, the abstraction of a fleeting scent or a stray butterfly—for this, stone is too heavy, the hand too clumsy, and the result not worthy of the effort. Let other arts take note of this and strive to capture *breath* and *speech* and the fugitive butterfly of wit and abstraction. For this the *statue* is too *true,* too *complete,* too *unified,* too *sacred.*

Shaping and creative Nature hates abstractions: she never gives everything to any one thing but accords to each what is proper to it in its own *proper* way. The art of form emulates Nature, and it must act in the same way or it is not worthy of the name. Sculpture does not form abstractions but *persons:* it gives us *this* person with *this* character, and *this* character is made present in *every* part of the body, in its placing and *position,* as if an enchanting wand had turned the living person into stone. It is never abstract *love* that stands before us, but the *god* or the *goddess* of love, not the female *divinity* or the virgin *virtue,* but *Minerva, Juno, Venus, Apollo,* and other highly specific names, forms, and persons. I can forgive the lazy mind that imposes allegory on the orator, the poet, or the painter; but whoever goes hunting after bats, after things that belong to neither art nor poetry, nor the soul, nor the body in sculpture, where everything is to the highest degree *substantial, true,* and *determinate*—such a person must seek forgiveness from the allegorized gods themselves.

If one art form is able to hold us fast to substance and to reality, it is sculpture. If sculpture is made into a phantom, what cannot be? The ancient artist could study different things in the most diverse subjects; it is only to us moderns that it appears strange that he could and must do so. But when he *created,* this diversity became a *unity;* he gave it relief and soul from out of his own soul. He spoke to the stone: change, become *this* person, live! This is how all idolatry understood art. The single particular god was *present* and hearkened. The Greeks *named* their statues. A statue did not represent Apollo in general terms, let alone as the beloved sun or as a personification of poetry: it was *the* Apollo *Smintheus, Delius, Pythius, Ἀγρεύς,*[26] as determined by the place and by his attributes. These attributes were no more allegorical (as we understand the word in its poetic sense) than Hercules' club or the noses on our own faces: they were *historical* and *individual characteristics* that served to describe *this* god *here and now.* They *signified,* but they did not signify abstractions; they portrayed an individual to the extent that this could be done without an inscription. If you examine the statues of the gods and the allegories that have been gathered from them, you will see that they are all of this kind.

This is not the place to investigate if, and to what extent, the sculpture of the Greeks was *passed on* from a foreign people.[27] Rather, we are concerned with what they *made* out of it and what they believed they were *doing* when they formed it into an art. In the age of art, the third eye on Jupiter's brow disappeared, for it was an allegorical and not a natural eye.[28] The form *itself* must be Jupiter; the rest could be left to poets, priests, or whoever else wished to speak about it.

The subtlety and complexity with which *attributes* are interpreted by commentators and expositors may well be valid as works of wit and poetry, but I doubt whether Greek priests, artists, or celebrants entertained such ideas. For the most part it was the *historical circumstance* that gave the god a particular name and was then specified through its own attribute. "You are not Jupiter, no, you are *my* Jupiter, *our* Jupiter, the Jupiter who was *here!*"—that is to say, an *idol.* Generally, the more subtle the interpretation given to an allegory the further it is from the truth.

Certainly there was little that surrounded a god or a hero that did not awaken ideas. In the case of the Greeks these ideas were natural and appropriate; they were not formed from *abstractions* or from *confabulated allegory*, but from the *circumstances of history*. The character of the gods and the heroes provided allegory enough and this was *given* to the artist. He sought to express this character: the rest served merely as its support and explanation or as an *interpretation of the particular history, location, or temple* in which the work was placed.

"Was allegory then so alien to the Greeks?" Not at all, but it was not their *principal concern*. The Greeks were too aware that it is not necessary to build a theater, compose an epic, or quarry blocks of marble in order to make an allegorical figure dance. They were too aware that if an allegory is to be beautiful and effective it must be small, simple, and easily circumscribed, such as on a precious stone in a ring. In short, it should not be given the form of a colossus, but is appropriate to *intaglios, coins, urns,* and *bas-reliefs,* such as were indeed dedicated to it.

May the goddess *Tyche*[29] come to me (for it is only fitting that I allegorize about allegory), may she grant me leisure and pleasure and love, which is more than leisure, so that I may draw together my patchwork of thoughts about *anaglyphics;*[30] I think with pleasure on the hours once bestowed on me by the simplest group in the world, *Greek allegory*. There we will discover the spirit of Greece in the most delightful figurative language; here, however, I fear it is too early. A Jupiter, a Hercules or an Apollo, a Laocoön or an Alexander are beings that are too *great* and too *determinate* for allegory to flutter around them. What the hand and the spirit encounter in them is allegory enough, that is, the *mind* and *spirit* of a heavenly being who is present. They were formed on the basis of a specific tradition and the story of their origin; the task of the artist was to give this *precision* where it was uncertain and to *ground it* in some detail of their personal existence, not to adorn it with allegory and so make it evaporate in the air.

What we encounter, however, is *Virtue* carved into stone, *Justice* as a woman, or the virginal figures of *Piety, Love,* and so forth. What do we receive from such things? Nothing! They are soap bubbles carved out of stone. I know what I should think in relation to their attributes. But what thoughts do the figures themselves produce? That they are good and delightful women, created out of a word, an abstract manner of speech, and that in general this is all they are worth? If such statues seek to express what they represent in its highest form, as they ought, they become intolerable; for the most rigorous justice, the most merciful mercy, the most passionate devotion, the sweetest charity, and the most radiant love cannot be borne either by man or stone. And yet it must be *eternally* borne! The figure stands there in the most unnatural, distorted, or abandoned condition and nothing can ever change it. Away with you, grimaces of stone! Transform yourselves back into what you once were, into words and syllables.

In general, however, the artist does *not* make himself strive so high: he does not want to force his block to repeat for eternity and without enthusiasm the *most elevated expression of all that is just,* that is to say, justice, or the *embodiment of all pious action,* that is to say, piety. Instead he remains in blessed mediocrity, and so says *absolutely nothing.* His *Pietas* is at most only a *pia* and his *Caritas* a *cara;*[31] both are indeterminate and lack individual form. Dear artist, this is a waste of marble, your chisel, and your time and effort! It would have been better if you had taken a *particular* pia and cara: at least the statue would have had some life in it, and at least one good woman in stone would have mourned and wept for the Holy Father. Instead He is mourned by a Nothing created from an allegory of virtue.

Allegory is, however, appropriate to *gravestones* and *memorials:* for these often take the place of bas-reliefs upon *monuments,* and like intaglios and coins they are not *independent works of art.* The Greeks, too, could depict Psyche and Cupid upon a gravestone, where, in part, they fulfilled an allegorical function (though they were more than this—they were a *myth*); the beautiful pair encounter one another again, and kiss and embrace like sisters.[32] If there is any place in which one expects to find an angel here on earth, then it is upon a grave above the beloved ashes of the dead, where everything is silent and no sound travels from the other world—but where we desire so fervently to meet with more than ashes. Here a weeping or consoling figure of *virtue* may be tolerated, but only in the form appropriate to the name, a *female angel.* If the dead man or woman can be depicted in the angel's features or shown standing alongside her, as we would wish to see them, all the better. Moreover, if the dead person's children or his lover or wife can be added to the scene, both art and the monument will gain in *truth* and be better for it. These sepulchral angels are permitted for humanity's sake as memorials to love and charity, but if they are made into the *principal feature* of art, into *learned* abstractions and allegories, they frighten everything else away like phantoms. Is it not a clear sign of our *neediness* and *poverty* that we possess nothing but allegories and that we do not know how to create anything else?

What becomes of the art of *bodily truth* when it no longer possess *bodily truth?* Instead of presenting a single ensouled whole, it seeks after the butterflies of *wit* and *meaning* that flutter *around, above,* or *alongside* it. It cannot reach this prize, no matter how small. It aims for something that it cannot express: for central to all literary and moral allegory is the *group,* and in the proper sense of the word this is not to be found in sculpture.

"Is this really so? Does sculpture present no groups? What then of Laocoön, Niobe, the two brothers?"[33] Indeed, I know all this and more. I know that a French writer has recently considered it worthy of the highest praise that "*his* nation has freshly rediscovered the grouping of statues; it is the first to group statues in a *painterly* fashion, as no ancient ever did."[34] Group statues in a painterly fashion? Listen to how the pipe whistles! Properly speaking, a *painterly* grouping of statues is a contradiction. Every statue is single and a unity. Every statue is self-sufficient and stands alone. What this writer criticizes in the ancients was, in fact, a *conscious and wise choice.* They chose not to group statues, and where a group was necessary they did everything they could to break it up.

This is why Laocoön's children are made so small, even though they are grown men. It is not, as Hogarth claimed, on account of his line of beauty, such that a packing case built around all three figures would take on the form of a pyramid or a flame.[35] The artist was not concerned with such carpenter's work. What did concern him and what had to concern him was that if the children were made the same size as their father, they would stand between him and the light even in the darkest night and the whole would thereby become three rather than one. If all three stood there and cried and wrestled in vain with the serpent, the spirit of the father's sublime suffering and his struggle against death would be lamentably dispersed and lost. Since the sculptor could not remove the two sons to allow his masterful work to stand *alone,* he made them smaller and limited them to *accessories.* The mouth of one is torn open (as every connoisseur of Greek art can see with horror),[36] and he is abandoned to his torment and the dominion of the serpent; this allows the sublime father to stand alone between his two sons as the hero and as the one who struggles and raises his cries to the heavens.

Where is the group of *Niobe* to be found? How far it is from being a group! And how distant and scattered are the figures that surround her! The youngest who takes refuge in her lap folds and hides herself there; it is precisely through this child that the mother is allowed to appear *alone* and *sublime* as the mother of such children.

Two fraternal friends that lean upon each other in the simplest of postures;[37] a pair that is unified with a kiss in the simplest of postures.[38] These are no more to be termed "groups" than *Leda* and the swan, or *Jupiter* and his eagle. The artist is aware of the eternal law, the essence of his art, that there can only be *one* and in this *one* there must be *everything.* The more his work is split into pieces, divided up, and then grouped and heaped together, the more impoverished it becomes. Until finally a dove is required to hover over the group as a whole with a message of stone in its beak in order to explain what this *forest of stone* means. For here the *individual statue* no longer means *anything* to the *gaze that looks* or to the *hand that feels.*

Approach the noble group of *Arria and Paetus,* presented alongside chamber women and servants.[39] Where should such a statue be placed? Which figure should be placed at the back? For the group is free on all sides in accordance with *painterly* conventions. If you call upon your sense of touch to help you, where should you begin? and where should you finish? Where is the spirit? Where is the *single soul that informs the work as a whole?* Everyone is in sorrow; all have heroic courage. Everyone has in their mouth the gentle words of Arria: *non dolcet Paete,*[40] though the hand can neither feel these nor would wish to. How simple, by contrast, is the *Paetus* of the ancients.[41] *Arria* sinks to his feet and he holds her and ends his life. Once again, we do not have a painterly group.

Can then a *story* not form a group in sculpture, so that each person *stands for himself on his own ground,* in his own world? Dear allegory, how would it be if you were to seek to fly forth like a butterfly or a dove from several persons or figures, each formed *complete* for themselves and yet *not* completely formed (only formed for *you allegory!*). I fear you would remain where you are, in the idle head of the artist. There is no path that leads from here to the working hand or the divided block that remains *single* only in the head of the artist.

Finally, why do we seek to contradict nature? Why do we not leave each art to do what it *alone* can do and what it *does best?* Where there is a *single ground,* on intaglios, coins, and panels, *nature connects everything together* through the *continuum of a surface.* Intaglios, coins, bas-reliefs, and gravestones can do little more than present an allegory. This is what they are for, and they do it inimitably. Why tear allegory from here? Why reduce it to a shadow? Why confuse and conflate it with the great images of *truth* and the *figures of gods and heroes* or with the enchanted panel of *historical truth,* with *painting?* An epic in which allegories act, a play in which abstractions take the stage, a history in which concepts perform for us an instructive dance, and a state in which ideals prevail—these are great and splendid ideas. But they are no more splendid than the art of form that sculpts them out of stone in order that they may not vanish from the world.

EDITOR'S NOTES

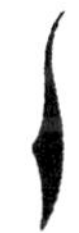

Title and Epigraphs

• "Pygmalion's Creative Dream." The story of Pygmalion is best known through the version told by Ovid (43 BC–AD 17) in his *Metamorphoses* (10.243–97). Pygmalion, a legendary king of Cyprus, carved a figure out of ivory and then fell in love with his own work. In response to his prayers, the goddess Venus allowed the statue to come to life under his touch. The myth enjoyed great popularity in the eighteenth century and was the subject of numerous retellings, including paintings, engravings, and an opera by Jean Jacques Rousseau (1712–78) that received its first performance in Paris in 1770. As Oskar Bätschmann has shown, this upsurge of popularity took place at a time when a new concept of art was beginning to take hold, one that emphasized the importance of the viewer's emotional response as a means of animating the work, or "bringing it to life." In contrast to the distanced contemplation of the antiquarian or the connoisseur, the appropriately responsive art lover was enjoined to enter into a more intimate relation to the object of his or her admiration. The myth of Pygmalion, who falls in love with and then succeeds in bringing to life the statue he so fervently admires, was represented as a paradigm of the ideal relation between viewer and work. See Bätschmann, "Pygmalion als Betrachter." In the course of the eighteenth century the Pygmalion myth took on a further significance through its incorporation into philosophical discussions concerning the relation of matter and spirit. In 1742, the French philosopher Boureau-Deslandes (1690–1757) published his *Pygmalion ou la statue animée,* in which he interpreted the myth in anti-Cartesian terms as revealing the coemergence of thought and sensibility. Materialist and sensualist philosophers such as La Mettrie (1709–51) and Condillac (1715–80) continued this practice and drew on the story of Pygmalion in order to oppose dualistic conceptions of the relation between the mind and the body. For a detailed discussion of the reception of the Pygmalion myth, see Blühm, *Pygmalion.*

• "Τί καλλος; ἐρώτηυα τυφλοῦ." Greek: "What is the beautiful? The question of a blind man," adapted from Diogenes Laertius (active first half of the third century AD), *Lives of Eminent Philosophers,* 5.20. In answer to the question, "Why do we devote so much time to the beautiful?" Aristotle replies, "That is the question of a blind man." The sensory experiences of the blind form the starting point for Herder's own reflections on art and beauty. The implication is that we stand to learn a great deal about beauty by asking someone who is blind.

• "anaglyphics." An anaglyph is an ornament in low relief; anaglyphics is thus the science or study of low reliefs. Herder had already begun to investigate the senses as the basis for understanding the arts in the fourth of his *Kritische Wälder* [Critical Groves], written in 1769 but published only posthumously, in 1846.

• "en! ille in nubibus arcus/mille trahit varios adverso sole colores." Latin: "Look! an arc in the sky that darts a thousand shifting tints athwart the sun," Virgil (70–19 BC), *Aeneid,* 5:88–89.—Herder added the first three words.

Part One

1. Denis Diderot (1713–84) published his *Lettre sur les aveugles, à l'usage de ceux qui voient* [Letter on the blind, for the use of those who can see] in London in 1749. There he gives an account of his visit to a congenitally blind man in the town of Puisseaux, some forty miles from Paris. See Diderot, *Oeuvres,* 1:139–85, especially pp. 140–47. A partial English translation of this essay appears in Morgan, *Molyneux's Question.*

2. The blind man Diderot questioned describes a mirror as a "device that puts things into relief at a distance, as long as they are placed in the appropriate position. It is like my hand, which does not need to touch an object in order to feel it" (Diderot, *Oeuvres,* 1:141). When the blind man is unable to feel the "relief copy" made by the mirror, however, he declares: "Here is a device that brings the two senses into conflict; a more perfect device would perhaps bring them into agreement, except that, even then, the objects would not be any more real; perhaps a third device that was even more perfect and less deceiving would make them disappear and would make us realise the error" (ibid., 1:141–42).

3. Nicholas Saunderson (1682–1739) became Lucasian Professor of Mathematics at Cambridge and a Fellow of the Royal Society despite being blind since infancy. His *Elements of Algebra in ten Books* (1740) contains a theory of "palpable arithmetic" based on tactile experience of space and number. Herder's information on Saunderson is largely taken from Diderot's *Lettre sur les aveugles,* where Saunderson's ideas are discussed at length. According to Diderot, Saunderson used the same device both for calculations and for drawing rectilinear figures. His calculating machine employed a system by which digits could be represented by placing one or more pegs in a matrix of holes.

In order to represent geometrical figures, Saunderson linked pegs together with silk thread so as to construct "palpable or tangible symbols." See Diderot, *Oeuvres*, 1:152–72.

4. William Cheselden (1688–1752) was an English surgeon and the author of *The Anatomy of the Human Body* (1713). He was the first to carry out an iridectomy (removal of part of the iris). In 1728 he published a report of an operation to remove a cataract from the eye of a thirteen-year-old boy in the *Philosophical Transactions of the Royal Society of London* entitled "An account of some observations made by a young gentleman, who was born blind, or lost his sight so early, that he had no remembrance of ever having seen, and was couch'd between 13 and 14 years of age." Herder's account of the case is taken from Robert Smith's *A Compleat System of Opticks* (1738), where Cheselden's report is cited verbatim.

5. Cf. the following passage of Cheselden's report: "Though we say of this gentleman that he was blind, as we do of all people who have ripe cataracts, yet they are never so blind from that cause, but that they can discern day from night; and for the most part in a strong light, distinguish, black, white, and scarlet, but they cannot perceive the shape of any thing: for the light by which these perceptions are made, being let in obliquely through the aqueous humour, or the anterior surface of the crystalline (by which the rays cannot be brought into a focus upon the retina) they can discern in no other manner, than a sound eye can through a glass of broken jelly, where a great variety of surfaces so differently refract the light, that the several distinct pencils of rays cannot be collected by the eye into their proper foci; wherefore the shape of an object in such a case, cannot be at all discerned, though the colour may" (Smith, *A Compleat System of Opticks*, vol. 1, bk. 1, pp. 42–43).

6. Herder takes this lengthy citation from Cheselden's report from the German edition of Smith's *A Compleat System of Opticks*, translated by Abraham Gotthelf Kästner (*Vollständiger Lehrbegriff der Optick* [Altenburg, 1755]). I have given the corresponding passages from Smith's work, which the German translation faithfully follows. The passages in Smith, the order of which Herder has changed somewhat, are in vol. 1, bk. 1, pp. 42–43.

7. "Ophthalmite" is Herder's coinage, based on the Greek word for "eye": *ophthalmos*.

8. Plato's analogy of the cave appears in the *Republic* (7:514a–18b). The cave dwellers have fetters on their necks and legs that constrain them to look forward. All they can see are the shadows of objects cast on the wall in front of them.

9. Herder plays on the sense of seizing or taking hold of something carried by the German word *Begriff* [concept]. Together with the cognate verb *begreifen* [to understand], *Begriff* is etymologically related to *greifen* [to grip or take hold of something] and *Griff* [the grip, grasp]. The English word "concept" enjoys a similar relation to the Latin verb *concipio*, which means both (1) to take hold of something and (2) to comprehend or think. The substantive *conceptus* describes both (1) a catching or taking hold of something and (2) a thought or idea in the mind.

10. The most celebrated example of a blind person who modeled in wax was the sculptor Giovanni Francesco Gonnelli (1603–64). Born in the town of

Gambassi, in Tuscany, he is sometimes referred to as "Gambassi the Blind." Despite losing his sight during the Austrian siege of Mantua in 1632, Gonnelli returned to sculpture, working in malleable materials such as wax and clay. He was particularly admired for his portrait busts, including a bust of Urban VIII, and his work excited considerable interest among his contemporaries. The French art theorist Roger de Piles (1635–1709) discussed his work in *Dialogue sur les coloris* (Paris, 1673, 19–23). One of the participants in the dialogue reports asking Gambassi "if he did not see a little, to copy so exactly as he did? He reply'd that he saw nothing at all, and that his Eyes were at his Fingers Ends. . . . My way is this; I feel my Original again and again; I attentively examine the Dimensions, the Risings and the Fallings; I imprint them on my Memory; then I take my Wax and by the Comparison which I make of one and the other by carrying my Hand [back and forth] several times, I finish my Work in the best manner I can" (*Dialogue upon Colouring,* trans. John Ozell [London: Daniel Brown, 1711], 13).

11. This is not a quotation from another author. Herder employs quotation marks to emphasize his own formulation.

12. Again, Herder employs quotation marks to emphasize his own formulation.

13. Herder's attempt to establish the etymology of the German term for beauty *(Schönheit)* in the words for "beholding" *(Schauen)* and "appearance" *(Schein)* is generally thought to be incorrect. It does not find any correlation in English.

14. The term Herder employs is *Hülfsbegriffe.* This appears to be his own coinage. Translated literally, it means "help-concepts." It is employed here to refer to concepts that are taken over from the other senses and that are no longer used in their primary context.

15. See John Locke, *An Essay concerning Human Understanding,* bk. 4, chap. 1, sect. 11. Locke argues that the "simple idea" of an object can only be gained through the appropriate sense, or "inlet," of the body. In order to know the taste of a pineapple, we must actually taste it; mere words or definitions cannot substitute for experience. Nor can ideas specific to any one sense be known through any another. This is demonstrated by the story of a blind man who claimed to know what scarlet was, but declared it to be "like the Sound of a Trumpet."

16. In his *Laokoön: oder über die Grenzen der Malerei und Poesie* [Laocoön: or on the limits of poetry and painting], published in Berlin in 1766, Gotthold Ephraim Lessing (1729–81) sought to identify the different laws governing painting and poetry by relating these two arts to the senses of sight and hearing, respectively. In what follows, Herder takes up Lessing's distinction between poetry as the art of "things that follow each other in time" and painting as the art of "things that coexist in space," but adds to it a third, "things that exist in depth." In doing so, he criticizes Lessing's assumption that the generic term "painting" can be used to describe the visual arts in general. For Herder, what is needed is not a two-fold distinction between poetry and painting, but a three-fold distinction between poetry, painting, and sculpture.

17. In Greek mythology, Argus is said to have possessed one hundred eyes. He was charged by Juno with watching over the mortal Io, whom Jupiter had transformed into a heifer. See Ovid, *Metamorphoses,* 1:622–723.

18. A corresponding passage in the fourth of Herder's *Critical Groves* reveals that he is primarily thinking here of the German art historian Johann Joachim Winckelmann (1717–68) and his celebrated description of the statue of the Apollo Belvedere (fig. 1) in Rome. See Herder, *Sämtliche Werke,* 4:65–66. Winckelmann's sensual and imaginative engagement with works of art, expressed in highly poeticized language, did much to stimulate the new enthusiasm for Greek art and culture. His description of the Apollo Belvedere was published in his *Geschichte der Kunst des Alterthums* (Dresden, 1764), 2:392–94). It appears in English in the translation of the second edition of 1776 by G. Henry Lodge, *History of Ancient Art,* 2:312–14.

19. Phidias (active c. 490–430 BC) is the most highly regarded sculptor of the Attic school. He is generally held to be responsible for supervising the design of the sculptures on the Parthenon, though this is now a subject of dispute. Herder refers to his late masterpiece, the colossal cult statue of Zeus (Jupiter), made for the god's temple at Olympia. Incorporating gold, ivory, glass, ebony, and hardstones, it was held to be one of the Seven Wonders of the Ancient World. Today it is known only through pictures on coins and the written testament of Pausanias (*Description of Greece,* 5.11.1–11), who describes a figure made of gold and ivory, seated on an ebony throne, wearing a mantle and an olive wreath; Zeus carries a figure of Nike (victory) in his right hand and a scepter topped by an eagle in his left. The source for Herder's claim that Phidias was inspired by Homer is the *Geographica* of Strabo (c. 60 BC–AD 20), 8.3.30. Strabo maintains that Phidias created his likeness of Zeus after the description in Homer's *Iliad:* "He spoke, the son of Kronos, and nodded his head with the dark brows,/and the immortally anointed hair of the great god/swept from his divine head, and all Olympus was shaken" (1.528–30). The same argument is taken up by Lessing in chapter 22 of *Laocoön:* "Phidias confessed that the lines [from Homer] served him as a model for his Olympian Jupiter, and that it was only through Homer's help that he succeeded in producing a divine countenance, *propemodum ex ipso coelo petitum* (almost brought down from heaven itself)" (p. 118).

20. An inscription on the base of the Belvedere Torso (fig. 2) in the Vatican Museum in Rome identifies it as the work of Apollonius, an Attic sculptor active in the first century BC. The massiveness of the figure and the fact that it is seated on an animal skin (thought to be that of a lion) led many experts, including Winckelmann, to interpret it as a Hercules. The Torso was particularly admired by Michelangelo, and for this reason is sometimes known as "the school of Michelangelo." Winckelmann published *Beschreibung des Torso im Belvedere zu Rom* [Description of the Torso in the Belvedere in Rome] in 1759, parts of which were subsequently incorporated into his *History of Ancient Art.* Herder's description of Hercules as a "giant conqueror" follows Winckelmann: "In that powerfully developed chest we behold in imagination the breast against which the giant Geryon was squeezed" (pp. 264–65). For the reception history of the statue, see Haskell and Penny, *Taste and the Antique,* no. 80, pp. 311–14.

21. Agasias of Ephesos signed the marble statue of the so-called Borghese Gladiator (fig. 3), now in the Louvre in Paris. The statue was particularly admired for its truthful rendering of anatomy. Winckelmann praised its "truth to nature" in the "Erläuterungen" appended to the second edition of his *Gedanken von der Nachahmung der grieschischen Werke in der Malerei und Bildhauerkunst* [Reflections on the imitation of Greek works in painting and sculpture], published in Dresden in 1756 (reprinted in Winckelmann, *Kleine Schriften,* 108). In the notes incorporated into the second edition of his *History of Ancient Art,* he argued that the statue was wrongly thought to depict a gladiator and that it was more likely to be of a warrior who had specially distinguished himself (see 2:312). This issue was taken up once again by Lessing in chapter 28 of *Laocoön.* The statue is now thought to be a Roman copy of a Greek original of c.100–75 BC. For the reception of the work, see Haskell and Penny, *Taste and the Antique,* no. 43, pp. 221–24.

22. Étienne Maurice Falconet (1716–91) was one of the foremost French sculptors of the mid-eighteenth century. He is best known for his small-scale pieces in marble and for the models he produced for the Sèvres porcelain factory. However, he is also renowned for his monumental equestrian monument to Peter the Great in St. Petersburg, executed during his long stay in Russia between 1766 and 1778. His *Réflexions sur la sculpture* was presented as a lecture to the French Royal Academy of Painting and Sculpture in 1760. It was published in Paris in 1761 and was subsequently incorporated into Diderot's *Encyclopédie* as the article "Sculpture." Herder's footnote refers the reader to the German translation, which appeared in 1765. Falconet identifies a series of differences between sculpture and painting: first, sculpture does not have "the advantage of shades, of backgrounds, of rounding, and of foreshortenings"; second, it has "as many points of view as there are points of space around it"; third, the sculptor must use his imagination to overcome "the disgust which the mechanism, the fatigue and the slowness of his operations must necessarily occasion"; finally, the sculptor is "deprived of the seducing charm of colours." See Falconet, "Reflexions on Sculpture," 14. Herder himself first sought to distinguish between the different arts on the basis of the contribution of the senses in the fourth of his *Critical Groves,* written in 1769 but not published until 1846.

23. The distinction between "natural signs," which possess an iconic resemblance to that which they represent, and "arbitrary signs," which possess a merely conventional connection, was first introduced by the Abbé Du Bos (1670–1742) in his *Réflexions critiques sur la poésie et sur la peinture,* published in Paris in 1719. Du Bos observes that "the signs with which painters address us, are not arbitrary or instituted, such as words employed in poetry. Painting makes use of natural signs, the energy of which does not depend on education. They draw their force from the relation which nature herself has fixed between our organs and external objects in order to attend to our preservation" (Du Bos, *Critical Reflections,* vol.1, sect. 40, p. 322). In Germany, the distinction between natural and artificial signs was taken up by Moses Mendelssohn (1729–86), who used it as the basis for a taxonomy of the arts in his "Betrachtungen über die Quellen und Verbindungen der schönen Künste und Wissenschaften" [Observations on the sources and interconnections of the fine

arts and sciences], first published in 1757 (reprinted in Mendelssohn, *Gesammelte Schriften,* vol. 1). Lessing also employs this distinction in chapter 17 of *Laocoön.*

24. Again, Herder is drawing on and taking issue with Lessing's *Laocoön* (see note 16 above). In chapter 16, the theoretical heart of the treatise, Lessing outlines his position as follows: "I reason thus: if it is true that in its imitations painting uses completely different means or signs than does poetry, namely figures and colours in space rather than articulated sounds in time, and if these signs must indisputably bear a suitable relation to the thing signified, then signs existing in space can express only objects whose wholes or parts coexist, while signs that follow one another can express only objects whose wholes or parts are consecutive./Objects or parts of objects which exist in space are called bodies. Accordingly, bodies with their visible properties are the true subjects of painting./Objects or parts of objects which follow one another are called actions. Accordingly, actions are the true subject of poetry" (p. 78).

25. Herder gives the Latin, Italian, and French terms for "painting" in order to make clear the connection between the painted image and the surface or "table." The German term, translated here as "image on a panel," is *Bildertafel.*

Part Two

1. In *History of Ancient Art,* Winckelmann interpreted the statue of the Apollo Belvedere (fig. 1) as showing the god in the moment after his victory over the giant serpent, Python (2:313). Ovid describes Apollo's slaying of the serpent "with a thousand arrows" (*Metamorphoses,* 1.438–51). The statue was termed the Apollo Belvedere after it was installed in the Vatican's Belvedere Courtyard early in the sixteenth century. It is now thought to be a Roman copy of a Greek original of c. 330 BC. For its reception history, see Haskell and Penny, *Taste and the Antique,* no. 8, pp. 148–51.

2. A statue of Laocoön and his sons wrestling with a serpent (fig. 4) was discovered in Rome in 1506 and was quickly identified as the work Pliny the Elder (23–79) describes in *Natural History* (36.37). Pope Julius II bought the statue and displayed it in the Vatican's Belvedere Courtyard. Pliny attributes the sculpture to the artists Hagesandrus, Polidorus, and Athenodorus of Rhodes. It is now thought to be a Roman copy of c. 20 BC to AD 20, after a Greek original of the mid-second century BC. Virgil tells the story of Laocoön (*Aeneid,* 2.199–24): While officiating at the sacrifice of a bull on the altar of Neptune to mark the apparent withdrawal of the Greeks from their siege of Troy, Laocoön and both his sons are killed by two huge serpents that emerge from the sea. The differences between the statue and Virgil's account were the source of much speculation in the eighteenth century. The expression of emotion in the two works of art received particular attention: whereas Virgil's Laocoön "lifts to heaven hideous cries," the statue was praised for its dignified restraint. In his book *Laocoön,* Lessing took these differences as the starting point for a sustained meditation on the respective limits imposed by the different media of poetry and painting. For the reception of the sculpture, see Haskell and Penny, *Taste and the Antique,* no. 52, pp. 243–47.

3. Latin: "fillets steeped in gore and black venom" (Virgil, *Aeneid,* 2.221). Lessing cites the same passage in chapter 5 of *Laocoön,* in which he considers why the priest and his sons are presented naked in the sculpture but not in Virgil's description. Lessing concludes: "In poetry a garment is not a garment; it conceals nothing; our imagination sees right through it. Whether Virgil's Laocoön wears robes or not, his suffering is just as evident in one part of the body as in another. To the imagination, his brow is encircled but not hidden by the priestly fillet. . . . [But if the sculptor had] left Laocoön so much as the fillet, he would have greatly weakened the expression, for the brow, the seat of expression, would have been partly covered" (p. 38).

4. Cybele was a Phrygian mother-goddess. Her chief sanctuary was in Pessinus in Anatolia, but her cult subsequently spread to Greece and Rome.

5. There are two important Greek philosophers named Zeno: Zeno of Elea (born c. 490 BC), a contemporary of Parmenides best known for his destructive arguments or paradoxes, and Zeno of Citium (334–262 BC), who founded the Hellenistic school of Stoic philosophy.

6. In Greek mythology, Niobe was the daughter of Tantalus and the wife of Amphion, king of Thebes, by whom she had seven daughters and seven sons. She was so proud of her children that she claimed to deserve the worship that the women of Thebes normally offered to Leto, the mother of Apollo and Diana. Leto punished Niobe's pride by asking her children to avenge the insult, whereupon Apollo slew with his arrows all of Niobe's sons, and Diana, all her daughters. In her grief, Niobe was turned to stone, but the stone continued to weep tears. The story is recounted by Homer (*Iliad,* 24.602–17) and Ovid (*Metamorphoses,* 6.146–313). A sculpted group including Niobe sheltering her daughter, together with statues of some of the other "Niobids," was discovered in Rome in the sixteenth century and displayed in the Belvedere Courtyard. Winckelmann maintained that it was one of "the most beautiful works of antiquity" and that "Niobe and her daughters are beautiful according to the highest conceptions of beauty" (*History of Ancient Art,* 1:251). The central statue of Niobe and her daughter (fig. 5) is now in the Uffizi in Florence. It is thought to be a Roman copy of a Greek original, perhaps by Skopas of Paros or Praxiteles of Athens, both of whom were active in the fourth century BC. For the reception of the sculpture, see Haskell and Penny, *Taste and the Antique,* no. 66, pp. 274–79.

7. Juno was the chief goddess of Olympia and both the sister and the wife of Jupiter. The term *matrona* (mother) identifies her as the protectress of wives and children. Alongside Venus and Minerva, she was one of the goddesses in the famous "judgment of Paris" in which the mortal Paris had to choose who was the most beautiful. Each offered him a different reward: Juno promised him power, Minerva, wisdom, and Venus, the most beautiful woman in the world. Paris's choice of Venus ultimately led to the Trojan War, for he was awarded as his prize Helen of Troy.

8. The phrase "character of the nation" derives from Montesquieu (1689–1755). In his *De l'esprit des lois* [The spirit of the laws], published in 1748, Montesquieu argued that climate was a significant influence upon the character of a people and its form of government.

9. In his *Gedanken von der Nachahmung der grieschischen Werke in der*

Malerei und Bildhauerkunst (Dresden, 1755), Winckelmann argued that "Greek drapery was usually modelled from thin and wet clothing which, as artists well know, clings to the skin and permits the naked outlines of the body to be seen. The entire outer garment of Greek women was of very thin material and was therefore called peplon, a 'veil.'" (*Reflections on the Imitation of Greek Works*, 32–33). In *History of Ancient Art*, he maintains: "The dress of women was partly of linen or some other light material. . . . This kind of drapery has been given to figures, not so much because artists imitated the moist linen with which they draped their models, as because the most ancient inhabitants of Athens, as Thuycidides and other Greeks also inform us, were accustomed to wear linen" (2:4). More recent studies suggest that Greek women were, in fact, extremely modestly dressed. The "peplos" was the standard form of dress throughout both the archaic (c. 600–c.480 BC) and the classical periods (c. 480–c. 320 BC). It was a long woolen tunic, pinned at the shoulders, girdled at or above the waist, and reaching down to the ankles. Whereas Herder recognizes drapery only as an impediment to sculptural form, recent studies emphasize the symbolic and expressive significance of clothing in Greek sculpture. Andrew Stewart, for example, maintains: "The study of Greek dress . . . is both coextensive with the study of Greek sculpture itself, and as necessary to our understanding of it as is a knowledge of anatomy" (*Greek Sculpture*, 1:76).

10. Homer maintains that the veins of the gods are filled with an ethereal fluid called "ichor," rather than blood. See *Iliad*, 5.340.

11. In his *Reflections on the Imitation of Greek Works*, Winckelmann claimed that Raphael had "sent young artists to Greece in order to sketch for him the relics of antiquity" (p. 61). The original source for this belief would appear to be Giorgio Vasari (1511–74), who claimed that "Raphael had draughtsman working for him throughout all Italy . . . and even in Greece" (*Lives of the Artists*, 310). Herder may also have in mind, however, the version of the story told by Roger de Piles. In his *Abrégé de la vie des peintres* (Paris, 1699), de Piles claims: "Besides the pains that Raphael was at in working after ancient sculptures he hir'd people in Greece and Italy to design for him all the Antique pieces that could be found, which, as opportunity offer'd, he made use of" (*The Art of Painting*, 110).

12. As Oskar Bätschmann has shown, the source of this anecdote is not, in fact, Winckelmann, but Hans Heinrich Füssli in a letter to Hans Conrad Vögelin, the translator of Daniel Webb's *Inquiries into the Beauties of Painting* (1760). The letter was published as a preface to the German translation, *Untersuchungen des Schönen in der Mahlerei* (Zurich, 1766). See Bätschmann, "Pygmalion als Betrachter," 183–224.

13. A marble statue of a hermaphrodite (fig. 6) was discovered in Rome in the early seventeenth century. Now preserved in the Louvre in Paris, it earlier formed part of the Borghese collection in Rome. The mattress is the work of Gianlorenzo Bernini (1598–1680). Winckelmann discusses the statue in his *History of Ancient Art* (1:208–9). It is now thought to be a Roman copy of a bronze original of the mid-second century BC. For its reception, see Haskell and Penny, *Taste and the Antique*, no. 48, pp. 234–36.

14. Chaerea is a character in the comedy *The Eunuch* by the Roman play-

wright Terence (c. 186–159 BC). Chaerea disguises himself as a eunuch in order to gain access to the house of a young girl with whom he has fallen in love. While spying on her preparations for a bath, he sees her looking at a picture on the wall that shows Jupiter appearing as a shower of gold to Danae.

15. Herder may have had in mind the highly erotic *Leda and the Swan* painted by Antonio Correggio (c. 1494–1534) for the Duke of Mantua, Frederico Gonzaga, in 1530/32. The painting was brought to Germany by Frederick the Great in 1755 to hang in his gallery at Sanssouci. It is now in the Gemäldegalerie, Berlin.

16. Titian painted two versions of *Danae.* The first, dating from c. 1545/46, is in the Museo Nazionale in Naples; the second, dating from c. 1554, is in the Prado in Madrid.

17. The opening pages of Winckelmann's *Reflections on the Imitation of Greek Works* describe the advantages afforded to artists by the Greek climate and way of life. Winckelmann argues that the high value the Greeks placed on beauty and their custom of participating fully naked in the games encouraged the cultivation of the body and allowed artists unrivalled opportunity to examine the human form. This theme is taken up again in *History of Ancient Art* in the chapter entitled "On the Grounds and Causes of the Progress and Superiority of Greek Art beyond That of Other Nations" (1:175ff).

18. The source of the belief that Raphael died young because 'he kept up his secret love affairs and pursued his pleasures with no sense of moderation' is Vasari. See, *Lives of the Artists, op cit.*, p. 320.

19. Praxiteles was an Athenian sculptor, active c. 370–330 BC. His masterpiece was the marble *Knidian Aphrodite,* supposedly modeled after his mistress, Phryne. Fully naked and viewable from every side, the statue was placed in a round temple dedicated to the goddess by the people of Knidos. Pliny the Elder discusses the statue in *Natural History* (36.4). In antiquity it was regarded as the greatest achievement of the late classic period, but it survives today only in a few poor copies. Lysippus was an exceptionally prolific Sikyonian sculptor, active c. 370–315 BC, who worked exclusively in bronze. He is reported to have made many statues of Zeus, including a colossal statue at Tarentum. No originals by either sculptor survive, but several Roman statues have been identified as copies on the basis of ancient descriptions.

20. A "houri" is a young and beautiful maiden who dwells in the Muslim paradise.

21. The final section of Falconet's "Reflections on Sculpture" (pp. 36–41) is dedicated to a discussion of drapery. There he argues that modern sculptors need not follow the Greeks in their manner of depicting clothing or in their choice of fine and diaphanous materials. By representing a variety of different materials the modern artist can give variety and depth to their sculptures and prevent the eye from becoming fatigued.

22. Herder is here paraphrasing Friedrich Riedel (1742–85), whose *Theorie der schönen Künste und Wissenschaften* [Theory of the fine arts and sciences] was published in Jena in 1767. In chapter 9 of this work, entitled "Similarity and Contrast," Riedel argues: "If a marble statue is clothed with colors, like a painting, the similarity becomes too complete and it no longer affects us. From a distance we can mistake it for a real human being. Although

we discover our error when we approach it, no other response is awakened in us than astonishment at what has deceived us" (pp. 133–34, my translation). Herder had already taken issue with Riedel on this point in the fourth of his *Critical Groves.* See Herder, *Sämtliche Werke,* 4:70–71.

23. Again, Herder is paraphrasing Riedel's *Theorie der schönen Künste und Wissenschaften.* In chapter 10, "On Imitation and Illusion," Riedel argues: "We take pleasure in looking at an animal carved out of stone. But if the artist Myron had covered his cow in hair, it would have looked too much like the original to give us pleasure, and it would always lose out by comparison" (p. 142). The Greek sculptor Myron, a contemporary of Phidias, was active in the fifth century BC. His sculpture of a cow is the subject of numerous epigrams preserved from antiquity, many of which comment on its realism. See *Greek Anthology,* bk. 9, nos. 713–44, 793–98.

24. The reference is to Winckelmann's description of the Apollo Belvedere in *History of Ancient Art:* "Neither blood-vessels nor sinews heat and stir this body, but a heavenly essence, diffusing itself like a gentle stream, seems to fill the whole contour of the figure" (2:313).

25. Quotation, slightly modified, from Winckelmann's description of the Apollo Belvedere, as above.

26. See 1 Corinthians 11:8–10. "For man was not made from woman, but woman from man. Neither was man created for woman but woman for man. That is why a woman ought to have a veil (ἐξουσία) on her head, because of the angels."

27. See Winckelmann, *History of Ancient Art,* 1:282.

28. In a footnote to the passage referred to above, Winckelmann observes: "In Tuscany, persons with such eyebrows are called *stupori,* 'dullards.'"

29. Herder's claims are not supported by modern scholarship, which recognizes extensive use of precious materials and the painting of statues throughout antiquity. See Stewart, *Greek Sculpture,* 33–42.

30. The background to Herder's discussion is Lessing's treatment of the same question in chapter 24 of *Laocoön.* Whereas Herder is concerned with the distinction between sculpture and painting, Lessing is concerned with the distinction between painting and poetry. Lessing concludes that poetry may represent ugly things that painting may not, since the representation of ugly things in painting cannot be a source of pleasure: "Painting as an imitative skill, can express ugliness; painting as a fine art refuses to do so. As a skill, it may take all visible objects as its subjects; as an art, it restricts itself only to those visible objects which awaken our pleasure" (p. 126).

31. Herder has in mind here *The Plague at Ashdod* of 1631 by Nicolas Poussin (1594–1665). Poussin's painting is based on the description of the plague at Ashdod given in 1 Samuel 5. In the foreground a man holds his nose as he stoops to lift a child from its dead mother's breast. Another onlooker approaching the scene does the same. The painting is now in the Louvre, Paris.

32. See Aristotle, *Poetics,* 4.1448b. Aristotle argues that "it is an instinct of human beings, from childhood, to engage in mimesis (indeed this distinguishes them from all other animals: man is the most mimetic of all, and it is

through mimesis that he develops his earliest understanding); and equally natural that everyone enjoys mimetic objects. A common occurrence indicates this: we enjoy contemplating the most precise images of things whose actual sight is painful to us, such as the forms of the vilest animals and of corpses. The explanation of this is that understanding gives great pleasure not only to philosophers but likewise to others too, though the latter have a smaller share of it."

33. In Greek mythology, Itys was the son of Procne and of Tereus, a Thracian king. Tereus raped his sister-in-law, Philomela, and then cut out her tongue to prevent her from telling anyone. She revealed the truth, however, by embroidering it on a cloth. As punishment, Procne killed and dismembered Itys, her own son, and served him as dinner to his father. See Ovid, *Metamorphoses,* 6.424–674.

Hippolytus, the son of Theseus and the Amazonian queen Antiope, neglected to worship Aphrodite. As punishment, she caused Hippolytus's stepmother, Phaedra, to fall in love with him. When Hippolytus rejected her advances, Phaedra claimed to Theseus that he had tried to rape her. In response to Theseus's calls for vengeance, Poseidon caused a sea monster to rise from the water, overturning Hippolytus's chariot and killing him. In the play *Hippolytus* by Euripides (480/4–406 BC), the battered body of the dying youth is brought onto the stage.

Medea was the daughter of Aeëtes of Colchis and his wife, Eidyia. She was gifted with magical powers and helped Jason to secure the Golden Fleece. When Jason deserted her in order to marry Creusa, the daughter of the king of Corinth, she killed the bride by giving her a poisoned robe and then slew her own children. Euripides presents the story in his play *Medea.*

In *The Iliad,* (2.716ff.), Homer recounts the story of Philoctetes, who is bitten on the foot by a snake on the way to Troy and is left behind on the island of Lemnos because of the stench of his festering wound. Sophocles (c. 496–405 BC) wrote a play on the subject entitled *Philoctetes.* In chapter 4 of *Laocoön,* Lessing discusses the treatment of physical pain in the play and points to Philoctetes' cries of anguish in order to show that the expression of suffering was not incompatible with the Greek nobility of soul.

34. Latin: "Praxiteles did not make me, but Marco d'Agrate," inscription on the base of a statue by Marco D'Agrate (c. 1504–c. 1574) still in situ in Milan Cathedral. The statue, a life-size *écorché,* depicts Saint Bartholemew with his flayed skin draped over his shoulder. He carries a knife and an open book. The inscription is thought to date from a later period.

35. In Greek mythology, Aesculapius is the god of medicine. He is depicted as a bearded man with a snake-entwined staff.

36. Pindar (c. 518–438 BC) was a Greek lyric poet. He is best remembered for his *Epinikia,* or Triumphal Odes, written in celebration of victories won in the Olympian, Pythian, Nemean, and Isthmian games. In the first Olympian Ode, dedicated to Hieron of Syracuse, winner in the horse race, Pindar praises the beauty of the horse Pherenikos, which also won in the Pythian games in 482 and 478 BC. See Pindar, *The Odes,* 64–70.

37. Job 39:19–25.

38. *The Greek Anthology* is a collection of epigrams put together in 1301

by Maximus Planudes, a Greek orthodox monk. The first epigrams were simply legends written upon an object to say who made it, who it belonged to, or to which god it is dedicated. By the fifth century the epigram had developed into an independent literary form, the subject matter of which included the satiric, the erotic, and the sympotic (drinking songs). The standard form remained the elegiac couplet, though other meters were occasionally employed. Epigrams on centaurs and on the Minotaur are to be found in bk. 16, nos. 115, 116, and 126.

39. Herder cites *The Greek Anthology* after a thematically ordered edition. His reference corresponds to the anonymous epigram in bk. 16, no. 115, "On the Centaur Chiron": "A horse is shed forth from a man, and a man springs up from a horse; a man without feet and a swift horse without a head; a horse belches out a man, and a man farts out a horse."

40. The story of Meleager hunting the Calydonian boars is told by Homer (*Iliad*, 9.529–49) and Ovid (*Metamorphoses*, 8.260–444). The epigram to which Herder refers is in *The Greek Anthology*, bk. 15, no. 51, "On the Calydonian Boar." It is attributed to Aulus Licinius Arcus and concerns a bronze statue: "It is of bronze, but see what strength he contrived to show, the sculptor of the boar, moulding a living beast with the bristles standing up on its neck, with sharpened tusks, grunting and darting terrible light from its eyes, all its lips wet with foam. No longer do we marvel that it destroyed a chosen host of demi-gods."

41. Herder's reference is to chapter 2 of Lessing's *Laocoön*. Lessing maintains that "among the ancients beauty was the supreme law of the visual arts" and that everything else was made subordinate to this highest command. It is for this reason that Greek artists refrained from depicting the contortions of the face and body that arise from extreme emotion or pain, and not, as Winckelmann had argued, because Greek "nobility of soul" did not allow the expression of suffering.

42. See Winckelmann, *History of Ancient Art*, 1:190ff. Herder's reference is to the chapter entitled "The Essential of Art," which is dedicated to a discussion of "beauty in general."

43. The sculptor Lysippus is said to have made several portrait statues of Alexander the Great. Plutarch (c. 46–c. 120) reports that "when Lysippus modelled his first statue of Alexander which represented him looking up with his face turned toward the heavens (as indeed Alexander often did look, with a slight inclination of his head to one side), someone engraved these verses on the statue, not without some plausibility: 'Eager to speak seems the statue of bronze, up to Zeus it gazes: / "Earth I have set under foot: Zeus, keep Olympus to yourself!"' " (*Moralia*, 335ab). This epigram also appears in *The Greek Anthology*, bk. 16, no. 120.

44. Greek: "to the worst," Aelian (c. 170–235), *Varia Historia* [Historical miscellany], 4.4. Aelian reports that "in Thebes a law was in force which instructed artists—both painters and sculptors—to make their portraits flattering. As punishment for those who produced a sculpture or painting less attractive than the original the law threatened a fine of a thousand drachmas." Both Winckelmann and Lessing refer to this law as evidence for idealization

in Greek art. See Winckelmann, *Reflections on the Imitation of Greek Works,* 15, and Lessing, *Laocoön,* chapter 2.

45. The source of this observation, cited by Lessing in chapter 2 of *Laocoön,* is Pliny the Elder He observes that it was the custom at Olympia "to dedicate statues of all those who had won a competition; these statues, in the case of those who had been victorious there three times, were modelled as exact personal likenesses of the winners—what are called iconicae, portrait statues" (*Natural History,* 34.9).

46. Herder's reference is to Patrick Brydone (1736–1818), *A Tour through Sicily and Malta.* The "enchanted palace" is the Villa Palagonia in La Bagaria, east of Palermo, which Ferdinando Francesco II, prince of Palagonia (1722–88). had decorated in a grotesque style. Brydone gives a description of what he saw in letter 22: "The amazing crowd of statues that surround his house appear at a distance like a little army drawn up for its defence; but when you get amongst them, and every one assumes his true likeness, you imagine you have got into the realm of delusion and enchantment: for of all that immense group, there is not one made to represent any one object in nature; nor is the absurdity of the wretched imagination that created them any less astonishing than its wonderful fertility" (p. 54). Brydone makes it clear that he considers the prince to be insane, declaring it "truly unaccountable that he has not been shut up many years ago."

47. One of Montesquieu's last works was "Essai sur le goût" (Essay on taste), which appeared in 1757 in Diderot's *Encylopédie.* An English translation is to be found in Alexander Gerard, *An Essay on Taste, with Three Dissertations on the same Subject by Mr de Voltaire, Mr D'Alembert, F.R.S., Mr de Montesquieu,* London and Edinburgh, 1759 (facsimile reprint, Scholar Press, 1971), 257–314.

48. In Greek mythology, Thetis is a sea goddess and the mother of Achilles. She is termed "silver-footed" by Homer (*Iliad,* 1.538). Ceres was a goddess of fertility and abundance. In *History of Ancient Art,* Winckelmann claims that she acquired the epithet "red-footed" from early painted clay statues (1:40).

49. Polykleitos was an Argive sculptor, active c. 460–410 BC. His most celebrated sculpture, the bronze *Doryphorus,* or Spearbearer, established a new paradigm for representing the human body and was acclaimed as the epitome of measure or good proportion. Stewart describes its impact on Western art as "incalculable" (*Greek Sculpture,* 160). Polykleitos wrote a book called the *Canon* in which he explained the principles of his art, apparently basing it on this statue. There are a number of Roman copies of the *Doryphorus,* but the text of the *Canon* has been lost apart from one or two fragments quoted by ancient authors.

50. In Virgil's account (Aeneid, 2.218), the serpents twice encircle Laocoön's waist and throat.

Part Three

1. The French Jesuit Louis-Bertrand Castel (1688–1757) devoted many years of his life to building an "ocular harpsichord" that would allow music to

be performed in the medium of light and color rather than sound. He produced various different prototypes between 1725 and 1755, but none was ever made fully operational. Aristotle's suggestion that there exists a profound connection between the principles of color harmony and the known principles of music harmony was revived by Newton in the speculative "Queries" section in book 3 of his *Opticks* (1730). Castel sought to realize these ideas in practice. His prototype of the 1730s used colored slips of paper that rose above the cover of the keyboard. In 1754, however, he exhibited a model that employed one hundred candles behind discs of colored glass. The ocular harpsichord suffered continued technical problems, and despite the creation of dedicated works by composers such as Jean-Philippe Rameau and Georg Philipp Telemann it was not considered a success. For further information on Castel, see Gage, *Colour and Culture*, 233–34.

2. The English painter and engraver William Hogarth (1697–1764) first introduced his "line of beauty" in a self-portrait of 1745 entitled *The Painter and his Pug*, which now hangs in London's Tate Gallery. Conspicuously situated in the foreground of this painting is a palette on which there rests a single serpentine line, labeled "The Line of Beauty and of Grace." Seven years later Hogarth published his only complete book on art, *The Analysis of Beauty* (London, 1753), in which he sought to explain his ideas to a wider public. The frontispiece to the book depicts the same serpentine line contained within the form of a pyramid. Hogarth argues that the line of grace and beauty is to be found both in art and in nature and that it lies at the basis of all beautiful forms. Whereas the prevailing standards of classicism emphasized symmetry and uniformity as the essence of beauty, Hogarth relishes the intricacy and variety that flows from the "curved" and "waving" lines. The "waving line" or "line of beauty" is composed of two contrasted curves and can be drawn with a pencil. The "serpentine line" or "line of grace," however, cannot be drawn on a flat surface but must be conceived as a fine wire twisted around a three-dimensional object, such as the figure of a cone. See Hogarth, *Analysis of Beauty*, chap. 7 and pp. 41–42. Just one year after its English publication, Hogarth's book was translated into German by C. Mylius as *Zergliederung der Schönheit, die schwankenden Begriffe von dem Geschmack festzusetzen* (Berlin and Potsdam, 1754).

3. This is a reference to the *Trattato dell'arte della pittura* [Treatise on the art of painting] published in Milan in 1584 by Giovanni Paolo Lomazzo (1538–1600). In the preface to *The Analysis of Beauty*, Hogarth cites approvingly Lomazzo's claim—which the Italian author in turn attributes to Michelangelo—that the painter "should alwaies make a figure Pyramidall, Serpentlike, and multiplied by one two and three" and that the form best fitted to express the "motion" or "spirite" of a picture is "the flame of fire" since it is "an elemente most active of all others." See Hogarth, *Analysis of Beauty*, 2–3.

4. The apparent contradiction between the arguments Hogarth put forward in his treatise on beauty and his own work as a painter and engraver was frequently remarked upon by his contemporaries. The point is expressed most succinctly by August Wilhelm Schlegel (1767–1845) in no. 183 of the "Atheneum Fragments" (1798): "Hogarth painted ugliness and wrote about beauty." See Schlegel, *Philosophical Fragments*, 41.

5. Physiognomy is the art of judging character from facial features. It attained great popularity in the last quarter of the eighteenth century through the work of Johann Kaspar Lavater (1741–1801). Lavater sought to raise physiognomy to the level of a science and raised ambitious claims for its rigor and usefulness to humanity. His *Physiognomische Fragmente zur Beförderung der Menschenkenntniß und Menschenliebe* [Physiognomical fragments for the promotion of human knowledge and human love] was published in four volumes in Leipzig and Winterthur between 1775 and 1778. The first volume begins with a long excerpt from Herder's *Älteste Urkunde des Menschengeschlechts* [Oldest document of the human race], an interpretation of the book of Genesis that Herder had published in 1774. Lavater's work is illustrated by a large number of profiles and silhouettes, including two of Herder. It is this reliance on the mere outline of the human face that forms the principal object of Herder's criticism here.

6. Italian: "sketch," but here employed in the sense of "silhouette."

7. According to Pliny the Elder, the art of modeling portraits out of clay was invented by Dibutades, a potter from Sicyon in Corinth: "He did this owing to his daughter, who was in love with a young man; and she, when he was going abroad, drew in outline on the wall the shadow of his face thrown by a lamp. Her father pressed clay on this and made a relief, which he hardened by exposure to fire with the rest of his pottery" (*Natural History*, 35.151–52).

8. The seven sons of the Jewish high priest Sceva seek in vain to imitate the miraculous healing carried out by Paul. When they attempt to exorcise an evil spirit, it answers them "Jesus I know and Paul I know; but who are you?" The spirit leaps upon them and forces them out of the house naked and wounded. This example leads the residents of Ephesus to give up all practice of "magic arts" and to burn their books.

9. Anubis is the Egyptian god of death, represented either in wholly animal form or as a jackal-headed human. Helmut Pfotenhauer (1995) traces this reference to Lavater's attempt to draw analogies between the heads of animals and of humans in his *Physiognomische Fragmente*, vol. 4, sect. 4, 1.

10. Shakespeare, *Hamlet*, 1.5.99–101. Herder offers his own translation in the text, but cites the original English in the footnote. The full passage reads, "Yea, from the table of my memory / I'll wipe away all trivial fond records, / All saws of books, all forms, all pressures past / That youth and observation copied there, / And thy commandment all alone shall live / Within the book and volume of my brain, / Unmixed with baser matter."

11. The story of Ymir is recounted in *Edda*, a collection of Norse mythological stories put together by the Icelandic poet, historian, and politician Snorri Sturluson (1179–1241). The giant Ymir is killed by the sons of Bor. Out of his body they make the earth, out of his blood the sea and the lakes, and out of his skull the sky. Sturluson cites the first verse of the ancient poem *Grimnismal:* "From Ymir's flesh was earth created, and from blood, sea; rocks of bones, trees of hair, and from his skull, the sky" (pp. 11–13).

12. Herder's reference is to the work of the Spanish doctor and philosopher Juan Huarte (c. 1529–88), *Examen de ingenios para las sciencias* (Baeza,

1575). This was translated into German by Lessing as *Johann Huarts Prüfung der Köpfe zu den Wissenschaften* (Zerbst, 1752). An English translation by Mr. Bellamy appeared as *Examen de Ingenios: or the Tryal of Wits* (London, 1698). Chapter 3 is concerned with the abilities a child requires in order to gain proficiency in knowledge.

13. See Homer, *Iliad,* 2.219: "his skull went up to a point with the wool grown sparsely upon it." Thersites is described as "the ugliest man who ever came beneath Ilion." He is viciously beaten by Odysseus for criticizing Agamemnon. In his frequent references to Thersites, Herder appears to endorse the Greek identification of physical ugliness and moral depravity.

14. In the *Odyssey* (9.375–400), Homer describes the blinding of the cyclops Polyphemos by Odysseus, who, together with his companions, thrusts a beam of burning olive wood into the giant's eye.

15. Quotation from 1 Corinthians 2:11.

16. Latin: "is impious to enquire into and to know," free after Horace (65–8 BC), *Odes,* 1.11.1. The preceding part of the sentence echoes 3.39.29–32: "With wise purpose does the god bury in the shades of night the future's outcome, and laugh if mortals be anxious beyond due limits."

17. See part 1, editor's note 19.

18. Greek: "angered / in his heart, carrying across his shoulders the bow and the hooded / quiver; and the shafts clashed on the shoulders of the god walking angrily" (Homer, *Iliad,* 1.44–47).

19. Alcides is another name for Hercules; it is sometimes considered to be his "divine" name.

20. Rhea is the Greek name of Cybele. See part 2, editor's note 4.

21. Herder connects the name Hamlet with "Hammel," the German word for a ram. The phrases in inverted quotation marks are in English in the original. See Shakespeare, *Hamlet,* 1.5.15–20: "I could a tale unfold, whose lightest word / Would harrow up thy soul, freeze thy young blood,/Make thy two eyes like stars start from their spheres, / Thy knotted and combinèd locks to part, / And each particular hair to stand on end / Like quills upon the fretful porpentine."

22. Shakespeare, *Hamlet,* 3.4.120–23. Herder cites the text in English, with minor variations.

23. Herder is referring to Zeus. See Homer, *Iliad,* 2.669, where Zeus is described as "lord over all gods and all men." For the shaking of Olympia, see *Iliad,* 1.528–30, and part 1, editor's note 19.

24. See Judges 16:13–14.

25. See Proverbs 16:31 and Ecclesiastes 12:5.

26. Plato, *Phaedo,* 89b.

27. The *Messiah* is an epic German poem by Friedrich Gottlieb Klopstock (1724–1803), begun in 1745 and finally brought to completion in 1773. Modeled on the examples of Homer, Virgil, and, above all, Milton, it was a self-conscious attempt to renew German literature. Its theme is Christ's redemption of mankind, told in a poem of nearly twenty thousand verses. Herder's

reference is to canto 15, verse 158, where it is Nephtoa and not an angel who plays with Benoni's hair.

28. See 1 Corinthians 11:14–15.

29. Song of Solomon 7:5.

30. Cuchillin is a character in *The Poems of Ossian* by James Macpherson (1736–96), based in part on the traditional Gaelic hero Cúchulainn. In book 4 of *Fingal: an Ancient Epic Poem in Six Books* (1765), Cuchillin uses his ancestral shield to sound the alarm. Macpherson's text is a free translation from early Gaelic sources and much debate has surrounded its supposed authenticity. The shield of Achilles is described in Homer, *Iliad,* 18.478–608. It is made by Vulcan (Hephaistos), the god of fire, at the request of Thetis and is embossed with rich figurative decoration. It is discussed by Lessing in chapter 19 of *Laocoön.*

31. Latin: "twin-peaked Parnasus," after Persius (34–62), *Satires,* prologue, 2–3: "never did I dream on the two-topped Parnasus, that I should thus come forth suddenly as a poet." To fall asleep and dream upon the summit of Parnasus was considered to presage poetic inspiration.

32. Cronos is the Greek name for Saturn. In Greek mythology, he is the son of Uranus (Sky) and Gaea (Earth), and the father of Zeus. Homer terms Zeus Cronion, thereby identifying him as Cronos's son. See *Iliad,* 5.522f. The "deep furrows" may refer to a later tradition in which Saturn is identified with the melancholy temperament.

33. Greek: "matter."

34. Latin: "universal catalog." Herder uses the Greek and Latin terms to identify the mere scholar, the person of empty learning. Giorgio Maragliano (1994) identifies a word play on the Latin "repertorium" (catalog) and the Latin "reperire" (to find).

35. Latin: "shameless brow," Martial (c. 40–104), *Epigrams,* 11.27.7. Its literal meaning is the "scrubbed brow"—scrubbed to remove the red blush of shame.

36. During his residency in Paris in 1665, the Italian sculptor Gianlorenzo Bernini (1598–1680) created a bust of Louis XIV that depicts the king with his forehead exposed. In the "Sendschreibungen" attached to the second edition of his *Reflections on the Imitation of Greek Works,* Winckelmann mockingly cites Bernini's words of justification: "Your Majesty . . . is King and may show his brow to the entire world" (*Kleine Schriften,* 71). A contemporary record of the commission and execution of the bust is given by Paul Fréart de Chantelou in *Diary of the Cavaliere Bernini's Visit to France.* See, in particular, the entry for July 22, 1665.

37. Giorgio Maragliano (1994) identifies this as an ironic allusion to Illuminism.

38. Latin: "horns given to the poor," free after Horace, *Odes,* 3.21.18. The "horns of the poor" are knots on the forehead caused by extreme physical exertion.

39. In the Sanskrit Puranas it is related that the demon Hayagriva stole the Vedas, the ancient holy books of the Hindus, from Brahma and hid them

at the bottom of the ocean. Vishnu in the form of a fish retrieved the holy books and killed Hayagriva. See Bhagavata Purana, 8.24.

40. In his description of the Belvedere Torso (fig. 2) in *History of Ancient Art,* Winckelmann suggests that the sculpture represents Hercules in an attitude of repose after his toils, "absorbed in lofty reflections" and meditating "with satisfaction on the great deeds he had achieved" (2:364).

41. Johann Jacob Volkmann (1732–1803) was a German travel writer and translator. His three-volume *Historisch-kritische Nachrichten von Italien* [Historical-critical reports from Italy] was published in Leipzig in 1770–71. It was one of the most widely read guides to the visual arts in Italy; Goethe took it with him when he set out for his Italian journey. A significant part of the work is made up of translations from other guide books, including Jerôme de Lalande's *Voyage d'un François en Italie* (1769) and Jean-Jacque Richard's *Description historique et critique de l'Italie* (1766). Jonathan Richardson (1665–1745) was an English painter and writer on art. His *Essay on the Theory of Painting* (1715) claimed for painting a status equal with poetry. It is considered the first significant work of artistic theory by an English author. Here Herder refers to Richardson's *An Account of some of the Statues, Bas-Reliefs, Drawings, and Pictures in Italy* (1722), which he wrote together with his son Jonathan Richardson Jr. (1694–1771). This work was best known on the Continent in the expanded, three-volume French translation that appeared under the title *Traité de la peinture et de la sculpture* in Amsterdam in 1728. The Richardsons were among the first to suggest that many of the surviving statues in Italy were in fact copies. Like Volkmann's, their guide book served as essential reading for those who embarked upon the Grand Tour.

42. For the importance of climate in Winckelmann's theory of art and his claim that the Greek climate offered ideal conditions for the development of art, see part 2, editor's note 17.

43. See Song of Solomon 7:4.

44. Ovid tells the story of King Midas, who is asked to judge in a musical contest between Apollo and Pan (*Metamorphoses,* 11.146–94). When Midas finds in favor of Apollo, the god punishes him by giving him ass's ears.

45. In Greek mythology, ambrosia and nectar are the food and drink of eternal life; they are thus properly reserved for the gods.

46. Latin: "lion's jaws," after Ovid, *Metamorphoses,* 4.97: "But see! here comes a lioness, her jaws all dripping with the blood of fresh-slain cattle, to slake her thirst at the neighbouring spring." The lion appears in the story of Pyramus and Thisbe.

47. Greek: "ring of the teeth," from the *Anacreontea,* no. 24: "Nature gave bulls horns, horses hooves, hares speed, lions a wide mouth full of teeth, fish power to swim, birds flight, men wisdom, women—she had nothing left. And so? She gives them beauty, strong as any shield, strong as any sword. A beautiful woman overcomes even steel or fire."

48. The Zohar (Hebrew for "brightness") is the chief work of the Spanish Kabbalah. Authorship is ascribed to Seimeon ben Yohai (second century), though some sections may be by other hands. Written in both Aramaic and Hebrew, it consists of a mystical and esoteric commentary on the Pentateuch

and parts of the Hagiographa (Song of Songs, Ruth, Lamentations). The section entitled "Idra' Rabba'" contains extensive meditations on the mystery of the beard.

49. Latin: "rough or shaggy chest," after Propertius, *Elegies*, 4.9. Propertius is describing Hercules.

50. See note 13 above.

51. See Qur'an 20:25–28: "He said: O my Lord! expand my breast for me: and make my affair easy to me: And loose the knot from my tongue: (That) they may understand my word."

52. See *Iliad*, 14.214–23, where Homer describes the girdle of Aphrodite.

53. In the preface to *History of Ancient Art*, Winckelmann declares, "I should have been able to say more if I had written for the Greeks, and not in a modern tongue, which imposes on me certain restrictions" (1:11).

54. In *History of Ancient Art*, Winckelmann describes a fragment of an antique statue of Bacchus in the Villa Albani: "I can scarcely refrain from tears, when I think of a Bacchus, once mutilated, now restored in the Villa Albani. . . . [H]is mantle, which is ample, has fallen down, and is gathered in rich folds about his hips. . . . No single figure gives one so high an idea of what Anacreon terms a belly of Bacchus" (1:220). The work described by Winckelmann is a Roman copy of the Satyr attributed to Praxiteles (see Helbig, *Führer durch die öffentlichen Sammlungen klassischer Altertümer in Rom*, vol. 4, no. 3286). The original is through to date from c. 350–330 BC. The finest copy of the torso is that preserved in the Louvre, Paris (fig. 7). A restored copy in the Capitoline Museum, Rome, reveals what the complete statue may have looked like (fig. 8). The large number of surviving copies of this work suggest that it enjoyed great popularity in antiquity. For Anacreon, see part 4, editor's note 9.

55. See Genesis 3:7.

56. In Greek mythology, Prometheus was one of the Titans, but he is also sometimes identified as the creator of man, whom he is said to have formed out of clay. See, for example, Pausanias, *Description of Greece*, 10.4.4, and Horace, *Odes*, 1.16.13–16. For Pygmalion, who brought his statue of Galatea to life, see editor's note to the title page, above.

57. Greek: "the Lord God formed man of dust from the ground, and breathed into his nostrils the breath of life; and man became a living being."

Part Four

1. Latin: "but I, queen of the gods," after Virgil, *Aeneid*, 1.46. Winckelmann describes Juno as "pre-eminent above the other goddesses" and claims that she may be known by her large eyes and imperious mouth. See *History of Ancient Art*, 1:233–34.

2. For Homer's description of Apollo "angered in his heart" and striding "down along the pinnacles of Olympus," see *Iliad*, 1.44–48. See, too, Winckelmann's description of the Apollo Belvedere (fig. 1) in *History of Ancient Art* (2:312–34). In chapter 11 of *The Analysis of Beauty*, Hogarth notes that the legs and thighs of the Apollo Belvedere are "too long, and too large for the up-

per parts," but he insists that this has been done on purpose in order to achieve an effect of greater nobleness.

3. See figs. 7 and 8 and part 3, editor's note 54, for Winckelmann's interpretation of the Praxiteles' Satyr as a statue of Bacchus.

4. See 1 Corinthians 2:9.

5. Nireus, who is described in the *Iliad* as "the most beautiful man who came before Ilion," is only mentioned once, in the catalog of the ships and their crews. See *Iliad,* 2.671–75.

6. Translation from the *Iliad,* 2.478–80.

7. See *Iliad,* 3.161–90. On the tower by the Skaian gates of Troy, Priam and the elders of the counsel look down on the surrounding army and consider its principal figures.

8. Herder combines elements of the speeches of Priam, Helen, and Antenor, who describe Ulysses (Odysseus) from their vantage point in the tower. See *Iliad,* 3.194–211.

9. Anacreon (c. 570–485 BC) was a Greek lyric poet. His style of writing is imitated in the so-called *Anacreontea,* a collection of poems in praise of love and beauty. Poem number 17 in this collection describes the beauty of the poet's lover, Bathyllus, by imagining how he might be depicted in a painting. See *Greek Lyric,* 2:185–87. The last lines of the poem suggest both that a depiction of Apollo could be turned into an image of Bathyllus and that a depiction of Bathyllus could be turned into an image of the god. Lessing discusses the poem in chapter 20 of *Laocoön* in support of his argument that poetry cannot rival painting in depicting beauty.

10. Herder is referring to the marble statue of a hermaphrodite (fig. 6), which formed part of the Borghese collection and is now in the Louvre in Paris. See part 2, editor's note 13.

11. For *The Greek Anthology,* see part 2, editor's note 41.

12. Latin: "not many, but much."

13. Daedalus was a mythical Greek artist, craftsman, and inventor; the father of Icarus, he made the wings with which his son flew too close to the sun. No archaeological remnants of his work remain, but the term "Daedalic" is conventionally used to describe the earliest Greek stone sculpture of the seventh century BC. Daedalus is described in later Greek and Roman literature as a *protos heuretes* ("first finder"). One of the fullest accounts is provided by Diodorus of Sicily in his *Library of History,* written in the first century BC: "In natural ability he towered far above all other men and cultivated the building art, the making of statues and the working of stone. He was also the inventor of many devices which contributed to the advancement of his art and built works in many regions of the inhabited world which arouse the wonder of men. In the carving of his statues he so far excelled all other men that later generations invented the story about him that the statues of his making were quite like their living models; they could see, they said, and walk and, in a word, preserved so well the characteristics of the entire body that the beholder thought that the image made by him was a being endowed with life. And since he was the first to represent the open eye and to fashion the legs separated in a stride and the arms and hands as extended, it was a natural thing

that he should have received the admiration of mankind; for the artists before his time had carved their statues with the eyes closed and the arms and hands hanging and attached to the sides" (4.76.1–3). The claim that the statues of Daedalus were able to move is a frequent topos in Greek literature. In Plato's *Meno,* for example, Socrates observes that philosophical opinions are like the statues of Daedalus: "if they are not fastened up, they play truant and run away" (97d).

14. Latin: "ruling prince."

15. In French, the uppermost tier of a theater is still termed *paradis;* the equivalent expression in English is "the gods."

16. Thought to refer either to Wilhelmsplatz in Berlin or the Parade Ground in Potsdam.

17. Pindar (518–438 BC). Cf. the opening of the fifth Nemean Ode, dedicated to Pytheas of Agina, winner in a trial of strength: "I am no maker of statues / Who fashions figures to stand unmoved / On the self-same pedestal./On every merchantman, in every skiff / Go, sweet song, from Agina, / And spread the news that Lampon's son, / Pytheas, sturdy and strong, / Has won the wreath for All Strength in the Nemean Games." Herder may also have in mind book 4 of Horace's *Odes,* in which Horace claims that when Pindar sings of the victories of athletes he "endows them with a tribute more glorious than a hundred statues" (4.2.19f).

18. For Hogarth's "line of beauty," see part 3, editor's note 2. Hogarth discusses the straight line and the circular line in chapter 7 of *The Analysis of Beauty,* (pp. 41–42).

19. The two forces are those of attraction and repulsion.

20. Plato, *Symposium,* 203 b–c. Herder translates the Greek πενία as *Bedürfnis* ("need") and πόπος as *Überfluß* ("superfluity" or "abundance"). The second term is sometimes rendered into English as "resource."

21. There is an echo here of 1 Corinthians 12:22–23: "the parts of the body which seem to be weaker are indispensable, and those parts of the body which we think less honourable we invest with the greater honour and our unpresentable parts are treated with greater modesty."

22. In Greek mythology, Atlas was one of the Titans. As punishment for participating in the revolt of the Titans against the gods, Zeus condemned him to support the heavens on his head and hands. In the Renaissance he was frequently represented as supporting the sphere of the earth.

23. See Lessing, *Laocoön,* chapter 2: "The scream had to be softened to a sigh, not because screaming betrays an ignoble soul, but because it distorts the features in a disgusting manner. Simply imagine Laocoön's mouth forced wide open, and then look!" (p. 17).

24. Here Herder may have had in mind two works of antique sculpture. A Leda, of which the most complete Roman copy is in the Capitoline Museum in Rome, depicts Leda semi-naked, with Zeus in the form of a swan sheltering on her lap (fig. 9). She holds her robe up with her left hand to protect the swan from a predatory eagle that Zeus has employed as a ruse in order to approach her. The lost original has been attributed to Timotheos of Epidauros (active c. 380–350 BC). Herder would have known the sculpture from a cast in

the sculpture gallery at Mannheim. The sculpture now known as the Baberini Suppliant (fig. 10) was previously interpreted as a representation of Danae visited by Zeus in the form of a shower of gold. The figure leans backward in a reclining pose and her left breast is bared. The statue, now in the Louvre, is a Roman copy of a bronze original of c. 430–10 BC.

25. Paul, 1 Corinthians 12:23.

Part Five

1. Herder visited the blind wife of a farmer in 1770 in order to learn more about the sensory experiences of the blind. He discusses the visit again in his *Kaligone* (1800). See Herder, *Sämtliche Werke,* 29:49.

2. For Nicholas Saunderson, see part 1, editor's note 3.

3. French: "Shame to he who thinks badly of it," motto of the Order of the Garter, the English order of knighthood founded by King Edward II in 1348.

4. The word "metagrabolise" was coined by François Rabelais (c. 1494–c. 1553) in his *Gargantua* (see chapter 19, "La harangue de maistre Janotous de Bragmardro"). It is formed from the Greek μάταιος, "vain," and the French, *grabeler,* to sift or examine. In this context it means "to discourse with excessive learning."

5. "Plastic": from the Greek *plastikos,* meaning "to mold or shape," used here to designate the art of sculpture in general (as in the title of Herder's book); "toreutic": from the Greek *toreutikos,* meaning "to bore," refers to artistic work in metal; ἄγαλμα and *signum:* Greek and Latin terms for "statue"; τόρευμα and *caelaturam:* Greek and Latin terms for "embossed and other fine metal work," including chasing and engraving; βαιτύλια: Greek for "meteor"; ξόανα: Greek for "images made of wood"; βρέτη: Greek for "wooden idols."

6. Herder's reference corresponds to Winckelmann's *Reflections on the Imitation of Greek Works* (pp. 51ff). The words in quotation marks are not a direct citation but give Herder's own interpretation of Winckelmann's argument. In the section to which Herder refers, Winckelmann attributes to Michelangelo the discovery of a novel technique for marking the traits of a wax model over to a block of marble. This involves immersing the model in water and then running the liquid off so as gradually to reveal its more prominent parts. Winckelmann maintains that "[i]n repeating this process [Michelangelo] attempted to transfer to his stone figure the motions and reactions of the muscles and tendons, the undulations of the smaller parts, and the most delicate artistry of his model. The water, touching even the most unobtrusive features, traced their shape with the greatest clarity and precision" (p. 55). The source for Winckelmann's argument is a passage in Vasari (see *Lives of the Artists,* 421). As Carl Justi first pointed out, however, this whole section of the *Reflections on the Imitation of Greek Works* is based on a misunderstanding of the metaphorical character of Vasari's comparison. See Justi, *Winckelmann,* 1:274–81.

7. See Mark 8:23–24: "And he took the blind man by the hand, and led him out of the village; and when he had spit on his eyes and laid his hand

upon him, he asked him, 'Do you see anything?' And he looked up and said, 'I see men; but they look like trees, walking.'"

8. For the patient cured of blindness by William Cheselden, see part 1, editor's note 4.

9. For Daedalus, see part 4, editor's note 13.

10. The term "foursquare" (Greek: τετράγωνος) is primarily associated with the statues of Polykleitos (see part 2, editor's note 52). According to Stewart, it "became a key element in Polykleitos' *Canon,* where it defined a physique that conformed to the golden mean, neither fat nor thin and ready for every eventuality" (*Greek Sculpture,* 80). The term "foursquare" is also used, however, in reference to sculptures produced during the Daedalic period (c. 700–600 BC), during which the shape of the quarried block still determined the appearance of the finished piece. Since the statue was drawn onto the sides of the block before carving began, the finished sculpture tended to look like a four-sided relief (ibid., 12).

11. See Job 4:15–16: "A spirit glided past my face; the hair of my flesh stood up. It stood still, but I could not discern its appearance. A form was there before my eyes; there was silence, then I heard a voice." Edmund Burke cites the same passage in his *A Philosophical Enquiry into the Origins of our Ideas of the Sublime and Beautiful* (London, 1757; part 2, sect. 4). Herder's discussion of the infinite sublime is much indebted to Burke's views.

12. The story to which Herder refers involves the Hindu deities Siva (Ixora), Visnu (Vistnum), and Brahma. Lambert Schneider (1969) identifies a number of possible sources, including the Vaya Purana 1.55 and Linga Purana 1.17, though both of these vary in the details and neither contains any reference to the three flowers which appear in Herder's version.

13. Jürgen Brummack (1994) refers to an epigram "On the Statue of Zeus at Olympia" by Philippus in *The Greek Anthology* (bk. 16, no. 81), which Herder translated in the first of his *Zerstreute Blätter* (1784): "Dir entweder ist Zeus vom Himmel hernieder gestiegen; oder du stiegest hinauf, Künstler, und sahest den Gott." In Paton's English translation it reads: "Either God came from Heaven to Earth to show thee His image, Phidias, or thou didst go to see God."

14. In the "Sendschreibungen" appended to the second edition of his *Reflections on the Imitation of Greek Works,* Winckelmann repeats the observation made by the first-century geographer Strabo that if Phidias's colossal statue of Zeus were to stand, it would unroof the temple that housed it. See Strabo, *Geography,* 7.3.30, and Winckelmann, *Kurze Schriften,* 66.

15. Milton, *Paradise Lost,* 1.589–91. The subject is Satan. Herder quotes the text in English. The same passage is also cited by Burke in *A Philosophical Enquiry* (part 2, sect. 4).

16. Quotation from the roman poet Statius (died after 96) (*Silvae,* 4.6.36): "A god he is, a god, and he granted you the privilege of gazing upon him, Lysippus, small in appearance and mighty in impression, and although his measure stands miraculously within a foot, nevertheless when you carry your gaze over his limbs you will want to explain: 'By this stout breast the scourge of Nemea was crushed.'"

17. Shakespeare, *A Midsummer Night's Dream*, 5.1.12–17.

18. For Minerva's stone, see *Iliad*, 21.403–5; for her helmet, see *Iliad*, 5.743–44; for Neptune's stride, see *Iliad*, 13.17–20; for Alcides' (Hercules') chest, see *Odyssey*, 11.609–12; for Jupiter's eyebrows, see *Iliad*, 1.528–30.

19. Flora was a Roman goddess and the mistress of flowers.

20. Latin: "horrible to relate."

21. Winckelmann had argued for the use of allegory in the visual arts in the final section of his *Reflections on the Imitation of Greek Works* (1755). In 1766 he published *Versuch einer Allegorie, besonders für die Kunst* [Attempt at an Allegory, especially for Art], a scholarly study of allegorical and symbolic subjects in ancient art.

22. At the beginning of his *Versuch einer Allegorie*, Winckelmann identifies Heraclides Ponticus (fourth century BC) as the author of a work entitled "On Allegory in Homer." This text is now generally attributed to Heracleitus (fourth century BC), about whom little else is known. The opening paragraph contains the definition of allegory that Herder discusses here.

23. Greek: "other." The Greek word for "allegory" is formed from ἄλλος and ἀγορεύω, meaning "to speak." Its literal meaning is "to say other things."

24. Occasionalist philosophers such as Arnold Geulincx (1624–49) and Nicolas Malebranche (1638–1715) attempted to solve the problem of the relation between mind and body by denying the existence of any causal relation between physical things, and between the human mind and physical things. Geulincx used the metaphor of two synchronized but unconnected clocks which strike simultaneously. On this view, what we take to be causes are in fact a consequence of God's will. The theory of pre-established harmony is primarily associated with G. W. Leibniz (1646–1716), who argued that although substances appear to interact their behavior is, in fact, determined by God at their creation.

25. Famed for his youthful beauty, Antinous was a favorite of the Roman emperor Hadrian. After Antinous's death in 122, Hadrian founded the city of Antinopolis on the banks of the Nile in his memory and enrolled him among the gods. Several important sculptures from antiquity are associated with his name, including the Belvedere Antinous (fig. 11), the Capitoline Antinous, and the Antinous Bas-Relief in the Villa Albani in Rome. However, the name Antinous is also used more generally to refer to figures of Greek youths. (See Haskell and Penny, *Taste and the Antique*, nos. 4–6, pp. 141–46). Here, the sensuous, almost feminine form of the youthful male body associated with Antinous stands in contrast to the more vigorous form of Mars, the god of war.

26. All names given to Apollo: *Smintheus* means "honored in Smintheus" (but also, "killer of rats"); *Delius* means "honored in Delos"; *Pythius* means "honored in Pytho" (or Delphi); *Ἀγρεύς* means "the hunter."

27. The Egyptians.

28. In his *Description of Greece* (2.24.5), Pausanias describes an image of Zeus with three eyes, "signifying that this same god rules in all three 'allot-

ments' of the Universe." Winckelmann refers to this passage in his *Versuch einer Allegorie* (p. 9).

29. Greek goddess of fortune or chance; her Latin name is "Fortuna."

30. Herder is referring to the third of his *Critical Groves*, published in 1769.

31. *Pietas:* Latin for "piety"; *Caritas:* Latin for "charity"; *pia:* Italian for "a pious woman"; *cara:* Italian for a "a dear or charitable woman."

32. The story of Psyche and Cupid is told in *Metamorphoses, or the Golden Ass* by Lucus Apuleius (second century). Psyche, whose name means "soul" in Greek, was visited each night by a mysterious lover, whose identity she was forbidden to discover. Driven by curiosity she lit a lamp and discovered Cupid himself asleep beside her, but she let a drop of hot oil fall on him and he fled. After a lengthy search and numerous trials, the two are finally reunited and married in heaven. The story has been interpreted as an allegory of the journey of the soul and of the soul's union with desire. In his essay "Wie die Alten den Tod gebildet?" [How did the ancients see death?], published in *Hannoverscher Magazin* in 1774, Herder interpreted the subject as an image of death and the soul. (See Herder, *Sämtliche Werke*, 5:667ff.) There he refers to a number of engravings after antique funerary monuments. He may also have had in mind, however, the celebrated antique statue of Psyche and Cupid, best known through the Roman copy in the Capitoline Museum (fig. 12). A second copy, which is now lost, was held in the sculpture collection at Mannheim. The original is thought to be a Hellenistic work of the second or first century BC. For the reception history of the sculpture, see Haskell and Penny, *Taste and the Antique*, no. 26, pp. 189–91.

33. The two brothers are Castor and Pollux, the inseparable children of Jupiter and Leda, who, after death, were transformed into the constellation "Gemini." Herder is referring to the antique sculpture of Castor and Pollux that was discovered in Rome in the seventeenth century and is now in the Prado, Madrid (fig. 13). He would have known it from a cast in the sculpture collection at Mannheim. The Prado sculpture, which is thought to date from the first century BC, was extensively restored, and doubts remain as to its subject. For its reception, see Haskell and Penny, *Taste and the Antique*, no. 19, pp. 173–74.

34. This is a reference to the work of Michel-François Dandré Bardon (1700–1783), whose *Traité de peinture* [Treatise on painting] was published in two volumes in Paris in 1765. In the "Essai sur la sculpture" included in the second volume, Bardon compares ancient and modern sculpture, praising the "diversity of groups, expressions, contrasts and effects" characteristic of the latter. Herder had already subjected Bardon's views to criticism in the fourth of his *Critical Groves*.

35. See *Analysis of Beauty*, chapter 4, where Hogarth argues that the author of the Laocoön "chose to be guilty of the absurdity of making the sons of half the father's size . . . rather than not bring their composition within the boundary of a pyramid. Thus if a judicious workman were employ'd to make a case of wood, for preserving it from the injuries of weather, or for the convenience of carriage; he would soon find by his eye, the whole composition

would readily fit and be easily pack'd up, in one of a pyramidical form" (p. 31). In one of the engravings accompanying the book, Hogarth depicts the Laocoön under the frame of a wooden pyramid.

36. See part 2, editor's note 2. Both Winckelmann and Lessing sought to explain why Laocoön cries out loud in Virgil's description in the *Aeneid* but is depicted with his features undistorted by a cry in the sculpture.

37. This is a reference to the antique statue of Castor and Pollux (fig. 13). See note 33 above.

38. This is a reference to the antique statue of Psyche and Cupid (fig. 12) See note 32 above.

39. This is a reference to the statue of Arria and Paetus (fig. 14) by the French sculptor Pierre Lepautre (c. 1659–1744), which Herder saw in the Tuileries Garden in Paris in 1769. The story of Arria and Paetus is best known from the account given by Pliny the Younger (62–113) in a letter to Maecilius Nepos (*Epistulae*, 3.15.1–7). After the Emperor Claudius condemned Paetus to death for his part in the conspiracy of Scribonianus (AD 42), his wife, Arria, persuaded him to take his own life. She first stabbed herself and then handed the dagger to her husband. Lepautre's statue was completed in 1691. Arria is in the center of the group with her breast exposed and the dagger in her hand. She is supported by a servant on her left and by Paetus at her right. At Paetus's feet there is a playful child, riding a dog.

40. Latin: "It does not hurt, Paetus," according to Pliny the words spoken by Arria to her husband after she had stabbed herself.

41. Herder refers to the antique statue Gaul Committing Suicide with His Wife (fig. 15) that was previously believed to represent the figures of Arria and Paetus. Modern scholarship identifies the subject as a Gaul killing himself after having stabbed his wife to prevent her capture. The statue is now in the Terme Museum in Rome. It is thought to be a Roman copy of a Greek original from the second half of the third century BC. See Haskell and Penny, *Taste and the Antique*, no. 68, pp. 282–84.

BIBLIOGRAPHY

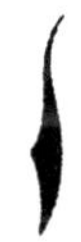

This bibliography is divided into two sections. The first lists sources referred to in the editor's explanatory notes. The second provides a selection of writings on Herder's *Sculpture*.

Selected Sources Referred to in the Editor's Notes

Aelian. *Historical Miscellany*. Trans. N. G. Wilson. Cambridge, Mass.: Harvard University Press, 1997.

Aristotle. *Poetics*. Trans. Stephen Halliwell. Cambridge, Mass.: Harvard University Press, 1999.

Bardon, Michel-François Dandré. *Traité de peinture*. 2 vols. Paris: Desaint, 1765.

Berkeley, George. *Works on Vision*. Ed. Colin Murray Turbayne. Indianapolis, Ind.: Bobbs-Merrill, 1963.

Blühm, Andreas. *Pygmalion: Die Ikonographie eines Künstlermythos zwischen 1500 und 1900*. Frankfurt am Main: Peter Lang, 1988.

Brydone, Patrick. *A Tour through Sicily and Malta, in a Series of Letters to William Beckford, Esq*. London: W. Strahan and T. Cadell, 1773.

Burke, Edmund. *A Philosophical Enquiry into the Origin of Our Ideas of the Sublime and Beautiful*. Ed. Adam Phillips. Oxford: Oxford University Press, 1990.

Chantelou, Paul Fréart de. *Diary of the Cavaliere Bernini's Visit to France*. Trans. Margery Corbett. Princeton, N.J.: Princeton University Press, 1985.

Cheselden, William. "An account of some observations made by a young gentleman, who was born blind. . . ." *Philosophical Transactions of the Royal Society of London*, 402 (1728), 447–50.

Diderot, Denis. *Oeuvres, Tome I: Philosophie.* Ed. Laurent Versini. Paris: Robert Lafont, 1994.

Diodorus Siculus. *Library of History.* 12 vols. Trans. C. H. Oldfather. Cambridge, Mass.: Harvard University Press, 1939.

Diogenes Laertius. *Lives of Eminent Philosophers.* 2 vols. Trans. R. D. Hicks. Cambridge, Mass.: Harvard University Press, 1925.

Du Bos, Abbé Jean-Baptiste. *Critical Reflections on Poetry, Painting, and Music.* 3 vols. Trans. Thomas Nugent. London: John Nourse, 1748.

Falconet, Étienne Maurice. "Reflexions on Sculpture." Trans. William Tooke. In *Pieces on Sculpture in General and particularly on the celebrated Statue of Peter the Great written by M. Falconet and M. Diderot.* London: W. Bowyer and J. Nichols, 1777.

Gage, John. *Colour and Culture: Practice and Meaning from Antiquity to Abstraction.* London: Thames and Hudson, 1993.

Greek Anthology. 5 vols. Trans. W. R. Paton. Cambridge, Mass.: Harvard University Press, 1916–18.

Greek Lyric, Volume II: Anacreon, Anacreonata, Choral Lyric from Olympus to Alcman. Trans. David A. Campbell. Cambridge, Mass.: Harvard University Press, 1988.

Haskell, Francis, and Nicholas Penny. *Taste and the Antique: The Lure of Classical Sculpture, 1500–1900.* New Haven, Conn.: Yale University Press, 1981.

Helbig, Wolfgang, *Führer durch die öffentlichen Sammlungen klassischer Altertümer in Rom.* 4th ed. Vol. 4. Ed. Hermine Speier. Tübingen: Ernst Wasmuth, 1963.

Hogarth, William. *The Analysis of Beauty.* Ed. Ronald Paulson. New Haven, Conn.: Yale University Press, 1997.

Holy Qur-án. Trans. Maulvi Muhammed Ali. Lahore: Ahmadiyya Anjuman-I-Isháat-I-Islam, 1920.

Homer. *The Iliad.* Trans. Richard Lattimore. Chicago: University of Chicago Press, 1951.

———. *The Odyssey.* Trans. Richard Lattimore. New York: Harper Collins, 1975.

Horace. *Odes and Epodes.* Rev. ed. Trans. C. E. Bennett. Cambridge, Mass.: Harvard University Press, 1968.

Huarte, Juan. *Examen de Ingenios: or the Tryal of Wits.* Trans. Edward Bellamy. London: Richard Sare, 1698.

Justi, Carl. *Winckelmann, seine Werke und seine Zeitgenossen.* 3 vols. Leipzig, 1866–72. Reprint, Cologne: Phaidon Verlag, 1956.

Juvenal and Persius. Trans. G. G. Ramsay. Cambridge, Mass.: Harvard University Press, 1918.

Lavater, Johann Kaspar. *Physiognomische Fragmente zur Beförderung der*

Menschenkenntniß und Menschenliebe. 4 vols. Leipzig and Winterthur, 1775–78.

Lalande, Jerôme de. *Voyage d'un François en Italie.* 8 vols. Venice and Paris, 1769.

Lessing, Gotthold Ephraim. *An Essay on the Limits of Painting and Poetry.* Trans. Edward Allen McCormick. Baltimore: Johns Hopkins University Press, 1984.

Lomazzo, Giovanni Paolo. *Trattato dell'arte della pittura.* Milan, 1584.

Macpherson, James. *The Poems of Ossian and Related Works.* Ed. Howard Gaskill. Edinburgh: Edinburgh University Press, 1996.

Martial. *Epigrams.* 3 vols. Trans. D. R. S. Bailey. Cambridge, Mass.: Harvard University Press, 1993.

Mendelssohn, Moses. "Betrachtungen über die Quellen und Verbindungen der schönen Künste und Wissenschaften." In Moses Mendelssohn, *Gesammelte Schriften: Jubiläumsausgabe,* vol. 1, ed. Fritz Bamberge, 167–90. Stuttgart: Friedrich Frommann, 1971.

Montesquieu, Charles de Secondat. "Essay on taste." In *An Essay on Taste, with Three Dissertations on the same Subject by Mr de Voltaire, Mr D'Alembert, F.R.S., Mr de Montesquieu,* trans. Alexander Gerard. London, 1759. Facsimile reprint, Menston: Scholar Press, 1971.

Morgan, Michael J. *Molyneux's Question: Vision, Touch, and the Philosophy of Perception.* Cambridge: Cambridge University Press, 1977.

Ovid. *Metamorphoses.* Trans. F. J. Miller. Rev. ed. 2 vols. Ed. G. P. Goold. Cambridge, Mass.: Harvard University Press, 1984.

Pausanias. *Description of Greece.* 5 vols. Trans. W. H. S. Jones and H. A. Ormerod. Cambridge, Mass.: Harvard University Press, 1919–35.

Piles, Roger de. *The Art of Painting [Abrégé de la vie des peintres].* Trans. John Savage. London: Thomas Payne, 1744.

———. *Dialogue upon Colouring.* Trans. John Ozell. London: Daniel Brown, 1711.

Pindar. *The Odes.* Trans. C. M. Bowra. Harmondsworth: Penguin, 1969.

Pliny the Elder. *Natural History.* Vol. 9, bks. 33–35. Trans. H. Rackham. Cambridge, Mass.: Harvard University Press, 1952.

———. *Natural History.* Vol. 10, bks. 36–37. Trans. D. E. Eichholz. Cambridge, Mass.: Harvard University Press, 1962.

Pliny the Younger. *Letters and Panegyricus.* 2 vols. Trans. B. Radice. Cambridge, Mass.: Harvard University Press, 1969.

Plutarch. *Moralia.* Vol. 4. Trans. F. C. Babbitt. Cambridge Mass.: Harvard University Press, 1936.

Propertius. *Elegies.* Trans. G. P. Goold. Cambridge, Mass.: Harvard University Press, 1990.

Richard, Jean-Jacque. *Description historique et critique de l'Italie.* 6 vols. Dijon and Paris, 1766.

Richardson, Jonathan, and Jonathan Richardson Jr. *An Account of some of the*

Statues, Bas-Reliefs, Drawings, and Pictures in Italy. London: J. Knapton, 1722.

Riedel, Friedrich. *Theorie der schönen Künste und Wissenschaften*. Jena, 1767.

Saunderson, Nicholas. *Elements of Algebra in ten Books*. Cambridge: Cambridge University Press, 1740.

Schlegel, Friedrich. *Philosophical Fragments*. Trans. Peter Firchow. Minneapolis: University of Minnesota Press, 1991.

Smith, Robert. *A Compleat System of Opticks*. 2 vols. Cambridge: Cornelius Crownfield, 1738.

Statius. *Silvae IV*. Ed. and trans. K. M. Coleman. Oxford: Clarendon Press, 1988.

Stewart, Andrew. *Greek Sculpture: An Exploration*. New Haven, Conn.: Yale University Press, 1990.

Strabo. *Geography*. 8 vols. Trans. H. L. Jones. Cambridge Mass.: Harvard University Press, 1917–32.

Sturluson, Snorri. *Edda*. Trans. Anthony Faulkes. London: Dent, 1987.

Terence. Volume 1: *The Lady of Andros; The Self-Tormentor; The Eunuch*. Trans. John Sargeaunt. Cambridge Mass.: Harvard University Press, 1912.

Vasari, Giorgio. *Lives of the Artists*. Vol. 1. Ed. and trans. George Bull. Harmondsworth: Penguin, 1987.

Virgil. *Ecologues, Georgics, Aeneid*. Trans. H. R. Fairclough. Rev. ed. 2 vols. Ed. G. P. Goold. Cambridge, Mass.: Harvard University Press, 1999.

Volkmann, Johann Jacob. *Historisch-kritische Nachrichten von Italien*. 3 vols. Leipzig, 1770–71.

Winckelmann, Johann Joachim. *History of Ancient Art*. Trans. G. Henry Lodge. 2 vols. New York: Friedrich Ungar, 1968.

———. *Kleine Schriften, Vorreden, Entwürfe*. Ed. Walther Rehm. Berlin: de Gruyter, 1968.

———. *Reflections on the Imitation of Greek Works in Painting and Sculpture*. Trans. Elfriede Heyer and Roger C. Norton. La Salle, Ill.: Open Court, 1987.

———. *Versuch einer Allegorie, besonders für die Kunst*. Dresden: Walthersche Hof-Buchhandlung, 1776.

Zohar. 5 vols. Trans. Harry Sperling and Maurice Simon. London: Soncino Press, 1931–34.

Selected Writings on Herder's *Sculpture*

Adler, Hans. *Die Prägnanz des Dunklen: Gnoseologie–Ästhetik–Geschichtsphilosophie bei Johann Gottfried Herder*. Hamburg: Felix Meiner, 1990.

Bätschmann, Oskar. "Pygmalion als Betrachter: Die Rezeption von Plastik und Malerei in der zweiten Hälfte des 18. Jahrhunderts." In *Der Betrachter ist im Bild: Kunstwissenschaft und Rezeptionsästhetik*, ed. Wolfgang Kemp, 183–224. Cologne: DuMont, 1985.

Braungart, Georg. *Leibhafter Sinn. Der andere Diskurs der Moderne.* Tübingen: Niemeyer, 1995.

Brummack, Jürgen, and Martin Bollacher, eds. *Schriften zu Philosophie, Literatur, Kunst, und Altertum, 1774–87,* by Johann Gottfried Herder. Vol. 4 of Johann Gottfried Herder, *Werke,* ed. Günter Arnold et al. Frankfurt am Main: Deutscher Klassiker Verlag, 1994.

Gessinger, Joachim, "'Das Gefühl liegt dem Gehör so nahe': The Physiological Foundations of Herder's Theory of Cognition." In *Johann Gottfried Herder: Academic Disciplines and the Pursuit of Knowledge,* ed. Wulf Koepke, 32–52. Columbia, S.C.: Camden House, 1996.

Grimm, Gunter E. "Kunst als Schule der Humanität. Beobachtungen zur Funktion Griechischer Plastik in Herders Kunst-Philosophie." In *Johann Gottfried Herder, 1744–1803,* ed. Gerhard Sauder, 352–63. Hamburg: Felix Meiner, 1987.

Hall, James. *The World as Sculpture: The Changing Status of Sculpture from the Renaissance to the Present Day.* London: Chatto and Windus, 1999.

Haym, Rudolf. *Herder nach seinem Leben und seinen Werken dargestellt.* 2 vols. Berlin: R. Gaertner, 1877–85.

Irmscher, Hans Dietrich. "Zur Ästhetik des jungen Herder." In *Johann Gottfried Herder, 1744–1803,* ed. Gerhard Sauder, 43–76. Hamburg: Felix Meiner, 1987.

Kemp, Wolfgang, ed. *Der Betrachter ist im Bild: Kunstwissenschaft und Rezeptionsästhetik.* Cologne: DuMont, 1985.

Koepke, Wulf, ed. *Johann Gottfried Herder: Academic Disciplines and the Pursuit of Knowledge.* Columbia, S.C.: Camden House, 1996.

———. *Johann Gottfried Herder: Language, History, and the Enlightenment.* Columbia, S.C.: Camden House, 1990.

Malsch, Wilfried. "Herders Schrift über die Skulpturkunst in der Geschichte der Unterscheidung des Plastischen und Malerischen oder Musikalischen in Kunst und Literatur." In *Johann Gottfried Herder: Language, History, and the Enlightenment,* ed. Wulf Koepke, 224–35. Columbia, S.C.: Camden House, 1990.

Maragliano, Giorgio, ed. *Plastica: Alcune osservazioni su forma e figura a partire dal sogno formativo di Pigmalione.* Palermo: Aesthetica edizioni Palermo, 1994.

Mülder-Bach, Inka. "Eine 'neue Logik für den Liebhaber': Herders Theorie der Plastik." In *Der ganze Mensch: Anthropologie und Literatur im 18. Jahrhundert* (DFG-Symposion 1992), ed. Hans-Jürgen Schings, 341–70. Stuttgart: J. B. Metzler, 1994.

Norton, Robert E. *Herder's Aesthetics and the European Enlightenment.* Ithaca, N.Y.: Cornell University Press, 1991.

Pfotenhauer, Helmut. *Um 1800. Konfigurationen der Literatur, Kunstliteratur, und Ästhetik.* Tübingen: Niemeyer, 1991.

Pfotenhauer, Helmut, and Peter Sprengel, eds. *Klassik und Klassizismus.* Bibliothek der Kunstliteratur, vol. 3. Frankfurt am Main: Deutscher Klassiker Verlag, 1995.

Podro, Michael. "Herder's *Plastik*." In *Sight and Insight: Essays on Art and Culture in Honour of E. H. Gombrich at 85*, ed. John Onian, 341–53. Oxford: Phaidon, 1984.

Potts, Alex. *The Sculptural Imagination: Figurative, Modernist, Minimalist.* New Haven: Yale University Press, 2000.

Saltzwedel, Johannes. *Das Gesicht der Welt. Physigionomisches Denken in der Goethezeit.* Munich: Fink, 1993.

Sauder, Gerhard, ed. *Johann Gottfried Herder, 1744–1803.* Hamburg: Felix Meiner, 1987.

Schings, Hans-Jürgen, ed. *Der ganze Mensch: Anthropologie und Literatur im 18. Jahrhundert* (DFG-Symposion 1992). Stuttgart: J. B. Metzler, 1994.

Schneider, Helmut J. "The Cold Eye: Herder's Critique of Enlightenment Visualism." In *Johann Gottfried Herder: Academic Disciplines and the Pursuit of Knowledge*, ed. Wulf Koepke, 53–60. Columbia, S.C.: Camden House, 1996.

Schneider, Lambert A., ed. *Plastik. Einige Warhnehmungen über Form und Gestalt aus Pygmalions Bildendem Traume*, by Johann Gottfried Herder. Cologne: Jakob Hegner, 1969.

Schweitzer, Bernhard. "J.G. Herders 'Plastik' und die Entstehung der neueren Kunstwissenschaft: Eine Einführung und Würdigung." In *Zur Kunst der Antike*, 1:198–252. Tübingen: Ernst Wasmuth, 1963.

Spemann, Wolf. *Plastisches Gestalten: Anthropologische Aspekte.* Hildesheim: Georg Olms, 1984.

INDEX

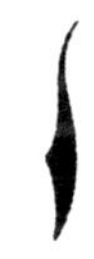

www.ingramcontent.com/pod-product-compliance
Lightning Source LLC
LaVergne TN
LVHW010619100826
845148LV00014B/3035

* 9 7 8 0 2 2 6 3 2 7 5 5 6 *